CITIZENSHIP, SECURITY AND DEMOCRACY
MUSLIM ENGAGEMENT WITH THE WEST

Selected papers from the **Citizenship, Security and Democracy** international conference held in Turkey on 1–3 September 2006. The conference was jointly organised by the Association of Muslims Social Scientists (AMSS UK) and the Foundation for Political, Economic and Social Research (SETA).

The **Association of Muslim Social Scientists** (AMSS UK) is an Association based in London committed to the development of Islamic thought through research, scholarship and publications. The AMSS (UK) aims to keep scholars informed about current conceptual, methodological, and analytical developments and promote greater interdisciplinary co-operation, in an effort towards generating informed, critical and creative views and opinions on topical and emerging issues of relevance to community relations and social cohesion.

The **Foundation for Political, Economic and Social Research (SETA Turkey)** is a non-profit research institute dedicated to innovative studies on national, regional, and international issues. Through its reports, policy briefs, panels and conferences, SETA seeks to foster collaborative and interdisciplinary research and provide decision-makers both in the public and private sectors with authoritative and independent information, analysis and proposals for action in Turkey and beyond. SETA publishes *Insight Turkey*, Turkey's most prominent English-language journal on Turkish and international affairs. Website: www.setav.org

CITIZENSHIP, SECURITY AND DEMOCRACY

Muslim Engagement with the West

Edited by
WANDA KRAUSE

ASSOCIATION OF MUSLIM
SOCIAL SCIENTISTS (UK)

SETA
FOUNDATION FOR POLITICAL, ECONOMIC AND SOCIAL RESEARCH

AMSS UK
P.O. BOX 126,
RICHMOND, SURREY, TW9 2UD, UK
WWW.AMSSUK.COM

ISBN 978–1–56564–443–4 paperback
ISBN 978–1–56564–444–1 hardback

Typesetting and cover design by Shiraz Khan
Printed in the United Kingdom by Cromwell Press Group

CONTENTS

PUBLISHER'S NOTE

On September 1–3, 2006, the Association of Muslim Social Scientists (AMSS UK) and the Foundation for Political, Economic, and Social Research (SETA Turkey) held a three-day international conference to explore the challenges of democracy and security with special reference to issues of citizenship and identity of Muslim communities in the West. Political discourse concerning Muslims has largely been dominated by a narrative that has wavered little beyond the context set by 7/7 and 9/11 and focus on the possibility of repetition, of a new terrorism that can strike at will, has come to govern much analysis of Muslim communities, governed primarily by issues of faith based radicalism and extremism. Further, increasing concentration on invasive and controversial security measures has curtailed civil liberties and strained relations globally, leading to rising levels of tension and a marked sense of alienation felt particularly by Muslims residing in the West. It is imperative therefore that a climate of mutual respect, safety and dialogue is nurtured, giving recognition to the 'other' and meeting the challenge of living and working together in diversity. The conference aimed to address these and other issues of relevance as well as to explore some of the many challenges faced by governments in this regard.

This conference marked a major milestone, bringing a large number of scholars and experts from a wide range of disciplines and professional backgrounds together to address one of the most important issues confronting society at the turn of the 21st century. In addition, the important academic and cultural collaboration between AMSS (UK) and SETA, underscored recognition of the convergence of the various issues and challenges facing both Muslims and governments throughout Europe, both East and West. The empty chair approach of former times is being effectively challenged and negotiated through conferences such as these, which allow good space for unique and valid perspectives to be brought to the table, and give impetus to initiatives focusing on strategic and confident dialogue.

PUBLISHER'S NOTE

AMSS (UK) and SETA would like to thank the Conference Secretariat as well as all those involved in organising the event for their hard work and professionalism. These include Dr. Fauzia Ahmad, Dr. Mehmet Asutay, Dr. Kamran Bokhari, Dr. Talip Kucukcan, Abdul-Rehman Malik, Dr. Fathi Malkawi, Dr. Mohamed Mestiri, Dr. Bobby Sayyid, Dr. Muhammad Siddique Seddon, Ahmet Selim Tekelioglu, and Umare Yazar. We also thank the Istanbul Metropolitan Municipality for hosting the Conference, as well as the International Institute of Islamic Thought (IIIT) for their strong support and collaboration. The publishers also wish to thank AMSS (France) and AMSS (USA), as well as the ICYF-DC, for their collaboration. Finally, we are indebted to El-Rahma Charity Trust for their support in publishing this work.

This book has been the result of a team effort, and we would like to thank all those involved in its production. Primarily we acknowledge the skilled and painstaking work of its editor, Dr. Wanda Krause, who had the difficult task of collating, editing, and reviewing the papers to produce a thorough and consistent manuscript. We also acknowledge the valuable editorial advice of Dr. Jeremy Henzell-Thomas and Professor Charles E. Butterworth. Finally thanks go to Shiraz Khan, Dr. Maryam Mahmood and Tahira Hadi, for copyediting the finished manuscript.

These papers have been published to widen discourse, stimulate debate, and hopefully pave the way for further research. Doubtless readers may agree with some of the issues raised, and disagree with others, but it is hoped that overall both general and specialised readers will benefit from the perspectives offered and some of the more focused issues examined in the book.

DR. ANAS AL-SHAIKH-ALI

Chair, AMSS UK
Academic Advisor, IIIT London Office

DR. IBRAHIM KALIN

Director, SETA, Turkey
Faculty Member, Prince Alwaleed
Bin Talal Center for
Muslim-Christian Understanding,
Georgetown University, USA

OCTOBER, 2009

CONTRIBUTORS

Tahir Abbas BSc(Econ) MSocSc PhD FRSA is an academic researcher, social commentator and consultant to government. He was Reader in Sociology and founding Director of the University of Birmingham Centre for the Study of Ethnicity and Culture, UK (2003–2009). His area of expertise is the study of race, ethnicity, multiculturalism and Muslim minorities. He has published over sixty single and joint authored articles in internationally respected journals and specialist edited collections. He is author of *Race, Ethnicity and Multiculturalism* (Sage, 2010), *Islamic Radicalism and Multicultural Politics* (Routledge, 2010), *The Education of British South Asians* (Palgrave-Macmillan, 2004); editor of *Islam and Education* (Routledge, 2010), *Muslim Britain* (Zed, 2005), *Islamic Political Radicalism* (Edinburgh University Press, 2007, ed.); and co-editor of *Islam, Honour, Violence and Women* (Routledge, 2010, with M.M. Idriss and R. Abbinnett) and *Immigration and Race Relations* (I B Tauris, 2007, with F.W. Reeves). In 2007–2008, Dr. Abbas was Visiting Fellow at the University of Oxford Centre for Islamic Studies. He is currently Fellow of the Royal Society of Arts and Honorary Fellow of the Exeter Centre for Ethno-Political Studies, Institute of Arab and Islamic Studies, University of Exeter.

Abdelwahab El-Affendi is Reader in Politics at the Centre for the Study of Democracy, University of Westminster and Co-ordinator of the Centre's Democracy and Islam Programme. Educated at the Universities of Khartoum, Wales, and Reading, he is author of *Turabi's Revolution: Islam and Power in Sudan* (1991), *Who Needs an Islamic State?* (1991), *Revolution and Political Reform in Sudan* (1995), *Rethinking Islam and Modernity* (2001), *For a State of Peace: Conflict and the Future of Democracy in Sudan* (2002) and *The Conquest of Muslim Hearts and Minds: Perspectives on U.S. Reform and Public Diplomacy Strategies* (2005). He has also contributed to many leading journals, and is contributor or co-author of works including: *The Routledge Encyclopedia of Philosophy* (1998), *Social Science and Conflict Analysis* (1993), *Islam and Justice* (1997), *Islam and Secularism in the Middle East* (2000), *Islamic Thought in the Twentieth Century* (2003), *Understanding Democratic Politics* (2003), *American Power in the 21st Century* (2004), *The Arab*

Human Development Report (2004), and *The Blackwell Companion to Contemporary Islamic Thought* (2006). Dr. El-Affendi was a member of the core team of authors of the *Arab Human Development Report* (2004) and a member of the Advisory Board and a contributor to the 2005 report. He is also a member of the Commission on British Muslims and Islamophobia, member of the Board of Directors of Inter-Africa Group, and a trustee of the International Forum for Islamic Dialogue, and on the AMSS UK Advisory Board. He is the 2006 winner of The Muslim News Allama Iqbal Award for Creativity in Islamic Thought.

IMAD AD-DEAN AHMAD graduated cum laude from Harvard in 1970 and in 1975 obtained a PhD in Astronomy and Astrophysics from the University of Arizona. He holds a position as Senior Lecturer teaching honours courses in Religion and Progress at the University of Maryland in College Park, MD. Dr. Ahmad is a frequent guest lecturer on Islam at the Foreign Services Institute and an Adjunct Lecturer for the Joint Special Operations University's Middle East Orientation course. He is currently President of the Minaret of Freedom Institute, an Islamic think tank in the Washington DC area, USA. He is the author of *Signs in the Heavens* and *The Islamic Rules of Order*. He is also co-editor of *Islam and the West: A Dialog*, and co-author of *Islam and the Discovery of Freedom*.

RAANA BOKHARI is a PhD student in Religious Studies. She has lectured on Islam and Muslim women in particular, and worked as a Research Associate at Lancaster University in education and social exclusion. She is the author of several articles in interfaith publications and on Gujarati Muslim women in Leicester in edited works.

CHARLES E. BUTTERWORTH is Professor Emeritus of Government and Politics at the University of Maryland, College Park. He specialises in medieval Arabic and Islamic political philosophy. Professor Butterworth's publications include critical editions of most of the Middle Commentaries written by Averroes on Aristotle's logic; translations of books and treatises by Averroes, al-Fārābī, and al-Rāzī, as well as Maimonides; and studies of different aspects of the political teaching of these and other thinkers in the ancient, medieval and modern tradition of philosophy. He has also written monograph analyses of the political thought of Frantz Fanon and Jean-

Jacques Rousseau. He is a member of several learned organisations and past President of the American Council for the Study of Islamic Societies (ACSIS) as well as of the Société Internationale pour l'Étude de l'Histoire de la Philosophie et la Science Arabe et Islamique (SIHSPAI).

HISHAM A. HELLYER is Fellow, Centre for Research in Ethnic Relations (CRER), University of Warwick, UK, Director, the Visionary Consultants Group (VCG), member, Oxford Centre for Islamic Studies (OCIS) of the University of Oxford, UK, Visiting Fellow, Institute of Strategic and International Studies (ISIS), Malaysia, Fellow of the Centre for Research in Ethnic Relations (CRER) at the University of Warwick (UK) and Principal Research Fellow at the Institute of Advanced Islamic Studies (Malaysia). Dr. Hellyer is an internationally acclaimed writer and commentator. Until recently Ford Fellow of the Saban Center for Middle East Policy at the Brookings Institution (USA), he also taught as Visiting Professor of Law at the American University in Cairo (AUC) (Egypt). A UN Alliance of Civilizations Global Expert, he received his PhD from the University of Warwick on a legal and political study on European minorities. He also holds a law degree from Sheffield's School of Law, and a Master's degree in international political economy from the University of Sheffield.

In addition to his academic contributions, he engages in popular mediums such as the Washington Post and the BBC Doha Debates, and also speaks authoritatively on his subject areas to forums such as the OSCE and the Royal United Services Institute for Defence. He was also an ESRC Placement Fellow at the UK Foreign & Commonwealth Office, examining state-minority community relations in Europe. At present, he focuses his research on Muslim minority communities throughout the globe and on Muslim world – West relations. His book on European Muslims ("The European 'Other'") is due to be published by Edinburgh University Press in 2009.

JEREMY HENZELL-THOMAS is Executive Director of the Book Foundation, a registered UK charity with worldwide projects working with partner institutions in the UK and the USA to improve understanding of Islam in the West. He was the first Chair of FAIR (Forum Against Islamophobia and Racism) and has served as a member of the Executive Committee and the Advisory Board of the AMSS (UK). He holds degrees in

English and Linguistics from London and Edinburgh universities, and a PhD in the Psychology of Learning from the University of Lancaster. He has worked at many levels in education both in the UK and overseas, as a teacher, academic director, curriculum development specialist, schools inspector, university lecturer, doctoral research supervisor and educational consultant. He speaks widely on the themes of education, society and spirituality, and writes regular columns for *Islamica* and *Emel* magazines. He is a member of the Advisory Board of *Islamica* and a contributing editor of *The American Muslim*. His recent international conference papers, including plenary addresses, have been delivered at the Gustav-Stresemann Institut, Bonn (2002), University of Surrey, Roehampton (2003), University of Indiana, Bloomington (2003), University of Edinburgh (2004), Institute for the Study of Muslim Civilisations, Aga Khan University, London (2005), and the University of Durham (2005). His keynote address, "Beyond the Tower of Babel: A Linguistic Approach to Clarifying Key Concepts in Islamic Pluralism" was delivered at the AMSS conference on Citizenship, Security and Democracy in Istanbul (2006).

ANWAR IBRAHIM is a former Deputy Prime Minister and Finance Minister of Malaysia. He is also one of the founders, together with the late Professor Ismail al-Faruqi, of the IIIT (International Institute of Islamic Thought). In 1998, *Newsweek International* named him Asian of the Year. He is currently a Senior Associate Member of St. Anthonys, Oxford University, and Visiting Professor in the Centre for Muslim-Christian Understanding, Georgetown University, USA. Anwar Ibrahim has published two books *Menangani Perubahan* (Managing Change, Berita Publishing, 1988), and *The Asian Renaissance*, (Times Publications, Singapore, 1997), and more than a dozen articles including: "The Ardent Moderates," *Time* magazine, August 1996; "Who Hijacked Islam?" *Time* magazine, October 2001; "We Muslims Must Reform our Own Politics," *The Asian Wall Street Journal*, October 2003; "There is So Much to Do" *Time* magazine, September 2004; and recently "The Quest for Social Justice" *Global Agenda* magazine (of the World Economic Forum Annual Meeting), January 2005.

WANDA KRAUSE is currently teaching politics at the School of Oriental and African Studies (SOAS), UK. Krause has a doctorate in Politics from the

University of Exeter, UK. Her research dealt with civil society development, gender politics, and Islamism. Her background studies, which she conducted in Canada, Germany, Egypt, and the UAE, include international relations, linguistics, social-psychology, and Arabic studies. Krause's recent book is *Women in Civil Society: The State, Islamism and Networks in the UAE*, (New York: Palgrave-Macmillan, 2008). Her current research focuses on the relationship between politics and spirituality.

LUCY MICHAEL received her PhD in the Research Institute for Law, Politics and Justice at Keele University. She graduated in Law from University College Dublin and then went on to complete a postgraduate degree in Criminology at Keele University. Her doctoral project is based on research in the Pakistani communities of Stoke-on-Trent and Manchester. Dr. Michael's research explores the nature and performance of leadership within ethnic minority communities facing problems of conflict and cohesion. The project has been supported by the Economic and Social Research Council UK, Office of the Deputy Prime Minister and Keele University.

ELMIRA MURATOVA is a Docent (Associate Professor) in the Department of Political Science at Taurida National Vernadsky University (Simferopol, Ukraine) where she teaches on the Islamic World in Modern Politics and Political Islam in the Post-Soviet Space. Dr. Muratova is also Director of the Crimean Institute for Peace which deals with interethnic and interfaith relations in the Crimea (Ukraine). In 2007 she was awarded the Erasmus Mundus Fellowship to conduct research on 'Ethnic Conflicts in Kosovo, Bosnia and the Crimea' at UCL. She holds a PhD in Political Science, thesis titled, "Political Analysis of Islam's Revival in Crimea" (2004). Her research areas include political Islam, ethnic and religious clashes, and Islam's revival in the post-Soviet space.

MOHAMMAD SIDDIQUE SEDDON obtained his PhD in Religious Studies at Lancaster University and is currently Lecturer in Muslim Studies at the Department of Theology and Religious Studies, University of Chester. He has previously worked as Development Officer at the Centre for the Study of Islam in the UK, Cardiff University. He is a former Research Fellow at the Islamic Foundation and is an Executive Member of the Association of Muslim Social Scientists (UK). His research interests are historical and contemporary issues relating to Islam in Britain and British Muslim communities. He has published a number of related works and books including, *British Muslims: Loyalty and Belonging* (2003), and *British Muslims between Assimilation and Segregation: Historical, Legal & Social Realities* (2004).

ANAS AL-SHAIKH-ALI has a PhD in American Studies and has taught Literature and Translation at universities in the Middle East. Dr. Al-Shaikh-Ali is a Founding member and current Chair of AMSS (UK), and Academic Advisor to the IIIT and Director of its London Office and Translation Department. He is a Founding Trustee of FED 2000 UK (Foundation for Education and Development), a Founding Trustee and former Chair of FAIR (Forum Against Islamophobia and Racism), former Chair of the Board of Governors of The Avenue School, and Founding Executive Director of Legacy Publishing Ltd. His research interests include Islam in Western Popular Culture, Islam and the Media, Muslim Education in Europe and Muslim Discourse in Europe. He has lectured and published in both Arabic and English on these topics. Among his recent papers being published is "Islamophobic Discourse Masquerading as Art and Literature: Combating Myth through Progressive Education." His expert advice was instrumental for the production of the joint British Council/AMSS UK publication *British Muslims: Media Guide*. He was awarded a CBE in June 2009 for Services to Community Relations. He is currently a Research Fellow at the Department of History, Royal Holloway, University of London, and member of the Management Board of the Prince Alwaleed Bin Talal Centre of Islamic Studies, University of Cambridge.

Introduction

THE EDITED BOOK ENTITLED, *Citizenship, Security and Democracy* provides greater analysis of and seeks solutions to the challenges of citizenship, security and democracy through fresh and more varied perspectives as is related to Islamic discourse and Muslim communities and their activism in the West. These concerns have never been more pressing than today. Democracy has been a global endeavour and concern, as in its ideal form, it gives promise to liberty, freedoms and rights. However, after especially 9/11 and 7/7, securitization has become a more immediate goal, making security the driving discourse today. But, both security and democracy are becoming ever less attainable in today's climate of increased division and cleavages along ideological lines and Islamophobia – an acute problem for citizenship in humanity.

On September 1–3, 2006, the Association of Muslim Social Scientists (AMSS) and the Foundation for Political, Economic and Social Research (SETA) held a three day conference to explore the challenges of democracy and security and, importantly, explore issues around citizenship and identity of Muslim diaspora. Given the backdrop to a growing political discourse on the Muslim 'Other', framed through the events of 9/11 and 7/7 and increased tension as a result of this discourse framing, the aim was to help discern causes to the major challenges facing governments and the safety, freedoms and dignity of individuals globally. This was attempted through the study of Islamic thought and on-the-ground case study research of Muslim societies and communities. This conference marks one of the major events to have been organised where such a large number of scholars, experts, and activists from a wide range of ideological positions and professional backgrounds come together in an

INTRODUCTION

ambitious attempt to resolve the most pressing issues at the turn of the 21st century. Concern was security and democratic rights of human beings within or in relation to an Islamic discourse.

This edited volume assembles selected contributions of these thinkers, academics, activists and faith leaders who not only analyzed but further interrogated the forces in historical and contemporary light that contribute to the greater lack of security and threaten democratic endeavours. How have constraints in government policy on community or group choices and opportunities influenced the political experience of these communities and groups? What political and economic choices have been made and what are their implications for governments, democracy, security, and the future of humanity? What options now exist to policy makers and affected communities and groups in these circumstances? The solutions put forward lie not in a single isolated variable, government, or group but in the complex interconnections between government and civil society, between domestic and external forces, historical legacies, and future strategies. Endeavouring to find solutions for ensuing problems of new transfigurations of citizenship and identity, the contributors draw on case studies, Islamic history, Islamic jurisprudence, and investigative analysis of historical and current political trends and contexts.

Citizenship entails membership in a community and this membership entails political rights of these individuals within the given society. Beginning this volume's discussion on citizenship, Anwar Ibrahim discusses the meaning of citizenship in both Western and predominantly Muslim countries. Notwithstanding the 'war on terror' and other failures in the practice of inclusive citizenship, he argues Western countries are indeed leading examples in the practice of democracy. Speaking from his own personal experience of imprisonment and about the problem of authoritarianism in Muslim countries, he argues for the implementation of the universalism of Islam in the sense that its values of justice, compassion and tolerance be practiced everywhere. He maintains human rights must be brought to the fore where condemnation against the violation of human rights must transcend race, colour and creed because one must never lose sight of the fact that humankind is one.

Illustrating the complexity of the notion of citizenship and Muslim communities in Western countries, H. A. Hellyer discusses how Muslim communities in the West understand citizenship as developed from the multiculturalism debate in mainly Europe. He shows that Muslim communities in the West are currently trying to cope with what Islam offers as guidance on the issues of 'belonging' and patriotism. They have not yet fully examined what the full weight of Islamic teachings has borne down on the concepts and values of the citizenship debate, as well as the integration debate. He argues for a more thorough deconstruction of these areas before a comprehensive understanding can begin.

Jeremy Henzell-Thomas considers the principles of citizenship in Islam through a discussion of the story of the Tower of Babel, and how contrary to the Biblical version, he argues plurality from the Qur'anic perspective as embodied in language is something to be celebrated. He discusses the problem of reality being dichotomized into competing unilateral or unipolar worldviews through these various mechanisms of transmitting 'truths', and as such, creating isolating pathologies of civilizational narcissism. He argues for the positive embodiment of the pluralistic Qur'anic vision of citizenship within diversity by embracing the best of all traditions through respectful co-existence, mutual recognition, active engagement, and transforming love.

Contexts having highly political and social import are, however, also found in what may be thought harmless entertainment. Anas Al-Shaikh-Ali argues popular fiction, in fact, serves as a powerful means in the shaping of public political opinion and in the intensification of Islamophobia. He illustrates how through fiction, consumed by billions and marketed globally, best selling authors routinely set the moral boundaries through which we are to view global confrontation. The paper examines not only the role of novels in shaping public opinion but how plotlines also appear to remarkably predict political/military events urging a deeper exploration of the complex relationship that oscillates between fiction and fact, writers and the intelligence services. Is the industry selling novels or marketing a worldview? These are some of the many issues the paper explores.

Illustrating, importantly, the agency of Muslim communities in negotiating citizenship and identity are Elmira Muratova and Mohammad Siddique Seddon with their case studies on the Tatars in the Crimea and British Yemenis, respectively. Muratova's work on Muslims in the Crimea contributes to the small, although growing, number of studies on

INTRODUCTION

Muslim diaspora in Russia and Eastern block countries. She discusses how the Tatars have developed their identity as Muslims through a cultural heritage different to Turks or Arabs and, furthermore, through their expulsion from modern Ukraine and return. She shows how they prove a striking example where people of different ethnic backgrounds and religion can co-exist harmoniously in a region where ethnic and religious differentiation has been marked.

Mohammad Siddique Seddon's paper also shows how a Muslim community has constructed its identity through migration. However, his case study illustrates how in the modern age it becomes impossible to associate a specific culture with a specific place as a symbolic guarantee of belonging. His study on Yemeni diaspora communities in Britain explores the facets of diasporic Yemeni identity by examining their translocal social networks and how this community preserves its distinct religious and cultural traditions in modern Britain, thus, disrupting expectations of the social integration, citizenry and 'belongingness' of minority Muslim communities.

Authors of this volume discuss the issue of citizenship and identity from a failed public policy angle, pointing to the effects of marginalization of minority populations, here Muslim communities, and the effects of the so-called 'war on terror'. Charles Butterworth discusses human rights violations under the US led 'war on terror' in the invasion of Iraq, treatment of persons seized abroad and imprisoned secretly, infringement of constitutional rights of US citizens, among other related issues. He looks at how these policies have been endorsed but importantly how these policies can be turned around. Tahir Abbas addresses these issues in terms of UK anti-terrorist legislation and policies towards the South Asian Muslim community in Britain. Through a more focused case study on policies experienced in Birmingham, he discusses the effect of marginalization and isolation. The larger argument Abbas makes is the ideological radicalization of British South Asian Muslims and formation of extremist identity as a result of government policies.

However, scholars also point to historical and contemporary examples to illustrate how alternative action to violence based on religion may be possible in the experience of imbalanced policies and injustice. Imad ad-Dean Ahmad examines the alternatives to violence in Muslim history. In view of contemporary challenges facing minority groups, Raana

Bokhari explores the practice of dissent as an alternative to violence and as a form of protest aimed at affecting social and political change. Ahmad considers the varied examples of the unauthorized pilgrimage to Makkah that led to the treaty of Hudaybiyyah, Abu Kalam Azad's role in the Indian resistance against the British occupation, and the first Palestinian intifada. He makes parallels between these Muslim examples and Western cases: Thoreau's resistance to the taxes supporting slavery and the Mexican War, the American civil rights movement, and the Vietnam War protests. He looks specifically at the role that religion played in these movements, the formation of alliances, how the movements dealt with issues of provocation, the role of publicity, and the role of the threat of violence. With this backdrop, he effectively makes a case for policy application in regards to contemporary challenges to individual liberties and broader security.

Raana Bokhari incorporates crucially a gendered perspective by studying dissenting voices among Muslim and non-Muslim women active in Leicester, UK, a model 'multicultural' city. Lucy Michael's work similarly focuses on the 'multicultural' city by studying Muslim communities in Manchester and Stoke-on-Trent, UK. After discussing the impact of exclusion and marginalization in terms of the resultant ordering of the city along ethnic and religious lines, she provides an analysis of how the Muslim communities develop a strong ethic of civility. This, she argues, has developed in response through greater community cohesion and social inclusion programmes in order to improve their capacity to access public institutions and mobilize effectively for a 'fair' share of social resources.

However, globally we witness also a resurgence of political Islam as a means through which groups larger than community level forms of organization or ethnic groups organized along religious lines organize and mobilize to action using Islamic rhetoric. Abdelwahab El-Affendi sheds new light on the causes and means through which this resurgence takes form and the implications political Islam has to global politics. El-Affendi re-examines the notion of the Islamic state by analyzing the Caliphate model, which revivalist movements seek to create. His argument of the impracticability of such an endeavor is supported by his analysis in regards to the problem of the autonomy of politics and lack of the 'ethical' state. The solution to the elusive ethical state, he argues, lies crucially in incorporating democratic values into Islamic political thought.

In this book, we concentrate on developments and challenges of citizenship, security and democracy primarily after the turn of the millennium in order to expose pressing problems of integration, co-existence and fast-widening cleavages along ideological lines as the greatest variables to consider. We offer this edited volume as a starting point to understanding the most pressing and difficult realities affecting security and democracy in the next decades to come. For those pondering how a shift in direction from conflict and fear to greater peaceful co-existence and security can begin, this book digs right into the heart of the most difficult dilemmas. With its varied angles to these problems it is also a starting point for finding critical solutions.

DR. WANDA KRAUSE

Islam and Principles of Citizenship

ANWAR IBRAHIM

Expanding our Intellectual Vision:
The Quest for a New Islamic Worldview

IMPRISONMENT, PARTICULARLY IF IT IS over a slightly protracted period of six years, is sometimes necessary – as a form of imposed *khalwah* – for politicians who get too caught up with affairs of the state. Speaking for myself, having been sent into solitary confinement, it enabled me to reread and reflect more deeply among others the works of some of the leading Muslim social scientists. I shall share with you the fruit of such contemplation.

At the turn of the last century, after the collapse of the last of the great Muslim empires, and Constantinople saw itself being partitioned between the imperial powers, Muslim intellectuals, politicians, and economists were adrift in a sea of contending theories as to what the Islamic worldview is or should really be. If it was a full sea, it is clear that they did not take the tide when it served, because until today, we remain faced with the same question: do we have that worldview, a lasting metaphysical paradigm, capable of solving not just the ills of the Ummah but mankind itself? Is this odyssey proving to be a search for the Holy Grail, or to bring home the metaphor, is this indeed a quest for the Red Sulphur?[1]

It is said that the key attribute of the Islamic social sciences in expounding a worldview must rest on the acquisition of knowledge through the rationality of the human mind. I share this view in as much as I believe that the Qur'an does not require man to deny his right to exercise his intelligence. The Qur'an speaks to the rational mind or as has been so well put by the late Professor Fazlur Rahman, "it alerts the intellect." Is that carte blanche for the wanton abandonment of faith on the altar of reason? The answer would be obvious if we consider too that the

Qur'an does not only lay out the order in the universe and the principles within it, but it throws out the challenge for mankind to critically examine them in order to attain certitude of the validity of its claims and message, which invariably would lead to the reinforcement of faith, not its rejection. It is therefore misconceived to imagine that alerting the intellect was a license to stray from the faith because this pursuit would inevitably lead to the realization of the eternal principles of the Divine Unity, which in turn springs forth from the Divine Laws. Because of its timelessness, knowledge premised on this acquires finality and absoluteness. The created order follows invariable laws, as the Qur'an says: "Such was the way of God in days gone by and you will find it does not change" (al-Fath, 48:23).[2] But eternal principles when they are understood to exclude all possibilities of change tend to immobilize what is essentially mobile in its nature, as in the immobility of Islam during the last five hundred years. As succinctly stated by Muhammad Iqbal, the structure of Islam embodies the principle of movement, and this is known as Ijtihad.[3] Unlike the Mosaic tablets, the Shariʿah was never cast in stone and evolves continuously through this dynamic process. To talk of finality and absoluteness is therefore to deny the dynamism that is central to the Shariʿah itself. In order to maintain a middle ground, the essential ingredients of an Islamic methodology in the social sciences must then be conceived not in a unipolar, nor even bi-polar, but a holistic perspective which will be universal and eternal in appeal.

The challenge to Muslim social scientists then is to articulate a coherent body of metaphysical thought on the basis of a unifying all-encompassing Qur'anic Weltanschauung. Though we do not believe that this is a quest for the Red Sulphur, we fear that the seekers may lose their way in the labyrinth – unless they remain faithful to the injunction to "travel through the earth and see how Allah did originate creation" (al-ʿAnkabūt, 29:20). No doubt, it is this Qur'anic imperative, which enables us to appreciate the diversity of the Muslim experience across geographical, ethnic, social and even denominational barriers. In formulating the fundamental principles and values of such a worldview, we shall stay on course if we remain faithful to the creed that in this diversity, the only absolute is the "unity of knowledge" and the meaning and orientation this unity gives to life.[4] The question is: Can this be possible without a transformation of the Islamic intellectual tradition?

Expanding Our Intellectual Vision

Muslim social scientists must resolve the long standing quandary, brought about by the ideological rigidity of anti-modern neo-revivalism, which remains tragically the stumbling block to progress and reform. Being still tied to its old practices of cliché-mongering and name calling, this failure to reform must not be seen as a completely new phenomenon, for indeed, it can be traced to the period of Islam after the death of the Prophet and that period of the Rightly Guided Caliphs. And since history tends to repeat itself, it may be useful to recall that the Kharijites tolerated no dissent of their view of Islam, and the view that I have just expressed at the start of this essay would have warranted a death sentence. Their intransigence as regards the outward espousal of the faith is correctly said to have sown the seed for the birth of the fundamentalist movements, which would eventually litter the Islamic geo-political landscape. But we would lay ourselves open to the charge of bigotry if we castigate fundamentalism merely because it sounds menacing. However, our objection rests on more solid ground in that it was this kind of intransigence which was fully adopted by Ashʿarite theology that had distorted the picture of Islam, and continues to do so today. One would have to concede that the excesses of Muʿtazilite rationalism might have contributed to this violent reaction, but the rigidity of orthodoxy also led to the rejection of even the moderates, and by this we mean the metaphysicians of medieval Islam. From al-Fārābī up until Ibn Rushd there is no doubt that a coherent worldview was expounded but from the start, this view was eyed with suspicion by orthodoxy. The argument against the formula of the Muslim philosophers continues to be that a truly Islamic Weltanschauung must be premised foundationally on the Qur'an and the Sunnah and not spring from the loins of Aristotelian and Neo-platonist metaphysics. Professor Rahman went further by suggesting that this 'borrowed grounds' worldview cloaked the approach with 'a more or less artificial character' and combined with the assault of orthodoxy, "Islamic intellectualism has remained truncated."[5] In this regard, Iqbal's *Reconstruction* as quoted earlier on the principle of movement in the structure of Islam, undoubtedly represented a tour de force in modern times, drawing sustenance from the primary sources and yet possessing an ecumenical sweep in its approach that would cut across cultural and geographical barriers. Yet, even though its articulation moved beyond tribal or parochial concerns, it was a creature of history born of the particular circumstances surrounding the collapse of empires and the final dissolution of the caliphate itself, and ipso facto, its structural elements remain period-bound.

Syed Naquib al-Attas made a commendable effort premised on the doctrine of '*dīn*' as *talbiyah, akhlāq* and *ta'dīb*. His intellectual assault was trained on the proponents of secularism, which regarded its integral components as the Weberian "disenchantment of nature" and the "deconsecration of values." Secularization is seen as the setting free of the world from religious blinkers, the dispelling of myths and sacred symbols, and with the "desacralization of politics," it purports to put back the power of destiny in man's hands. But al-Attas's target was not secularism per se but Christianity.[6] Alas, today the thematic thrust would seem to have lost its edge because the Western challenge to Islam today can no longer be seen as being solely cast in the Christian mould, though at one time it provided the raison d'être for mounting Islam's intellectual offensive. The late Isma'il al-Faruqi expounded his now legendary doctrine of the Islamization of knowledge as a comprehensive intellectual response to the challenge of modernity but the follow through on his ideas has been uninspiring.[7]

The Intra-civilizational Clash

Much as we are getting tired of mentioning it, the 'clash of civilizations' specter seems to be the metaphor that appeals to the imagination of historians and political scientists. Many scholars have fallen into this quagmire. It would be well to accept that the discourse between Islam and the West is indeed subject to various predilections, civilizational clash being one. However, all resulting views are essentially influenced by the enormous historical baggage that accompanies this discourse. The upshot is a clash of visions of history, perceptions, and images, which in turn brings about differing and often opposing interpretations, not just of history, but worldviews. Muslim social scientists should disabuse themselves of this notion of the clash between civilizations and refocus their attentions on the clash that has been brewing within the Ummah. We see a more dangerous and portentous clash as one that is intra-civilizational – between the old and the new, the weak and the strong, the moderates and the fundamentalists and between the modernists and the traditionalists. In recent times, over the dissonance of

4

competing demands, Muslims are said to be caught between the centrifugal forces of modernity on the one hand, with its secularizing and liberating tendencies, and centripetal forces of traditionalism on the other, with its predisposition to sacralize and control.

One approach out of this conundrum is to formulate a universal Islamic Weltanschauung by expanding the Muslim intellectual vision, not just by raising his intellectual standards but by radically reorienting his mindset. This begs the question: What is the language of our discourse? Are Muslim intellectuals merely engaging themselves and running the risk of descending into a mutual admiration club? It is well and good that we are able to articulate our views coherently in seminars and symposiums, but are we doing enough to broaden the discourse to make it truly inclusive? This is a question that addresses the very role of Muslim social scientists themselves.

Modernity Revisited

In the 19th century, Rifāʿah Rāfiʿ al-Ṭahṭāwī asserted that patriotism – *ḥubb al-waṭan* – was the condition *sine qua non* for the establishment of a civilized community.[8] The stress on *ḥubb al-waṭan* as a modern conception of territorial patriotism is significant, and marked a departure from the religion-bound notion of the Islamic Ummah, which hitherto represented the main reason for the Khaldūnian notion of ʿaṣabiyyah. Ibn Khaldūn rightly pointed out that it was this notion, which gave rise to the ascent of a new civilization; but membership was exclusive to Muslims. In attempting to open up participation to other faiths, Ṭahṭāwī's approach, though not entirely secular, nevertheless broke new ground by breaching the time honoured religious connotations of the term, Ummah. To my mind, this no doubt was among the earliest calls to plurality. He also advocated that Muslims learn all the modern sciences, and that should not be seen as borrowing from the Europeans because they had originally borrowed from Muslims themselves. To his detractors, Ṭahṭāwī had fallen prey to the allure of the French Enlightenment. However, there were others who saw him as one of the earliest progressive reformists in Islam. Even today, it may be reasoned that it was only natural that one already steeped in the tradition of Islamic political thought could find affinity with some of the Enlightenment's leading ideas – the principle of justice being essential for a good society, and the

5

theme of virtue and liberty. A common fallacy carried even until today has been the characterization of the Enlightenment as the promotion of unbridled liberty. On the contrary, as is clear from Montesquieu's *Persian Letters*, for example, the best life is not the hedonistic, libertine existence, but the virtuous one. Liberty and virtue are invariably linked and in *The Spirit of the Laws* he asserts that virtue is the dominating principle in a republican form of government; where virtue fails, freedom disappears into the hands of a despot.

When Muhammad Abduh came on the scene, the pursuit of knowledge in Egypt had fallen into the intra-cultural and intra-religious divide heading for an inevitable clash – the traditional versus the modern, the old religious schools with al-Azhar at the pinnacle versus the European mission schools. The religious schools came under attack by Abduh himself. They could only impart religious knowledge while knowledge needed for survival in the modern world was as good as abandoned. Missionary schools appeared to have the upper hand in this, but were viewed with suspicion because of their proselytizing tendencies. Abduh saw the European light but was not dazzled by it, advocating instead reform through the lens of an Islamic renaissance. We have alluded to his theology of unity earlier. Essentially, he saw the clash within Islamic society and knew that the only way to bridge the chasm was not by a mere return to the past, but to the principles of Islam that could justify the introduction of modern Western learning. Scholars tend to gloss over this aspect of Abduh in their eagerness to pin the blame on him as one of the founding fathers of fundamentalism which would morph into radicalism and extremism of various forms.

Syed Ameer Ali, perhaps the first of the apologists, sought to show that there was nothing inherently different between predominantly Muslim societies and the societies in western Europe. He contended that the ideals and history of Islam show that it was fully compatible with the Victorian notions of individual choice, private property, and regard for rationality. After all, Muslim societies were at one time far more advanced than European societies in scientific endeavors.[9] They fell behind because of the self-imposed intellectual inertia brought on by a complete misunderstanding of the foundational principles of the religion. This led to the stagnation and intellectual slavishness of the age of *taqlīd*. Europe was the answer. Apologetic writings in this mould culminated in Taha

Husayn's no doubt valiant but entirely misconceived attempt to prove that Egypt was essentially a western land in terms of cultural orientation.[10] Taha Husayn's philosophy of history and society, under the influence of the French masters, such as Comte, Renan, Anatole France and Andre Gide, was a complete transformation of the worldview with Europe becoming the epicenter, symbolizing modernity and progress, and a perfect metaphor for Egypt's transformation: to be modern Egypt must therefore become part of Europe.

This was the last straw; this European obsession, thrown into harsh relief against the backdrop of oppression felt by Muslims under the yoke of colonialism, triggered the violent reaction which brought forth the likes of Rashid Reda, Hassan al-Banna, Sayyid Qutb and Maududi. Tracing its genealogy to Jamal ad-Din al-Afghani and moulded and ameliorated by Abduh, this started as pan-Islamism with a benign face which was prepared to integrate the old with the new and more particularly traditional Islam with the progressive features of the West. But the disciples broke ranks from their masters because they could not see how any middle ground could be attained with a morally reprehensible and decadent West. Qutb for example came to believe that only a truly Islamic State that was firm in its application of the divine law could counter the West and anything short of that was prone to evil and corruption.[11] Together with Hassan al-Banna and Maududi, Qutb transformed pan-Islamism from modernist reformism to radical fundamentalism.

On the other hand, in Southeast Asia, particularly for the Malay-Indonesian archipelago, a pre-Pan Islamist modernism prepared the way for Muslims to embrace more readily Arab modernism than its reception at its own place of birth. While Abduh's project in the Arab world lost steam by the second half of the last century it was more readily embraced into mainstream Islam in Southeast Asia avoiding the intra-civilizational clash unfolding in the Middle East. Modernity and moderation came hand in hand for the region. Muhammad Natsir, the former Prime Minister and leader of the Masyumi party and Abdul Malik Karim Amrullah, the scholar and novelist known to many as Hamka, were leading exponents of what they felt to be the Islamic worldview, which included the love of knowledge, promotion of democratic values and inclusiveness. Their ideas were readily and widely embraced. The writings of Sutan Takdir Alisyahbana, and Soedjatmoko among the most ardent advocates of Westernization were also well received after separating the wheat from the chaff: ideas about modernizing the education system were accepted while outright adoption of Western ways was rejected. I daresay that it is this feature of Southeast Asian Islam, and particularly Indonesian Islam, that has enabled Indonesia recently to make its quantum leap from dictatorship to democracy. Muslim social scientists could draw invaluable lessons from this rapid accommodation of Southeast Asian Islam to modernity, and perhaps better appreciate why Islamic radicalism has gained far less footing in Southeast Asia than other parts of the Muslim world. This is not to deny that radicalism can and does in fact pose a serious challenge to the region but for radically different reasons, political repression and marginalization being the chief causes – as we witnessed in Aceh until recently, and which remains a major problem in southern Thailand and the southern Philippines.

Nonetheless, back in the Arab world, as well as in the Indian subcontinent, the assault by the traditionalists struck at the very core of modernity itself – the concept of democracy. There was no question that taken to its logical conclusion, the demands of reform in the path to modernity would also warrant the adoption of democratic principles of governance. Reformist advocates cited scriptural authority and the practice of *shūrā* as well in the election of the Rightly-Guided Caliphs and asserted that the sanctity of the majority vote was not even a Western construct. Traditionalists, on the other hand, led by Sayyid Qutb, countered with even 'higher' scriptural authority – Western democracy was a usurpation of God's sovereignty and was tantamount to idolatry. It was a matter of *tawḥīd*, which gave Islam its distinctive feature of cohesion binding all Muslims within a universal Ummah. It was further argued that the moral foundations of the Ummah would be undermined by this elevation of man's rational thought over God's sovereignty. According to Maududi, democracy slowly developed its positive idea of claiming the absolute freedom of the people to legislate and to select governments accountable to their interest and ambitions. However, once the will of the majority is acknowledged as the ultimate source of law, there is question as to whether that majority will remain faithful to the principles that should govern the just Islamic society. A majority unbounded by the constraints of the *'ulamā'* would inevitably lead to chaos and corruption. Whereas secularism detached people from the restraining bonds of religious morality, and nationalism made them intoxicated with arrogant selfishness, democracy opened the floodgates to uncontrollable acts of plunder, aggression and tyranny.[12]

We could gloss over this historical perspective and consign it to the realm of academia on the ground that we are already in the 21st century. I have consistently cited Turkey and Indonesia as the best two examples of democracy in action among the most populous Muslim nations; there indeed is life after military dictatorships. The impending accession of Turkey into the European Union is another statement as to the level of liberal democracy attained while in the race for democracy in Southeast Asia, Indonesia has already reached the finishing line leaving its Muslim neighbours still stuck at the starting block. As such, I would hesitate to dismiss the historical perspective as merely academic for indeed varying interpretations may be given to these events as well as valuable lessons may be drawn. Montesquieu made a great impression on the Egyptian reformists in advocating the theory of the rise and fall of great nations but we would have thought that the same lesson was imparted by Ibn Khaldūn centuries earlier. As Iranian scholar Abdolkarim Soroush has argued, the history of Islam is fundamentally a history of different interpretations, of the different schools of thought, and of the different approaches of what Islam is.[13]

It is true that secularism has seen a major retreat in the West, if not already altogether passé. Nationalism in Europe is all but dead. There is no doubt that the West is seeing a revival of spiritualism. Yet in the Muslim world, there still prevails the fear that the spirit of individual reason and free inquiry will undermine the Ummah, and this fear is compounded by the activities of ultra liberal Muslims who profess an ideology even more secular than their Western counterparts. These new zealots brandish their cultural theology and advocate that Islam has little to offer as a guide to life in this globalized world, and that religious knowledge has resulted in a narrow Muslim vision of knowledge and is singularly responsible for the decline of the Islamic civilization. Under the weight of such incessant attacks, the resultant backlash in Muslim predominant countries is renewed fundamentalism with an increasingly hostile face. Being no longer a response to colonial conquest or military confrontation, this neofundamentalism becomes a response to acculturation, exacerbating intra-societal tensions.[14]

For Muslim social scientists of the modernist persuasion, there seems validity in the argument that the Islamic worldview as articulated by the traditional 'ulamā' continues to be divorced from contemporary realities, still plagued by the fear that the spirit of individual reason and free inquiry will undermine the moral fabric of the Ummah. We shall not attempt to reenter the ancient polemics between the Ash'arites and Mu'tazilites, but suffice it to say that the Qur'an reminds us that Allah will exalt to higher ranks those who believe and those who have knowledge, "[and] God will exalt by [many] degrees those of you who have attained to faith and, [above all,] such as have been vouchsafed [true] knowledge" (al-Mujādilah, 58:11).

Democracy, Jihad and Complicity with Tyranny

Throughout the last century, there have been attempts to create a truly Islamic state, its ultimate objective being the attainment of a just polity premised on the Qur'an and the Sunnah. However, being essentially a reaction to Western imperialism, these attempts invariably were linked to the concept of jihad even though we know that primarily jihad is a doctrine of sacrifice for the preservation of faith. Traditionally, jihad was interpreted to sanction war against enemies of the religion and had provided a moral framework for regulating the ensuing conflicts. What about rebellion against the state? The conventional view grounded on a hadith points to the principle that if a ruler orders something that is contrary to the Shari'ah Muslims were at liberty to rebel. This view has been extended to justify acts against all forms of oppression. Today, jihad has been invoked by certain quarters to legitimize acts of violence in varied forms and guises, blurring the line between jihad and terrorism.

With the exception of Turkey, the post-war experiments of Muslim countries with democratic institutions ended in unmitigated failure, returning to power instead corrupt regimes of tyranny and repression. We are by now familiar with the United States policy of ambivalence both prior to and now in the era of the war on terror, supporting autocrats in the Muslim world on the one hand, and championing the cause of freedom and democracy on the other. But why point the finger at the United States alone when we know that we ourselves share in the blame. As Shaykh Muhammad al-Ghazali puts it, it is telling, to see how Muslims are treated in Muslim countries and under Muslim governments and how other countries, such as Israel or Britain or the United States, for instance, treat their own citizens. Human life and the dignity of man appear to have a much lower value and command less respect in Muslim countries ... it is difficult under current conditions, to see how Muslims can expect to earn God's support and fulfill their task as leaders of mankind.[15]

We are only too familiar with the 1992 bloodbath in Algeria, which saw the banning of the FIS (Front Islamique de Salut) just as it was becoming certain that the Islamist party was about to be legitimately brought to power. Thousands are known to have been abducted by "eradicators." And notwithstanding a protracted civil war, the oligarchs continue their stranglehold on power. Morocco has likewise used the bogey of terrorism and fundamentalism to resist political reform and the powers that be continue to brook no dissent. The banning of the Muslim Welfare party in Turkey is another instance of the denial of political liberty, though thankfully this is one country which has been able to walk through the storm and come out even stronger and more vibrant. Thus, as an aside, to talk of a "democratic arena of citizenship" is therefore anathema because we know that the existence of free democratic thought is not possible without the active support of the State. And we have just iterated beyond doubt that most Muslim states, secular or sacred, have displayed a notorious history of tyranny and oppression.

We can go on ad nauseam about this appalling state of affairs in our own backyard but the fact is that the West has also to blame. It too has a long track record of supporting military dictatorships during the past half century. We know too that Mohammed Mossadegh, for example, was legitimately elected by the people in Iran but was removed from power in a coup led by British and US intelligence agencies. Even in Lebanon and the Palestinian state today, the United States is complicit in the aggression against these two nascent Muslim democracies. And now one-third of the Muslim population who live in non-Muslim countries, are getting the short end of the stick on account of democracy being eroded at their expense for the sins of terrorists.

Still, there is no denying that the West offers at least in theory freedom and democracy – fundamental liberties, civil society, and representative government. But if we cast the net wide over Muslim countries, it will be a small catch indeed – we have already alluded to Turkey being the first and until recently the only Muslim nation with clear democratic institutions, a market economy and a free society, notwithstanding its ups and downs. Indonesia of course is now a respectable second entrant into this arena. If democracy is about giving dignity to the human spirit, then freedom is the *sine qua non*. Within Islam, freedom is considered one of the higher objectives of the divine law in as much as the very same elements in a constitutional democracy become moral imperatives in Islam – freedom of conscience, freedom to speak out against tyranny, a call for reform and the right to property. The recent victories by Islamist radicals have caused certain quarters to be alarmed about the future of democracy. They say it means the rejection of democracy and freedom. But we already know that all but two Muslim nations ruled by secular regimes are tyrannies and dictatorships of varying degrees on the one hand and autocratic regimes and sham democracies on the other, and as such have been the breeding ground for precisely those radical elements that we hope to diffuse by establishing democratic societies.

Undoubtedly, democracy and freedom are at the core of our discourse and, to my mind, acquire greater significance around the presence of substantial Muslim communities in the West, whose democratic institutions are under attack all in the name of the war on terror. 'National security' has now ominously taken on the hue of political persecution even in established democracies, and there are legitimate concerns to be addressed as we see the increasing tendencies to allow the erosion of fundamental liberties, not just because they are occurring in places with the presence of significant Muslim minorities, but because they should not be condoned anywhere. If the notion of the universalism of Islam is to mean anything, it would require that its values of justice, compassion and tolerance be practiced everywhere. Can we remain blind to the injustice perpetrated in non-Muslim countries? Should we not also relate to the suffering of other minorities in Muslim countries? Needless to say, our condemnation against the violation of human rights must transcend race, colour or creed.

An Islamic worldview cannot be articulated without giving preeminence to the heart of the Islamic message, which is first and foremost a message of love and understanding, of compassion and tolerance and of peace. It tells us to strive for justice, fight oppression and oppose tyranny. There are many tribes and communities, cultures and languages, and all these will impinge directly on our worldview. Yet we must never lose sight of the fact that humankind is only one.

REFERENCES

ʿAbduh, Muhammad, *Risalat al-Tauhid* [*The Theology of Unity*] (Allen and Unwin, 1966).

Addas, Claude, *Quest for the Red Sulphur – The Life of Ibn Arabi*, trans. Peter Kingsley (Cambridge: The Islamic Texts Society, 1993).

Ali, Syed Ameer, *The Spirit of Islam – A History of the Evolution and Ideals of Islam* (London: Chatto & Windus, 1974).

Al-Attas, Syed Muhammad Naquib, *Islam and Secularism* (Kuala Lumpur: International Institute of Islamic Thought and Civilisation, 1993).

Al-Faruqi, Ismaʿil R., *Islamisation of Knowledge* (Herndon: International Institute of Islamic Thought, 1982).

Al-Ghazālī, Shaykh Muhammad, *A Thematic Commentary on the Qur'an*, trans. Ashur A. Shamis (Herndon: International Institute of Islamic Thought, 2000).

Hourani, Albert, *Arabic Thought in the Liberal Age, 1798–1939* (Cambridge: Cambridge University Press, 1983).

Husayn, Taha, *Mustaqbal al-Thaqāfah fī-Miṣr* (Cairo: 1938).

Iqbal, Muhammad, *The Reconstruction of Religious Thought in Islam* (Kazi Publications, 1999).

Maududi, Sayyid Abul A'la, *The Islamic Way of Life*, 11th edn. (Lahore: Islamic Publications, 1979).

Qutb, Sayyid, *Maʿālim fī al-Ṭarīq* [Milestones].

Rahman, Fazlur, *Islam and Modernity – Transformation of an Intellectual Tradition* (Chicago: The University of Chicago Press, 1982).

Roy, Oliver, *The Failure of Political Islam*, trans. Carol Volk, (Cambridge: Harvard University Press, 1996).

Soroush, Abdolkarim, *Reason, Freedom, and Democracy in Islam* (Oxford University Press, 2000).

Al-Ṭahṭāwī, Rifāʿah Rāfiʿ, *Al-Murshid al-Amīn li al-Banāt wa al-Banīn* (Cairo, (1872–1873).

H. A. HELLYER

From Tolerance to Recognition to Beyond: The Dynamics of Defining Muslim Space in Europe

Introduction

THE CITIZENSHIP DEBATE has followed from the multiculturalism debate in Europe and elsewhere, bringing us to the point where Muslim communities, particularly in the 'West' are trying to cope with what Islam offers as guidance on the issues of 'belonging' and patriotism. However, the Muslim community has not yet fully examined what the full weight of Islamic teachings has borne down on the concepts and values of the citizenship debate, as well as the integration debate; a more thorough deconstruction of these areas is required before comprehensive understanding can be begun. Such a deconstruction is an encyclopedic endeavour, but some initial thoughts can be given here.

The Perpetual 'Other': Muslims in Europe and the Multi-Culturalist Experiment[1]

> Whether the hyperrealistic 'Other' of urgent history is controlled or feared, remains to be seen, but what is for sure, is that in the foreseeable future, Europe's 'Other' will remain undoubtedly Muslim.[2]

It is difficult to find a country in the world that has absolute uniformity in terms of religious identity. Whether this is the self-proclaimed Jewish state, the heartlands of Islam, or the Catholic states of southern and western Europe, no state today is completely devoid of religious diversity. The reality on the 'ground'[3] is very clear; Europeans live in societies that are multi-cultural and multi-religious, even if they are not run according to multiculturalist principles or a universalist religious philosophy. Saying a country is multicultural is a statement of empirical observation;

saying a country is multiculturalist is an identification of political ideology. Germany was also 'multicultural' in a certain manner in the era leading up to the Holocaust, but it is rather obvious that Nazism was not a multiculturalist philosophy.

Ideologies such as Nazism and other extreme forms of ethno-nationalism heavily affected the development of political philosophy in Europe, and on the issue of multiculturalism as a philosophy, the debate became heated and multi-faceted. This took place, it must be noted, during a time when European identities were heavily contested notions; contested by their own internal sub-European dimensions, as well as European integration (the intra-European dimension) and beyond Europe (the supra-European dimension).

The basic question that theorists involved in this debate pose themselves is relatively simple: are the claims of minority groups just? If the arguments involved were simplified for purposes of discussion, and viewed some decades ago, the answers to this question dividing the 'multiculturalists' and their opponents would be neatly distinct from one another. The 'multiculturalist' would answer 'yes' and their opponents would answer 'no.'

Critics of multiculturalism would have generally insisted that justice demanded that the state act 'colour-blind' and by extension, treat every single individual precisely the same, with little or no regard, positive or negative, for the different attributes of the individual. Any other course of action would be considered to be necessarily discriminatory, and *hence*, unjust. These criticisms would generally belong to the nationalist and, to a greater degree, a particular take on the liberal theory of governance.[4]

The multiculturalists also formulated support for their position in the language of justice, and insisted that differential treatment was sometimes not only permitted by the concept of 'justice' but also *demanded* by it. To treat every single individual precisely the same would necessarily result in, in some cases, injustice. The multiculturalists noted that in fact no state institution was remotely 'procedural' (i.e., culturally neutral) but was actually favourable towards the majority group, consciously or unconsciously, and might therefore discriminate against minority groups, even if unintentionally. The standard pluralist position within the multiculturalist school noted that with the growth of diversity in terms of language, identity and culture in modern states, typical notions of justice could not cope adequately.[5]

The Current Debate: Moving beyond Respect for Difference

However, as Kymlicka notes insightfully,[6] the debate has shifted. Few thinkers, if any, in contemporary 'Western'[7] political philosophical thought, promote the idea that justice can be achieved through 'difference-blind rules.' This is no longer, by definition, the dividing line *per se*; few thinkers, if any, argue that justice can be achieved through 'difference-blind rules.' The debate has moved on and political thinkers, as well as politicians, know that the rules of the game have changed. Arguing about political philosophy without having a modicum of respect for diversity and difference is a losing combination in today's European scene. The proponents of multiculturalism have, to date, effectively made their case. How much respect is required, however, is still a subject for discussion. It should be noted very clearly that this article is not entirely concerned with abstract theoretical discussions of what normative political theory should be; rather, what is described is contemporary civil society. If it was a purely theoretical discussion, then the normative basis might be something quite different, but politics is, after all, the art of the possible.[8]

Critics have generally accepted (passively, if not by conviction) that injustice is likely if notice of pluralism is not taken, but they now focus 'on the way that the general trend towards multiculturalism threatens to erode the sorts of civic virtues, identities and practices which sustain a healthy democracy.'[9] Such erosion would be likely under an extreme form of the procedural model,[10] which is in itself a radical position from within the multiculturalist school. Some level of commonality, it is argued, is necessary for social cohesion, which is necessary for a viable and healthy European democracy. What level of commonality: that is the new basic question.

> The last ten years have witnessed a remarkable upsurge of interest in two topics amongst political philosophers: the rights and status of ethno cultural minorities in multi-ethnic societies (the 'minority rights-multiculturalism debate), and the virtues, practices and responsibilities of democratic citizenship (the 'citizenship-civic virtue' debate).[11]

From Tolerance to Recognition to Beyond

The critics of multiculturalism no longer articulate their arguments on the basis of justice. The detailed censure of multiculturalism now takes place on a different field of argument: the citizenship-civic virtue debate. Likewise, the reverse is also true. The two debates operated in parallel before; they could now even be mistaken for the same debate, linked inextricably together. Any debate where multiculturalism becomes criticised leads to the citizenship-civic virtue discussion, and any debate where an inclusive citizenship is proposed inevitably discusses multiculturalism. The 'citizenship-civic virtue' and 'minority rights-multiculturalism' debates are precisely where the rights of the minority over the majority and vice versa are now discussed.

In the debates, it is now admitted that numerically minor communities have specific needs and requirements that should be significantly considered. The first arena of discussion, the 'citizenship-civic virtue debate' has two tendencies, which Modood describes in the following way, each of which emphasises certain rights:

(i) The right to assimilate to the majority/dominant culture in the public sphere and toleration of 'difference' in the private sphere alone.
(ii) The right to have one's 'difference' (minority, ethnicity, etc.) recognized and supported in the public and the private spheres.

The first is generally portrayed as the 'assimilation' tendency, whilst the latter would be called the 'integration' tendency. This is certainly oversimplifying matters but the basic parameters are thus laid down, showing how the debates have shifted. Classical assimilationist thought would assume that even in private spaces, a degree of assimilation should take place. Yet in this debate, both tendencies recognise that those who are different from the majority may be considered as accepted by the mainstream, but they differ on what this might mean in practice. How far must the minority go before being accepted? What differences should the majority accept? What sort of compromises should each side make, and on what basis should they be made? In other words, what are the bare requirements of citizenship?

The first approach might also be called 'liberal' but its important feature is the assumption, as Modood notes, 'that participation in the public or national culture is necessary for the effective exercise of citizenship, the only obstacle to which are the exclusionary processes preventing gradual assimilation.' Modood insists, with a compelling case, that this should be supported to a point, with a confirmation that one may keep one's distinct ethnic identity as it becomes included as part of the national culture through time: 'Grounding equality in uniformity also has unfortunate consequences. It requires us to treat human beings equally in those respects in which they are similar and not those in which they are different.'[12] Hence, to scholars, such as Modood, equal treatment does not mean assimilation to the national culture in all things, and the national culture should gradually change to incorporate the culture of ethnic minorities as time goes on.

In the EU specifically, there are currently two main expressions of this liberal model, with some variations. The first has a good example in the French dominant paradigm, and it found its most recent and poignant manifestation in the *l'affaire du foulard* in September 1989. For those who demanded that the Muslim schoolgirls take off their headscarfs, France was 'a single and indivisible nation based on a single culture.'[13] The state was to aggressively and positively pursue a policy of assimilation; differences were to be accepted only if they were not judged to be against the principles of French culture, which are universal (sic). To follow a different path would be to deny the universal nature of French culture, and further, to invite a threat against it. In practice, this meant the French state banning 'ostentatious symbols' being worn in school; what 'ostentatious' referred to, however, was well known. Yet, until December 2003, individual schools were given the freedom to choose or not to choose to enforce this particular interpretation; the French state then formally decided to ban the headscarf in public schools, with ten federal states in Germany following suit shortly thereafter.

Another example of the liberal model leaning towards an assimilationist interpretation rather than a pluralistic one was found in the UK, albeit with slightly different reasoning, more pluralistic in nature. Until recently, the UK government had consistently rejected funding Muslim schools, although thousands of Anglican, Catholic and Jewish schools are so funded. Some of those that defended this disparity insisted that the state should not be funding religious schools in general or that to fund Muslim schools would be to fund a reactionary religion that would then attack the state. Furthermore, whilst other religious schools managed to come to a balance of secular and religiously inspired knowledge after a long struggle, Muslim schools would not be so able.

It is important to note that in most of these cases, and other similar cases, students of Muslim background were not forbidden education. On the contrary; they were invited, on the whole with enthusiasm to participate in education, but only on the terms acceptable to the authorities. They might look different and in their private capacities behave differently, but in the eyes of the state, they would be the same as their non-Muslim counterparts and be treated 'equally.' Those who made such arguments often thought they were indeed being fair, as they did not ask the minorities to pursue a course they would not be willing to pursue. In the UK, this argument was slightly different, for there the arguments were based on a particular discriminatory attitude; non-Anglican schools had been funded for many years, so it was not merely a question of how narrow the vision of the national culture was. There was indeed educational pluralism, for Catholics and Jews, but not for Muslims.

Theoretically, from a particular standpoint (that of the majority), the idea of equality might seem like a perfectly just concept on which to base educational policy. What the French in particular were offering was indeed equality but on the basis of uniformity, a typical liberal model. Practically, however, as the pluralistic critique emphasises, the world is most certainly not uniform. Were the world, the EU or a single state, homogenous in every way, equal treatment would involve identical treatment; yet, in every state, not least the EU, there are differences according to sex, ethnicity and religion, as well as a number of other characteristics. Once this is taken into account, identical treatment does not result in equal treatment; rather, it provides for a situation where certain members are 'more equal than others.' In political theory, as can be seen above, the discussion has moved on; in politics as well, the scene has changed.

'Europe will Succumb': The Fears of the European Political Centre

As noted earlier, Britain and the rest of Europe are at a new stage of the discussion: the definition of 'citizen.' It is no longer a question of agreeing on how important it is to respect diversity: it is a question of 'what brings us together and makes us special' as Britons, Europeans and so forth. The citizenship debate is in full force, and the discussion as to what defines a Frenchman, a Briton, a German and so on, is raging on.

In that discussion, a centre-ground where Left and Right congregate seems to have been established on two points. The first is that diversity should be respected; justice demands it. The second is that there must be a common idea of self and belonging; justice demands it. Beyond the idea of justice, there is a deep-rooted fear involved as well, making the discussion fairly urgent, and likely to be *the* political issue of the majority of the political spectrum for the coming decades. This is a fear that goes beyond the right wing; this is a fear that crosses ideological boundaries in certain ways. The European Union is a place where identities have become contested, on the individual and the collective level, not simply on the Right, but in society in general.

For those who hold this fear, terrorism is not particularly the main issue. It is a side effect, a short-term problem of a wider concern – the fear that Islam will become a force that will eventually displace modern Western civilisation in Europe, and cause the end of Europe as it is known.

Europe is treading a very dangerous path. Two things can happen in Europe:

1. 'Islam is left alone to grow unchecked, which means Europe will succumb to Islamism before the end of this century. Or
2. The Europeans sense the danger too late, panic, and give birth to Eurofascism to counter Islamofascism.'

This is how Ali Sina, a former Muslim, analysed the future, and it is an analysis that seems to be gaining adherents. In this context, the European Union is seen as pandering to an 'Islam' and a Muslim community that is bent on destroying Europe from the inside. The European Union, as the upholder of European institutions, is seen as aiding and abetting in that aim (naively), an attitude described as 'dhimmitude.'[14] Websites, such as 'jihadwatch.org' and 'faithfreedom.org,' are radical in content, but they are not as marginal as they might appear. The fear of the end of Europe in the future owing to a Muslim presence is one shared by many of the left as well as the right and in the centre, across the EU. Whether it is Oriana Fallaci[15] in Italy or Melanie Phillips in the UK,[16] there is a common thread at work here. Europe as we know it is under threat from a large Muslim European presence, and multiculturalism, cultural relativism and appeasement in Europe is assisting in the fulfilment of that threat.

The collapse of old European identities is due to the European Union project, and it is creating a ripe, fertile ground for the Green Menace. Europe will either succumb to Islam by becoming Muslim or by becoming *dhimmī*s (free non-Muslim subjects living in Muslim countries who in return for paying capital tax enjoyed protection by the state), or it will destroy itself through civil war.

There is an inordinate amount of websites out at the moment that detail a composed fear of Islam and Muslims, with regards to the future of Europe. As far as they are concerned, Europe is committing suicide by allowing Muslims to remain in such high numbers there. One of the websites is actually called 'suicideofthewest.com.'

Large sections on the right and the left, growing in momentum, are united on this fear that Islam will become a force that will eventually displace modern Western civilisation in Europe, and cause the end of Europe. In this context, the European Union is seen as pandering to an 'Islam;' an attitude of 'dhimmitude,' strengthened by treasonous philosophies such as multiculturalism. The collapse of old European identities is due to the European Union project, and it is creating a ripe, fertile ground for the Green Menace. Here it can be seen how a fear of Islam (precisely Islamophobia) combines with a rejection of multiculturalism, and a desire to scapegoat Muslims vis-à-vis the modern European identity crisis.

The Main Political Actors: The Centre and the Right
The most populist visions in this debate are being put forward by the Centre-Right and the Far-Right. Whereas the Left was able to put forward strong critiques of national identities that allowed for multiculturalism to flourish in the 80s and the 90s, as of yet, it has fallen to the Right and the Centre Right to put forward strong critiques of multiculturalism in the context of building up cohesive national identities. The centre at present tends towards the Right, not the Left.

Huge swathes of Europe are going through an identity crisis, in the context of demographic changes owed to migration patterns, Europe integration, modernity, globalisation and the US-EU relationship. In that background, and the background of a set of European states that are built on national identities with long historical pedigrees, without much of a history of inbuilt pluralism (at least on the scale necessary), the discussion of 'what it means to be a European' has taken on a sense of urgency. This will likely be the most pertinent political issue for decades to come. It is for this reason that the Far-Right has begun to find popularity again in Europe. Those sections of the political spectrum have always taken these issues in the context of nationalism quite seriously. The Far-Right is stigmatised in Europe, and thus their popularity is relatively low; the amount of interest that issues they campaign on, on the other hand, is quite large.

It is clear from the above that the political debate in this arena has shifted in two ways – ideationally/theoretically and politically. From the perspective of ideas and theories, respect for diversity is now taken for granted, but the new battleground of ideas is where the limits of diversity are to be delineated. From the perspective of politics, it is evident that the Right and the Centre-Right are most actively engaging with the delineation process. These are shifts of significant proportion. What has not changed, however, is the lack of a strong Muslim element as a proactive component.

The Lack of an Active Muslim Element in the Discussion

In the 80s and early 90s, Muslims were a part of the discussion – as subjects, not as actors. As mentioned above, the result of that phase of the discussion did not turn out too badly, but it was done in spite of the Muslim non-contribution, not because of it. The Left essentially carried their interests.

Part of this has remained the case in the current phase of the discussion. Historically, the sections of society that Muslim communities have heavily engaged with are *not* the sections that are most involved in this debate. The example of Britain is used as an example, but similarities can be seen all over Europe. The Left, the Centre-Left, the Far-Left – these are the sections that Muslim communities have been most active within, or engaged with. The old bastions of the British Labour Party, to a lesser extent the Liberal Democrats, the Stop-the-War movement, and so forth, although the centre Left 'New Labour' has begun to engage within this discussion (notably the Fabian Society),[17] it is the more right wing sections of British society that are most active. The largest proportion of British society is on the centre and the Centre-Right; not on the left where Muslims are active, and it is the Centre/Centre-Right that has been and is likely to remain the most involved in this discussion about defining the parameters of national identity.

There are a few exceptions – Tariq Ramadan, for example, is often quoted. His discourse of universal common values[18] is sometimes more abstract than locally or nationally based, but it is constructive and relevant. In general, however, there has been either silence or responses that do not resonate on the centre-ground at all. In the aftermath of the Home Secretary's pronouncements on English needing to be a requirement of British citizenship, one Muslim commentator insisted that this was absurd. When pressed about what he would require for citizenship, he answered 'five years residency, no criminal record.' This was a model that would be rejected out of hand by the mainstream, without any consideration, in the present political climate, and for the foreseeable future. The result in such a scenario would be the expulsion of a Muslim element to the debate.

This example is obviously extreme. In Muslim community organisations, there is not a rejection of an integration process, but the general trend appears to be more towards a defiant reassertion of identity politics, which may be connected to the mainstream, but ultimately, is distinct and separate from a mainstream indigenous identity. It is not wholly unsurprising, considering the discrimination and social prejudice that presently exists. Nevertheless, that ideational trend carries less than significant currency with the centre and Centre-Right, where the real discussion is ensuing for the future of national identities in Britain specifically and Europe as a whole.

This bears deep consideration because if the discussion becomes exclusively an extreme right-wing affair without direct Muslim input that is both meaningful and sustainable (and thus taken seriously), the results could be greatly debilitating to a sustainable Muslim presence. In short, Muslims could be doubly affected if the Eurabia paranoia continues. The current intellectual framework does not make this discussion particularly easy. The 'elephant' in the 'room' where citizenship is discussed and argued about remains the same: racism. That notion remains destructive and ruptures the progress that might take place if it is not recognised and correctly resolved. At some point, however, the discussion may have to transcend the point where it currently is.

Current Muslim Identity Political Formation

The following does not purport to be a structured ten-point plan for locating a Muslim response and engagement to the current European identity crisis. It is only meant to be an articulation of what *some* of the relevant questions might be in a discussion relating to identity politics.

For pre-modern Muslims, to be a Muslim was to follow the principles of the Qur'an and the Sunnah. This was a spiritual connection that certainly permeated through all fields, including how to filter identities. This was the extent of its 'value' as an 'identity': it is difficult to prove that it was ever thought of as an identity *per se*, at least vis-à-vis how identity is commonly defined in political and ethnic-identity discourses. The opposite anti-thesis of classical Muslim 'identity' was also about principles: injustice, unethical actions, ungratefulness and so forth. The condemnations that took place in the Qur'an applied to Muslims as well as non-Muslims when they partook of these attributes. The Muslim 'group' *per se* did not exist as an ethno-cultural category but as an ideational one based on principles. Culture was derived from those principles and thus a group could emerge; neither culture nor 'the group' was the basis for 'Muslimness,' but both were natural outcomes.

Modernity places a high value on the concept of a unique cultural identity; this is true the world over, and in every community. It is not a uniquely Muslim trait. Amin Maalouf[19] notes a patently obvious fact in his book *In the Name of Identity*, that human beings have a multitude of identities, ranging from cultural to local, that simultaneously exist. The Prophet himself had a clear Arab cultural identity, as can be seen from the biographies of the period, but this did not detract from his clearly human identity, which can also be seen in the same material. What Maalouf has not noted is that while human beings in general should respect the reality of pluralistic identities, an identity of 'Muslim' was not necessarily part of that discourse historically. Again, keeping in mind what 'identity' generally purports to relate to in modern identity politics.

Assuming there is a 'Muslim identity' is tantamount to assuming that the concept of a 'Muslim' is comparable to the idea of an ethno-cultural identity such as 'English' or 'Pakistani,' and can thus be placed in a hierarchical relationship to each another. In other words, they are both in the same category of analysis. This assumption about the philosophy of these concepts should not be taken uncritically: identities are typically ethno-cultural; whereas the basis of the Muslim 'identity' historically was ethical and spiritual, not ethnic or cultural. As such the Muslim 'identity' cannot quite be analysed in that context; it is on a different level of enquiry and category of analysis.

Pre-modern societies seem to have understood this very well, and as such, the question of 'Muslim first' and thus the construction of a 'Muslim identity' did not take place. This is not to say that the concept of 'Muslim' is non-existent, which would be non-sensical, but that it has been defined as a concept according to the law of Islam (the Shariʿah), not as an identity that can serve as a substitute or competing cultural identity. It is on another level, as it were, of identification.

The same can be said for the political cause of Muslims, which exists just as the early prophetic community existed as a political force. Human beings are, as Aristotle said, political animals. It is only natural, therefore, that moral human beings will seek answers to political problems and issues that are congruent with their moral sanctuaries – in the case of Muslims, the precepts of the Divine Word and the Messenger.

A relationship between Islam and culture cannot be denied, a topic that U.F. Abd-Allah has explored,[20] but Islam itself is not a culture *per se*. In the spreading of Islam across the globe, different cultures arose, all 'Islamic' in so far as they adhered to the Shariʿah, but not all part of the same culture. If it were otherwise, all Muslims would all look and sound like Qurayshi Arabs (the tribe of the Prophet); they do not and their tradition did not argue for that. Rather, Islam filters and sieves cultures according to whether aspects of the culture are *ḥalāl* or *ḥarām*.

Nor need it be said that identities themselves are in and of themselves necessarily harmful, for every human being partakes in multiple identities based on his or her circumstances, ranging from gender, social class, place of birth, place of residence and so forth. The Qur'an and the prophetic example do not appear to deny that multiple identities, and multiple *types* of identity may exist within a single individual, but includes a caveat and a prescription from the point of view of Muslim canon law: that the spiritual matrix of the Shariʿah guides them, and if necessary, overrides their concerns.

Nationalism, Identities and Muslim Identity Politics
With the advent of modern nationalism, culture and political identity

became interwoven with one another. Many Muslim political movements, led by political elites, were not immune to that type of discourse and logic, leading to two of the great ironies of modern Islamist politics. Comparing the discourses, the reasoning and the postulates of various nationalist and Islamist political movements reveals some parallels, even while *ʿaṣabiyyah* (tribalism) was condemned in a virulent way from the pulpit and the presses. They share the common desire to define a group, and to define the concerns of that group as a group even if in a Machiavellian manner, rather than according to moral precepts. Just as tribalist discourse will argue 'my nation, right or wrong,' so too will 'identity merchants'[21] propound a similar statement: my Ummah, right or wrong, my *ṭarīqah*, right or wrong, my *madhhab* co-affiliates, right or wrong.

This impulse is particularly problematic from classical Islamic teachings, which indicate ethics about group concerns (see the Qur'an chapter 4, verse 135). Hence, al-Awzāʿī, a legal scholar who founded his own school of law (similar to the extant schools that were founded by Abū Ḥanīfah, Mālik, al-Shāfiʿī and Aḥmad), declared that God would give victory to a just non-Muslim country over an unjust Muslim one. The criterion was justice (an ethic), not religious affiliation (a group mentality). Medieval discussions on the subject denounced all kinds of tribalism (*ʿaṣabiyyah*) and *taʿaṣṣub* (partiality). 'What is ethical' trumps all else, even the political needs of the Ummah; what is ethical *is, par excellence, the political need of the Ummah*.

The second irony of modern Islamist politics is that this methodology has a historical precedent amongst a people bound by faith. Some Jewish interpretations of nationalism beget Zionism, the erstwhile adversary of all Islamist political movements.[22]

Muslim Nationalism, Jewish Nationalism, Nationalism and Islam

As noted earlier, there is already a historical precedent for a nationalist movement based on religious affiliation, which is Jewish nationalism, otherwise commonly known as Zionism. The Jewish nation, the Children of Israel, exists, much as the Muslim nation, the Ummah of Muhammad, exists. But whereas classical Orthodox Jewish scholars defined the Children of Israel to be those who follow the precepts of the message of the prophets of Israel, and thus of God, dominant interpretations of modern Zionism (and there are different strands that should be kept in mind) has altered the paradigm. As far as classical Judaism was concerned, to be a Jew, one had to follow the Torah. If one renounced it, as many have done, then membership in the Jewish nation was rescinded; one might not fulfil the precepts, but this made one a sinner, not necessarily a disbeliever.

Some forms of modern political Zionism, despite the rigorous opposition of classical Orthodox Judaism, disagreed. The message of the Israelite prophets, the guidance of God, was no longer what defined membership in the Jewish Ummah; rather, the Jewish people defined membership. Thus, God and His message were placed at an inferior basis to the nation; the equation had been reversed. The Ummah of the Jews now possessed the *dīn*, rather than the *dīn* being the guide to their own Possessor: the Almighty Divine.

De Haan, an associate of Muhammad Asad (the translator of the Qur'an) said once:

> We Jews were driven away from the Holy Land and scattered all over the world because we had fallen short of the task God conferred upon us. We had been chosen by Him to preach his word, but in our stubborn pride, we began to believe that He had made us a chosen nation for our own sake and thus we betrayed Him.[23]

The 'Chosen People' had a meaning in classical Judaism 'those who had been chosen to serve,' rather than 'those who had been privileged.' There was certainly a group mentality that emerged as a side effect to there being a group from amongst humanity who were chosen, but this group mentality had its place. The omnipotence of God and the precepts of His message were above and beyond the 'group.' Many Jewish thinkers construed any association between the two as idolatry, a betrayal of Him, as de Haan notes.

If this is considered in the light of modern discourse amongst Muslims, there are some salient congruencies to be observed. As one author long ago realised, whereas pre-modern Muslim communities would think along the lines of 'God and His Prophet say,' today the speech of many Muslims is filled with statements such as 'Islam says,' which leads to 'We the Muslims say,' perhaps laying the groundwork for a democratic conception of belief that will eventually do away with the need for a Divine altogether, as what happened in some followings of modern Jewry.

The message of the Qur'an is clear that it is not 'group membership' that defines one's being a Muslim, regardless of one's actions on behalf of one's co-religionists, or one's distinctness vis-à-vis other groups (a group mentality). Rather, it is the act of submission to the will of God (an idea) that defines one's being a Muslim. *Aṣabiyyah* (tribalism), on the other hand, is one quality that the believer is defined in contradistinction to by the Prophet as related in the corpuses of his statements: 'He that calls for *asabiyyah* is not one of us; neither the one who fights for *asabiyyah* is one of us, nor the one who shows anger out of *asabiyyah*.'

The contemporary Shāfiʿī jurist, Muhammad Afifi al-Akiti, recounts the following hadith from the Prophet that sits uncomfortably with any type of superior group dynamic, laden with religious vocabulary or not:

lā yu'minu aḥadukum ḥattā yuḥibba li-akhīhi mā yuḥibbu li-nafsihi [None of you believes until he wants for his brother what he would want for himself.]

Imam Najm al-Dīn al-Ṭūfī, the Ḥanbalī commentator, more plainly than any other medieval interpreter of this hadith, used the expression *maḥabbat al-insān* [the love for mankind]; not love of Muslims, or 'the group.'

'Muslim identity' as 'Islamic Transformation'

Beyond the injunctions against tribalism above that make the entire discourse from Muslim 'identity-merchants' awkward, there is one other critical concern. How does this discourse impinge on the concept of *niyyah* (intention) for Muslims, which is a core concept of Islam?

The totality of the inheritors of the Prophetic message, the Ummah, clearly has defining features. There are obviously rites and rituals that apply only to them, and not necessarily to others. The five pillars of Islam are pillars of Islam, and not applicable for human beings who are not Muslim. As such, in the modern age, where rites are used (or misused) as symbols, the outward practices of Islam are commandeered to certify and secure a 'Muslim identity.'

Nevertheless, this misappropriation can bypass the point of those rites. The canon law of Islam, the Shariʿah has one purpose: 'to help the notoriously absentminded human race to remember its Maker.'[24] There is a story in the classical collections of prophetic statements that mentions a man who is being questioned in the grave by two angels. They ask him three questions: "Who is your lord? What is your religion? Who is your messenger?" He finds himself tongue tied and unable to answer that which every believer is expected to be able to answer. The angels ask: 'How is that possible? We saw you praying with the people who pray, paying zakah with those who pay zakah, fasting with the people who fast, and going on Hajj as well.' His answer to them is, 'I just did what I saw other people doing.'

Ultimately, his intention was of no value to him, even though it may have appeared otherwise, as it was not for God. Even though the acts were acts of worship, the acts were nullified because the intention made for them made reference to people. One of the classical jurisprudential authorities, Imam al-Shāṭibī noted that for the believer there were two possible motivations of intentions. One was revelation (i.e., an intention in line with fulfilling the remembrance of God and His Commands). The other was *hawā*, the whims and lower desires of the base ego, and only one was judged to be pure by medieval authorities.

Hence the supplication of the Prophet as related in the collection by Ibn Mājah:

> *Allāhumma ḥajjatan lā riyā'a fīhā wa lā sumʿah*
> (O Allah, (enable me to make) Hajj with no *riyā'* [showing off with the desire that others witness one's good acts] or *sumʿah* [showing off with the desire that others hear about one's good acts].

This is an injunction against seeking fame in conjunction with explicit acts of worship. Seeking fame in general is condemned by many authorities, whether personal or communal:

> You should know – may Allah bestow uprightness upon you – that the basis of status is reputation and fame, both of which are blameworthy. By contrast, anonymity is praiseworthy, except for him whom Allah, Exalted is He, has given fame in the spread of His *dīn* without him making an effort to procure it. [25]

Nevertheless, seeking fame is the basis of modern identity politics, including within the Muslim community.

This is not to say that seeking public recognition, as a community or otherwise, is unnecessary. Indeed, it may very well be necessary to provide protection for the Muslim community from various forms of discrimination. Some sort of public organisation is required, if only to be a reference point for the state when legal and civil service (not necessarily political) institutions require it. Discrimination and Islamophobia, along with legitimate questions of what Islam does and does not require of its adherents, demand such points of interaction. But at present, it appears that such organisations are entertained as a perpetual aim in and of themselves, rather than as a practical 'as needed' basis.

If the intention is any principle sanctified by God (justice, freedom, and so forth), and fame follows as a result, then it is clearly not censured. If the intention was representation, even for the representation of that principle, then representation itself tends to override the transforming nature of the principle in question, and that is reproachable. Herein lies the kernel of 'Islamic identity': sincere character and a continual transformation of self for the sake of God alone. It is difficult to see how current identity politics follows this model.

Conclusion

The above is not a definitive discussion by any means, but rather an attempt to draw attention to certain ideas and concepts that may have been assumed uncritically by present Muslim discourse. If, as Professor Yahya Michot notes,[26] the Muslim community is called to be *shuhadā' 'alā al-nās* (witnesses unto the people), then how they locate themselves within these discussions of identity, recognition and belonging is the a *priori* question.

Ibn Taymiyyah, the 11th century Ḥanbalī *faqīh*, wrote that Muslims should take on the culture of the majority non-Muslim populations that they happened to find themselves for two reasons: their continued survival, and the facilitation of the spreading of the invitation to God. The historical precedent has been that when this occurred, Islam renewed cultures that were undergoing great challenges. The challenges are quite obvious in Europe. Whether Muslims will renew them is something that has yet to be decided.

Ultimately, they have a choice between two models: being another piece of 'salad' in the 'salad bowl' of modern Europe or being the vinegar that freshens it all. Vinegar might ferment, but as readers of classical

Muslim literature will know, some types of 'wine' are not just permissible but laudable.[27]

REFERENCES

Allen, Christopher, "Endemically European or a European Epidemic? Islamophobia in a Post 9/11 Europe," in *Islam & The West: Post 9/11*. Eds. Ron Greaves, Gabriel Theodore, Yvonne Haddad, and Jane Idleman Smith (Aldershot: Ashgate, 2004).

Commission on the Future of Multi-Ethnic Britain (CFMB). The Report of the Commission of Multi-Ethnic Britain (London: Profile, 2002).

al-Ghazālī, Imam Abū Ḥāmid, Book VIII of his *Iḥyā' ʿUlūm-ud-Dīn* [The Revival of the Religious Sciences]: *The Condemnation of Status and Ostentation*, abridged by Shaykh Ahmad al-Shami, http://www.masud.co.uk/ISLAM/misc/MISC-Ghazali_status.htm

Kymlicka, Will, *Contemporary Political Philosophy: An Introduction* (Oxford: Oxford University Press, 2002).

Maalouf, Amin, *In the Name of Identity: Violence and the Need to Belong* (Arcade Publishing: USA, 2001).

Murad, Abdal Hakim, "Bombing without Moonlight" (October, 2004), http://www.masud.co.uk/ISLAM/ahm/moonlight.htm

Ramadan, Tariq, *Western Muslims and the Future of Islam* (Oxford: Oxford University Press, 2004).

Parekh, Bhikhu, *Rethinking Multiculturalism: Cultural Diversity and Political Theory* (London: Palgrave Macmillan, 2000).

Phillips, Melanie, *Londonistan* (London: Encounter Books, 2006).

Shakir, Zaid, *Scattered Pictures: Reflections of an American Muslim* (USA: NiD Publishers, 2005).

Sina, Ali, "The Fall of Europe" (2005), http://www.faithfreedom.org/oped/sina50525.htm

Talbot, Margaret, "The Agitator" (2006), http://www.newyorker.com/fact/content/articles/060605fa_fact

Abd-Allah, U.F., "Islam and the Cultural Imperative" (Nawawi Foundation, 2004), http://www.nawawi.org/downloads/article3.pdf

Ben-David, Amir, "Leopold of Arabia" (2001), http://www.haaretz.com/hasen/pages/ShArt.jhtml?itemNo=95213

"A Look at the Five Pillars of Islam," http://www.islam-australia.com.au/revert/five_pillars.htm

JEREMY HENZELL-THOMAS

Beyond The Tower of Babel: A Linguistic Approach to Clarifying Key Concepts in Islamic Pluralism

I AM SURE MOST OF US KNOW some version of the Biblical story of the Tower of Babel from the Book of Genesis[1] and even those of us who do not may be familiar with the metaphorical application of the word 'Babel' to denote a confused medley of sounds or the din of mutually incomprehensible speech.[2]

According to the Genesis account, the Tower of Babel was erected by the descendants of Nūḥ (Noah) in Shinar in a presumptuous attempt to reach up to heaven. As a punishment for their arrogant hubris, God confounded them by making the builders unable to understand each other's speech; hence, according to legend, the fragmentation of human speech into the various languages of the world, and also the dispersion of mankind over the face of the earth.

My starting point is to question the legendary belief that God's punishment was the fragmentation of human speech into different languages and the dispersion of humankind into separate races. The Qur'an does not support the idea that the diversity of languages and races is a punishment or a burden placed on mankind. On the contrary, the Qur'an is unique among the revealed scriptures of the world in the explicit manner in which it divinely ordains unity in diversity, not only in terms of culture, language and race, but also in religion.[3] Pluralism, quite simply, is part of the *fiṭrah*, the essential nature or primordial condition of the human being.

The key verses of the Qur'an are well known, but let me repeat them, because they cannot be repeated enough:

> And among His wonders is the creation of the heavens and the earth, and the

diversity of your tongues and colours: for in this, behold, there are signs indeed for all who are endowed with knowledge! (Qur'an 30:22)[4]

Unto every one of you have We appointed a [different] law and way of life.[5] And if God had so willed, He could surely have made you all one single community: but [He willed it otherwise] in order to test you by means of what He has vouchsafed unto you. Vie, then, with one another in doing good works! Unto God you all must return and then He will make you truly understand all that on which you were wont to differ. (Qur'an 5:48)[6]

Furthermore, the Qur'an tells us that we must go beyond the unchallenging mediocrity of mere tolerance of diversity and seek to "know one another."

We ... have made you into nations and tribes, so that you may come to know one another. (Qur'an 49:13)[7]

Now, we cannot truly *know* one another if our relationship with each other is little more than a kind of sullen tolerance, a "passive form of hostility," a "shaky truce," or, as is sometimes the case, an "expression of privilege."[8] Omid Safi reminds us that "the connotations of 'tolerance' are deeply problematic ... the root of the word *tolerance* comes from medieval toxicology and pharmacology, 'marking how much poison a body could "tolerate" before it would succumb to death.'" He asks: "Is this the best that we can do? Is it our task to figure out how many 'others' we can tolerate before it really kills us? Is this the most sublime height of pluralism we can aspire to?"[9] Like him, I don't want merely to 'tolerate' my fellow human beings, "but rather to engage them at the deepest level of what makes us human, through both our phenomenal commonality and our dazzling cultural differences." It is this active and open-hearted encounter and dialogue between different cultures for the purpose of affirming universal values as the urgent task before us. "The diversity of my people is a blessing,"[10] the Prophet Muhammad is reported to have said.

And it is this quality of active engagement which distinguishes the authentic Qur'anic spirit of pluralism.[11] As Diana Eck passionately argues, pluralism is a "truth-seeking encounter" which goes well beyond the passive acknowledgment or tolerance of the mere existence of plurality or cosmopolitanism, or even the celebration of it, as the cliché goes.

Tolerance "does not require us to know anything new, it does not even entertain the fact that we might change in the process."[12]

And neither can we know one another if we are indifferent to each other, or ignorant of each other's existence. Diana Eck relates how, in the Elmhurst area of Queens, a suburb of New York, a New York Times reporter found people from eleven countries on a single floor of an apartment building. There were immigrants from Korea, Haiti, Vietnam, Nigeria, and India – all living in isolation, and fear – each certain they were the only immigrants there. Diversity in a cosmopolitan city, to be sure, but not pluralism by any stretch of the imagination.[13]

Last year I went to the USA a number of times to participate in an initiative to improve education and reframe perceptions about Islam and Muslims in the USA. On the day I arrived in Washington DC on my latest trip there, there was an article in the *Washington Post* which described how mental health professionals in the USA, including psychiatrists, are finding such an increase in extreme fear and suspicion of the "other" that they believe it has reached a stage in the national consciousness where it has become an identifiable pathology which needs to be described and treated as a mental illness. Its main symptoms are irrational prejudice, a constant feeling of threat, and an incapacitating sense of isolation.

In *Perelandra*,[14] the first book of his remarkable science fiction trilogy, C.S. Lewis describes how a Cambridge philologist is kidnapped by a fellow professor and is taken on a fantastic voyage to Mars with the intention of offering him to the native population as a 'ransom' in exchange for gold. Our hero, however, makes friends with the beings that inhabit the red planet and discovers that they live a life infinitely more civilised than their counterparts on earth. The three races of conscious beings which inhabit the planet[15] are reminiscent of Norse and Germanic mythology, but there is something strikingly different about Lewis' conception. In the Norse tales, there is often conflict, rivalry and division between the different races and orders of beings, whether gods, giants, humans (both heroic and villainous), mythical beasts and dwarves, fuelled by mutual contempt, suspicion and lust for wealth and power. But on C.S. Lewis's Mars, the three races live together in perfect harmony, sharing their talents and their provisions, and never exploiting each other or the planet's resources. They acknowledge and appreciate their differences and see them as a source of strength. Their need for otherness

34

is satisfied by their mutually supporting and interdependent relationship with the people of other races. Any other agenda is simply not in their hearts. This is the primordial condition.[16]

Nancy Kline has written: "Diversity raises the intelligence of groups. Homogeneity is a form of denial."[17] Let us highlight this point that pluralism, the willingness to embrace diversity, is matter of intelligence. As we have already noted, the Qur'an tells us that in the diversity of tongues and colours, *there are signs indeed for all who are endowed with knowledge*! And what then are the signs of ignorance? Bigotry, division, dichotomisation, one-sidedness, isolationism, exclusivism, intolerance, the self-sufficient and self-interested solipsism which dismantles relationships, triumphalism, self-aggrandisement, and the fear, suspicion and hatred which demonise the "other." Already in 1882, the British diplomat, W.S. Blunt, published the book, *The Future of Islam*, which called for the need to establish a new relationship between Europe and the West based on mutual respect and recognition and the renunciation of policies and ideologies of conquest and conversion. Has there ever been a time when the revival of such vision was more sorely needed? Let us hope that Martin Luther King's vision of a world in which "our loyalties must become ecumenical rather than sectional" will be realised.

Some, however, may agree with Chandra Muzaffar's assessment that "the centres of power in the West ... are not interested in a multi-civilisational world that is based on justice, equality and respect for diversity."[18]

But wait a minute. Let us not polarise this argument into categorical generalisations about East and West which support the pernicious doctrine of the Clash of Civilisations. Are religious exclusivists hostile to other faiths and other cultures, whether of the East or the West, whether Muslim, Christian or Jew, any more interested in a multi-civilisational world than the supremacists Muzaffar sees as occupying the centres of power in the West? There are schools in London, and I am sure elsewhere in the West, which are beacons of pluralism, while there are schools in the Muslim world which openly teach the children in their charge "not to greet" the *kāfirūn*, by which, with no justification in the Qur'an, they mean people of other faiths.

Let us take stock for a moment. I am questioning the conventional interpretation of the Tower of Babel story which holds that the diversity of languages and races is a punishment visited on mankind by God for arrogance and presumption. On the contrary, the Qur'an tells us that diversity is a gift, an element of man's primordial condition, a sign for the intelligent, an opportunity to know one another and to vie with one another in doing good works.

So what is meant then by the confusion of tongues which arises from human presumption and arrogance?

Let me illustrate the answer with a story from a classic of Islamic spirituality.[19] Four travellers, a Persian, a Turk, an Arab, and a Greek, are quarrelling about how best to spend a single coin, which was the only piece of money they had between them. They all want grapes, but they do not realise this because each of them has a different word for the fruit. A traveller hears them quarrelling, realises that they all want the same thing, and offers to satisfy all their needs with the one coin they possess. He goes off and buys them a bunch of grapes, and they are all astonished to discover that their different words were referring to the same thing.

Now, like all parables, this is a multi-layered story. On the surface, the confusion is caused by language differences, and it takes a multi-lingual traveller, a translator, to unravel the confusion of tongues. And this literal level is the level represented by the conventional interpretation of the Tower of Babel story, where mutual incomprehension is the result of everybody speaking different languages. The meaning of the parable of course goes much deeper than this. We all yearn to remember the divine unity (*tawḥīd*) but we give it different names and have different conceptions of what it is. Only the sage, represented here by the traveller-linguist, can show us that what we yearn for is, deep down, the same thing.

True, many misunderstandings do arise from poor understanding of foreign terms, from translation problems, such as the impossibility of capturing the full range of connotations of a foreign word,[20] and so on, but there is a much deeper level here. It goes far beyond the cacophony and strife caused by people who mistakenly believe that Allah is different from God, because He has a different name,[21] or that the word *fatwa* means a death-sentence (yes, it's true – even many distinguished and influential policy-makers believe this), or that *jihad* means holy war, or that *mushrik* means a polytheist or that *kāfir* means a non-Muslim.[22] It also goes beyond the more subtle imbalances caused by the difficulty in capturing in translation all the associations of a particular word.

The remedy for these kinds of misunderstandings and distortions can be provided to a large extent by properly informed and corrective education which brings to light the authentic meanings of key terms in any tradition. This requires both deep scholarship, a long-term commitment to engage with mainstream curriculum development agencies and teachers, and communicative competence in making concepts accessible to the contemporary mind so that they impact effectively on dedicated programmes of inter-cultural and inter-faith education. The parallel training of teachers of excellence is also a pressing priority. There is a "diversity" strand, for example, in the Citizenship programme within the British National Curriculum, and this requires teachers to promote respect for diversity in culture, race, ethnicity and religion. They can only do so, however, if they themselves are informed and open-hearted, and this applies not only to teachers who may be called on to teach about religions of which they are not adherents, but also those who teach about their own faith. I see from Farid Panjwani's abstract that he will emphasise the importance of education about one's own religion in preparing students for "active, responsible and critical citizenship." And this need for informed and enlightened role models applies in all directions. I could give you many examples of where such education has failed, both in the West and the East,[23] but I will reserve my comments on education until the end, when I will not dwell on failure but give a shining example of success.

My main purpose today is to explore a different level of the Tower of Babel story, the symbolic level which points to a deeper and more elusive level of confusion and mutual incomprehensibility than the diversity of languages. This is the confusion caused by the degradation of authentic concepts. And this is not a matter of different languages, but of words in the *same* language understood by people in different ways.

Let me give an example. We would all agree, I am sure, that there is a serious derangement in the relationship between man and the created order at the present time, and that one form this takes is a sustained assault on diversity from many directions. For example, globalisation threatens cultural and linguistic diversity, and rampant exploitation of the earth in the service of "growth" and "development" is causing the extinction of many species of animals and plants. Recent research indicates that the rate of extinction of the world's languages is faster even than the alarming rate of extinction of species. This destruction of diversity is a travesty of the concept of unity, for the universe was created as a manifestation of unity *in diversity* and not as a uniform entity. When a sacred conception of what is beyond the visible is lost to a culture, then the reflection of unity in the human soul is transposed to the forms themselves. The outcome is the need to make things uniform, to homogenise. The homogenising impulse springs from the denial of the Unseen which is a denial of God. This confusion between *unity* and *uniformity* is a typical example of the confusion caused by the distortion and degradation of key concepts and this is what the Tower of Babel story is telling us at a symbolic level. A Tower built by people who sought to usurp the eminence of God symbolises the arrogance which seeks to impose uniformity on a plural world. It is the Promethean theft of what belongs to God alone, bringing it down to a base level where its reflection is distorted beyond recognition.

We can identify many other key concepts which are also subject to this degradation and distortion. Just as *uniformity* is a travesty of *unity*, so the *division* caused by tribalism, sectarianism and narrow identity politics is a corruption of *diversity*. At the same time we need to distinguish *conformation* to a divine pattern[24] from uncritical *conformity* to human constructions; the *authority* of divine revelation which liberates the human soul from the *authoritarianism* imposed by narrow human formulations which imprison it; and the existence of *absolute* and timeless truths from the tyranny of an *absolutism* which obliterates all context. The process can be carried further to distinguish *standard*[25] from *standardisation*, *community* from *communalism*, *science* from *scientism*, *relationship*[26] from *relativism*, *individuality* from *individualism*, *liberty* from *libertarianism*,[27] *religion* from *religiosity*, *morality* from *moralism*, and the true *democracy* assured by an informed populace[28] from the *demagoguery* which thrives on repetitive rhetoric directed at the ignorant or those kept from the truth by biased media.

There are many more pairs of related words, and I only touch on them here. There are problematic pairs too, such as *tradition* in the sense of perennial wisdom and *traditionalism* in the sense of a conservative, orthodox and even anti-progressive and reactionary outlook. The same applies to the distinction between a vision of *progress* rooted in innate human values (such as concern for the advancement and welfare of our fellow human beings) and that brand of rootless *progressivism* which is dogmatically inimical to the past or merely synonymous with the blind worship of technological advancement. The confusion over what is meant by the words *tradition* and *progress* is perhaps the best example of the Tower of Babel at this time. We all tread carefully around these terms, lest we be labelled in the wrong way. How many people have the insight to see that one can be wedded to tradition and progress at the same time, and that the espousal of one does not entail the rejection of the other?

We need to build a lexicon of authentic concepts and distinguish them from their forgeries. The preponderance of the abstract noun *–ism* suffix on the negative side should alert us to the fact that many of the degraded meanings are not authentic *ideas* in the original Platonic sense but the product of human *ideology,*[29] – abstract systems of doctrine and belief constructed by human minds rooted neither in revealed wisdom nor in higher human faculties.

It is linguistic precision which is one of the foremost conceptual keys to avoiding the Clash of Civilisations. This is because without the recovery of the authentic primordial concepts,[30] we can only ever confound ourselves in the mutually uncomprehending hostility of competing ideologies.

And this is the core of the problem, this tendency of the human mind to dichotomise. This impulse to engage in adversarial argument is ingrained in us because we inhabit a world of duality.[31] The gift of language, given to man alone by God when He "*imparted unto Adam the names of all things*"[32] itself has two sides, mirrored in two levels of the faculty of human reason *(ʿaql)*. The root meaning of the word *ʿaql* is to 'bind' or 'withhold," indicating the human capacity for separating, defining and differentiating meanings so as to arrive at precise and distinct concepts. This is one level of "reason." If well developed, it is an indispensable cognitive tool for advancing the mature dialogue and dialectic which fosters the critical refinement of ideas, and as such it ought to be the foundation all education in thinking skills. If poorly developed, or if contaminated by ideology, the same innate faculty of differentiation can easily become a negative force, one which reduces the positive process of dialectic to the irreconcilable dichotomies and polarised positions of adversarial debate, and ultimately to a destructive us-versus-them mentality which can only lead to war.

I said there were two levels of the faculty of ʿaql, and I want to refer briefly to the higher level which goes beyond even the positive differentiation which enables us to think with clarity and precision. Al-Niffari reminds us that the letter (i.e. language) is a veil that separates us from unity precisely because it is a tool of endless diversification and multiplicity.[33] As well as being given the Names that enable us to differentiate, we are also endowed with fiṭrah, that innate disposition which enables us to remember the unity of our primordial condition. It is that common yearning for that essential unity, however it is defined which is the inner meaning of the story of the Travellers and the Grapes. To go beyond dichotomies, to see through this veil, we must realise that the gift of ʿaql is not only one of intellectual definition but also a faculty of deeper intelligence and discernment resident in the human heart. As the ḥadīth qudsī tells us: "Only the heart of My faithful servant can encompass Me."

Conclusion

So let me conclude with a call to the Heart. I would like to tell you about a model of pluralism in an English primary school which totally vindicates my confidence in the fiṭrah of young people if only they can be given strong, positive, visionary leadership. We can continue to argue about the extent to which Chandra Muzaffar is right when he claims that "the centres of power in the West ... are not interested in a multi-civilisational world," but we must never forget that in democratic states it is the people who elect such centres of power, and that it is the people who often uphold core values in the face of their betrayal by those very centres of power. Above all, it is young people to whom we must entrust the revival and embodiment of those values. We do this, or we should do it, through a process of education which gives ample space for respectful co-existence, mutual recognition, active engagement, and transforming love.

Roland Barth, Professor of Education at Harvard University, has said:

> I would prefer my children to be in a school where differences were looked for, attended to, and celebrated as good news, as opportunities for learning ... I would like to see our disdain for differences among students replaced by the question, How can we make use of the differences for the powerful learning opportunity they hold ....What is important about people – and about schools – is what is different, not what is the same.[34]

40

On 26 July this year there was a remarkable picture which took up the whole front page of *The Independent* newspaper in the UK. The headline above it reads: "26 Pupils. 26 Languages. One Lesson for Britain." The picture showed 26 smiling, happy children from Uphall Primary School in Ilford, England, with their headteacher. I have it here if you want to see it and it will warm your hearts. The children depicted speak 26 different languages, including Arabic, Hindi, Urdu, Punjabi, Gujerati, Somali, Swahili, Russian, Polish, Bengali, Shona, Yoruba, Tamil, Turkish, Dari, Pashto, Lingala, Xhosa, Filipino, Dutch, Lugandan, Mina, and Bravanese. Three out of ten of these children are asylum seekers or refugees. The total number of languages spoken by all the children in this school is 52, and 90 percent of them speak a language other than English at home. When they leave almost 100 percent of them are bilingual.

Is this a Tower of Babel? Absolutely not, although those poor souls crippled by fear of the "other" will have it so. As the headteacher, Andrew Morrish, said: "The racial harmony in school is marvellous – children do not see anyone as different. In 20 years' time if some of these children were world leaders, the world would be a better place."

An OFSTED inspection report described the school as "outstanding." Despite the fact that almost all the children have English as an additional language, 79 percent of them reach the expected standard in English in National Curriculum tests for 11-year-olds, and results in general are in line with the national average.

The caption under the picture reads: "These children come from all over the world. Some say they reflect an immigration crisis. But as ministers unveiled a crackdown [on immigration], their school was being lauded. Shouldn't this teach us something?"

Yes, indeed it should. It should teach us that the Tower of Babel is not the multilingual, multicultural, world which we increasingly occupy. This is the hopeful future, and the vanguard is our young people. The Tower of Babel is the mutual incomprehension fomented by those whose goal is to divide us along national, cultural, religious or ideological lines. Whether of the East or the West, their impoverished mono-cultural attitudes, masquerading as superior civilisational principles, dichotomise reality into the either/or of competing worldviews and fixed unilateral positions, and ultimately into the isolating pathologies of civilisational narcissism and cultural autism. This self-righteous attribution of goodness, truth or civilisation only to a single perspective is a sclerosis of the spirit, a failure of the heart, and we owe it to our children and their children to expose it for what it is. It is a dying paradigm, and the people who try to sell it to us are people of the past, not of the future. I want to head off into the future with the children of Uphall Primary School, and I urge others to do the same.

REFERENCES

Abou El Fadl, Khalid, *The Place of Tolerance in Islam* (Boston: Beacon Press, 2002).

Arberry, A. J., ed. and trans. *The Mawaqif and Mukhatabat of Muhammad Ibn 'Abdi 'l-Jabbar al-Niffari* (Cambridge: CUP, 1935).

Ayoub, Mahmoud M., "The Qur'an and Religious Pluralism" in *Islam and Global Dialogue, Religious Pluralism and the Pursuit of Peace*, ed. Roger Boase (Aldershot: Ashgate, 2005).

Ayto, John, ed. *Bloomsbury Dictionary of Word Origins* (London: Bloomsbury Publishing, 1990).

Barnhart, Robert K., ed. *Chambers Dictionary of Etymology* (Edinburgh: Chambers, 1988).

Barth, Roland S., *Improving Schools from Within* (San Francisco: Jossey-Bass, 1990).

Book Foundation (www.TheBook.org).

Eck, Diana L., *Encountering God* (Boston: Beacon Press, 1993).

Genesis 11:1–9.

Halliday, Fred, "The 'Clash of Civilisations?': Sense and Nonsense" in *Islam and Global Dialogue, Religious Pluralism and the Pursuit of Peace*, ed. by Roger Boase, (Aldershot: Ashgate, 2005).

Haydon, Caroline, *The Independent* on 9/10/03.

Henzell-Thomas, J., *The Challenge of Pluralism and the Middle Way of Islam* (London: AMSS UK, 2002).

_____ "Going Beyond Thinking Skills: Reviving an Understanding of Higher Human Faculties" presented at the 10th annual conference of the International Association of Cognitive Education and Psychology, University of Durham, England, July 2004. Book Foundation, www.TheBook.org.

Hofmann, Murad W., "Religious Pluralism and Islam," in *Islam and Global Dialogue, Religious Pluralism and the Pursuit of Peace*, ed. Roger Boase (Aldershot: Ashgate, 2005).

Kline, Nancy, *Time to Think: Listening to Ignite the Human Mind* (London: Lock, 1999).

Lewis, C.S., *Perelandra* (London: HarperCollins, 1943).

Morris, James, "Ibn 'Arabi's Rhetoric of Realisation," *Journal of the Muhyiddin Ibn 'Arabi Society*, vol. XXXIV, (2003).

Perry, M., *On Awakening and Remembering* (Louisville: Fons Vitae, 2000).

Qur'an translation: Asad, Muhammad, *The Message of the Qur'an* (Bath: The Book Foundation, 2003).

Shah-Kazemi, R., "The Metaphysics of Interfaith Dialogue: Sufi Perspectives on the Universality of the Qur'anic Message," in *Paths to the Heart: Sufism and the Christian East*, ed. James Cutsinger (Bloomington, IN: World Wisdom, 2002).

Safi, Omid, ed. *Progressive Muslims on Justice, Gender and Pluralism* (Oxford: Oneworld Publications, 2003).

Negotiating Citizenship and Identity

ANAS AL-SHAIKH-ALI

Public Opinion and Political Influence: Issues in Contemporary Popular Fiction[1]

THIS PAPER FOCUSES ON THE ROLE OF popular fiction in relation to public opinion, political influence, and Islamophobia, exploring the political and social contexts of novels, paying attention to the ways in which best selling authors routinely set the moral boundaries through which we are to perceive the dynamics of global confrontation. Often overlooked as harmless entertainment popular fiction is big business. Marketed globally and consumed by billions it defines cultural identity and shapes public opinion to an extent that is self-evident and to a degree that is alarming. Far more than just spinning a good yarn, novelists reinforce and develop our deep-rooted fears, subtly transpose our perception of the 'other,' and can affect political understanding and shape popular perceptions through a series of plot lines that often appear, interestingly, to predict future events through a fictionalised present. So how seriously should we take what the industry is doing?

The range and proliferation of this type of fiction, with its multifarious subgenres, (that is under the more general category of "popular fiction") is bewildering and indicative of the mass appeal which the genre enjoys. Some 80 percent of the bulk of fast-selling paperbacks fall into this category.[2] Statistics, for instance, suggest that espionage fiction (alternatively, the spy thriller) has a large global readership with one out of every four new works of fiction published in the United States belonging to this subgenre[3] alone. However, and no matter what the standard of the novel is or is not, popular fiction seems to have always enjoyed wide-spread popularity even in the nineteenth and early twentieth centuries. This popularity increased beginning in the 1960s. Reeva Simon relates this to the "paperback publishing explosion" of the 1950s and the

47

Ian Fleming novels and the Bond phenomenon.[4] She points out that "during the years Ian Fleming wrote the Bond books ... more than 25 million copies in eighteen languages were sold. Sales figures more than doubled after Fleming's death."[5]

It may not be very difficult to discover why popular fiction goes down so well with the public. As with other forms of modern entertainment (say, films, songs, etc.), it is, among other things, light, racy, topical, gossipy, casual, and morally and dramatically simplistic; not only is it packed with "action" but also with a dose of violence and gore, as well as exotica and sex, the last ranging from the titillating to the explicit. Popular fiction and entertainment go virtually hand in hand. It is also cheap to buy, especially in paperback. Interestingly, to cater for such popular taste, even

> Shakespeare and other classic drama productions are being sold as Hollywood-style sex-and-violence epics by the Royal Shakespeare Company to woo young audiences .... The RSC poster at the Barbican Theater, London has a blood-soaked face with the punning slogan 'A Natural Born Killer Too'. The nod towards Oliver Stone's graphically violent movie has clearly worked. The run at the Barbican has sold out .... The *Pulp-Fiction*-style advertising is also being used for the six-hour adaptation of Goethe's *Faust*. It warns titillatingly that the production contains nudity.[6]

Another secret to its huge appeal is that popular fiction is almost as easily available to the public as newspapers. In her important study, *The Middle East in Crime Fiction*, Simon points out that these books are sold not only at traditional outlets such as bookstores but also at non-traditional ones like supermarkets, drugstores, bus stations, and airports.[7] In Europe they are available at petrol stations and newsagents. Moreover, a large number of these titles are translated and published almost immediately into European and other languages.[8] For instance, during a visit to the 1994 Frankfurt book fair, I noticed that Frederick Forsyth's *The Fist of God* had already been translated into several European languages within a few months of having been published in its original English edition. There have also been cases where the traffic has flowed from other European languages into English.[9]

In 1980 I began to collect popular fiction titles published since 1970 dealing wholly or partially with the Middle East, Islam and Muslims, to explore the ways in which Islam and Muslims were being projected to a target audience envisaged as global. The collection now amounts to over 1300 titles and the subgenres on which the research is based include detective fiction, thrillers (sometimes labeled "political thrillers"), techno-thrillers, spy fiction (or secret-agent fiction), "futuristic" fiction, romances, historical romances, historical fiction, nuclear (alternatively chemical and biological) holocaust fiction, missionary fiction, evangelical fiction, young people's fiction, children's fiction, and even adult fiction. The collection, does not, however, include fantasy titles (namely, the sword and sorcery type, covered in an article by Riad Nourallah[10]), or literary fiction and science fiction.

The choice of 1970 as the point of departure is not arbitrary. The 1967 and 1973 Arab-Israeli wars, the oil embargo, the Lebanese civil war, the Iranian revolution, the hostage crisis, the recession of the early eighties, the two Gulf wars, as well as the tragic events of September 11, and the invasion of both Afghanistan and Iraq, focused global attention on the Middle East and Islam and Muslims as never before. More importantly, they brought national (and individual) egos and interests in various parts of the world on a noisy, tragic and no doubt costly collision course, in both human and financial terms. Nor should we forget that worldwide, religious sentiments, hitherto entombed under the great pyramids of modern ideologies and the dazzling, techno-colour mantle of materialism, saw an astonishing revival for reasons ranging from despair to over satiety.

The transition of traditional imagery forms that once symbolised the face of the enemy, often camouflaged in the language of politics, to the portrayal of a power hungry Islam attempting to assert its once historical might, speaks volumes for the relationship between authors, their motives, political expediency, and propaganda. In the earlier fiction of the fifties and sixties fictional or potential perpetrators of a nuclear holocaust were invariably mad scientists, deranged generals, and frustrated Nazis (Dr. Strangelove, Dr. No, etc). Mainly of German, Chinese or Russian extraction they tended to reflect the political theatre of the times. Occasionally, Arab terrorists, mainly Palestinians, and oil "sheikhs" would also surface, contemptuously portrayed as uncivilised, filthy-rich womanizers, and backward savages. Since the seventies this balance began to shift with far greater attention being paid to "anti-

Islamic" or Islamophobic portrayals than Communist/Fascist denunciation. In fact, this critical trend in contemporary popular British and American fiction has been growing by leaps and bounds reaching unprecedented levels in the late nineties to an almost climactic burst after 11th September. In many recent works it is not only Muslims that are being depicted as arch villains (or the enemy), but Islam itself with some of its most basic elements coming under heavy censure; and there is no attempt to disguise this.

The question of interest is why Islam and some of its icons have been chosen for fictional pillory, and why the "instant TV Arab kit" (to use Jack Shaheen's shrewd phrase)[11] has rather adroitly been metamorphosised into the "instant TV Muslim kit." Exploitation of political events to boost sales is an obvious but not altogether accurate answer. Daniel Easterman explores some of the reasons in an article entitled "Demons and the New Dogs of War." He stressed the dilemma faced by novelists when the Cold War finally came to an end and the curtain fell on a dark fantasy which had until then allowed them to indulge in a world of "evil empires and Stalinist plots":

> So what do we do now, those of us who depend for our living on the thrills and spills of international skullduggery? Where in the world may we find the scenarios and characters on which our continued existence – and the pleasure of our readers – must depend?

> The answer is, I fear, all too simple. Even before the Cold War ended and the second Gulf War began, the old East-West skirmish between capitalism and socialism was already giving ground to a renewed state of tension between older enemies – the West (including Russia) and Islam ...

> It is a division that has never gone away... both sides have got on with the business of prosecuting a cold war through propaganda and the making of myth .... On our side it was sustained by the threat of an "Islamic peril" – oriental fantasies, ... a harsh God, a debauched prophet, bearded fanatics, oil sheikhs, ayatollahs, and terrorists.

Inevitably, he continues, thriller writers will be attracted in increasing numbers to "the theme of an embattled West hand-in-hand with a decaying Soviet imperium threatened from without and within by the hordes of militant Islam." As evidence he goes on to list several titles already published: James Clavell's *Whirlwind*, Ken Follett's *On the Wings of Eagles*, Leon Uris's *The Haj*, A. J. Quinnell's *The Mahdi*, and himself with *The Last Assassin* and *The Seventh Sanctuary*.[12]

However, fiction responds to realities, and it would now appear, and as writers such as Samuel Huntington would have us believe (*The Clash of Civilizations and the Remaking of World Order*), this new reality concerns an imminent conflict between civilizations, notably Islam and the West. In other words, layers of convoluted allusion identify Islam as the new enemy to be fought and contained.

Novels claim to give us a clear picture of what is, and what is to be. When the "red evil" or in the words of Ronald Reagan, the communist "evil empire" imploded, a new enemy needed to be found.[13] And who, for many historical, economic, and religious reasons, could better fit the bill and be more readily available than Islam and Muslims? For political expediency the "red evil" was conveniently and seamlessly replaced with the "green" one. This binary definition of the world is intellectually bankrupt but fits in well with the simplistic language and uncomplicated structure of particularly political novels, which ostensibly are nothing if not formulaic.

The erstwhile British Foreign Secretary, Douglas Hurd, a novelist in his own right, could not, in his double capacity, have missed noticing the new trend. Reviewing Gerald Seymour's *Home Run*, he wrote:

> Mr Seymour describes two establishments, one familiar, the other new but certain now to come at us in novel after novel. As the traditional Cold War thriller loses credibility we shall certainly be exposed to countless mullahs and ayatollahs, with heroes and villains criss-crossing the Gulf and the Turkish frontier as resolutely as they did the Berlin Wall.[14]

Even ordinary readers felt the new pulse, and one Elspeth Huxley wrote to the editor of the *Sunday Telegraph*:

> I don't think Mr. Eric Major of Hodder and Stoughton will have to look far to find a "new evil" for our spy writers to tilt at, as suggested in last Sunday's story about John Le Carre's dilemma. I have been wondering for some time what he and his fellow spy men will do now that their horses have been shot under them by Mr. Gorbachev.

Muslim fundamentalists are the answer, the book burners of Bradford. Nor should we forget that their ancestors conquered all Spain and Portugal and were only turned back from the rest of Europe at the gates of Vienna.[15]

In the same year in which Ms Huxley wrote her letter (1989) *The Times* commissioned a poll on popular expectations for the second millennium. Of those polled, 49 percent cited "Islam" in response to the rather leading question: "who would be the most likely enemies of Britain in 2000?" The Russians came second with only 11 percent. A year later, R. W. Johnson, writing in *The Independent*, commented on the exercise:

> But one can hardly write off as ignorant bigots the 49 per cent who thought Islam would be our enemy. Indeed, it could be argued that they were remarkably prescient – just a year later the West stands poised on the brink of a war against a Muslim state. (The fact that Saddam Hussein runs a secular regime, which allows the sale of alcohol, counts not a fig in popular perception.) And those prejudices have great political and military significance. In the West, at least, modern wars cannot be fought without popular backing.[16]

However, even some well-known novelists who have used Islam and Muslims in best selling works have felt the danger that such a trend could pose. Daniel Easterman warns:

> But we court disaster of a sort in all this ... turning Muslims (or Pakistanis, or Arabs or Iranians) into the new enemy of the American (or British or French) way of life threatens to bring in its wake dangers of a new kind. The Soviets were an enemy 'out there', unknown to most of us, lost in a sort of mist of space and ideology. Muslims however, are not just out there: they are, increasingly, here with us, as immigrants, as refugees, and even as converts from within our own society.
>
> So what is the thriller writer to do? There can be no denying the appeal of Islam and the Middle East as locales within which the suspense novelists may find rich material for decades to come ...
>
> Perhaps we can rise to the challenge. Perhaps we can provide the thrills without the stereotypes, the blood without the blood libels, the criticisms without the insult. Sadly, recent reporting of events in the Gulf gives little room for hope. The demons of the new cold war have been Khomeini, Ghadhafi, Arafat, and now Saddam Hussein. Demons call for demonologists. I fear it is a call that will not go unanswered.[17]

In "The New Anti-Semitism," Easterman further warns:

> There is no question that [Edward Said] is correct, that the stereotyping of Arabs and Muslims in the modern West is ugly, distorted and widespread. Europeans and Americans are (largely) sensitive to anti-Semitism, but unfaltering images of Arabs, Iranians and other Middle Easterners still crowd our newspapers and television screens. None of this matches the excesses of, say, Nazi anti-Jewish propaganda – and God forbid that it ever should – but it is dangerous and pernicious for all that.[18]

The role of thriller writers is further explained by Easterman in the following quotation which appeared in a full page advertisement in *The Independent* entitled "20 Things You Should Know About Daniel Easterman":

> We ignore thriller writers at our peril. Their genre is the political condition. They massage our dreams and magnify our nightmares. If it is true that we always need enemies, then we will always need writers of fiction to encode our fears and fantasies.[19]

In both "The Thriller in an Age of *Détente*," and "The New Anti-Semitism" Easterman seems to straddle a dual position; on the one hand warning against stereotypes and calling on thriller writers to rise to the challenge by producing thrillers without blatant stereotypes,[20] yet on the other seemingly neglecting to do so in some of his own novels (i.e. *Day of Wrath*). Easterman felt disturbed that although he had attempted to meet this more ethical standard in his novel *The Seventh Sanctuary* (1987), where he felt he had been sensitive to anti-Arab prejudice, he was nevertheless accused of being "a racist, anti-Arab and of having received funds from Mossad."[21]

Political Influence

Grant Hugo in his article "The Political Influence of the Thriller," is surprised to find that even as late as 1972 the political influence of the thriller had received "little notice," since as a means of communication, he suggests, "the thriller offers greater opportunities than any of the conventional methods of disseminating political ideas."[22] He further also observes that readers are usually accustomed to "accept much information on trust from their writers, because it is necessary for ... [the] enjoyment of the story." Readers who opt for a good read are at the receiving end:

> To them the thriller seems less suspect, a surer source of the pleasures of unadulterated escapism. This is precisely its attraction for the modern propagandist, who no longer alienates his audience by assertion and argument but, whether it is a cigarette or a politician he is selling, seeks to project an 'image' by appealing to emotions, prejudices and cravings as potent as they are often unconscious or unavowed.[23]

Hugo also wonders whether the "authentic *romans policiers* of television owe only their factual knowledge, or also their ethos, to official assistance." He suggests that such questions may be interesting for the student of politics, but asserts that "to the sociologist they offer opportunities for research." As to why the thriller offers an unsuspecting vehicle for political propaganda Hugo says:

> Indeed, overtly political ideas do not always attract attention even among the minority actively interested in politics, many of whom are positively repelled by any expression of opinion which differs from their own. Exceptional talents or opportunities are needed if explicitly political propaganda is to exercise much impact beyond the narrow circle of party workers and others already committed ....Thrillers have been shown to command a wide audience and to be suitable vehicles for the unobtrusive dissemination of the political concepts that are at least implicit in most of them.[24]

It is argued that "the reader of espionage tales of the future must be on his guard against blatant propaganda heavily disguised as spy fiction."[25]

In the early 1990s I was requested to assess a paper for publication in the *American Journal of Islamic Social Sciences* (AJISS) entitled "The Muslim Image in Contemporary American Fiction and its Effect on Decisions Concerning the Holy Land of Palestine." I felt, at the time, that the paper was somewhat too ardent and ambitious for the eleven novels written between 1977 and 1988, on which the paper focused, to have feasibly influenced decisions made by the American administration with regard to a complicated and major issue such as the question of Palestine. Such policies had surely been decided much earlier and had never changed in substance! However, there is enough data now to show that popular fiction can – in both the short and long runs and with other conditions permitting – generate political influence by shaping public sentiment and preparing public opinion for whatever action is intended or planned.[26] It can also create new prejudices and strengthen old ones, and – assisted by other media – help induce public support for, or at least defuse any possible opposition to, certain policies or actions. This does not have to happen through collusion. It can, and does operate more usually through a silent, even unconscious consensus – or common interest – on the part of writers, publishers, and others.

Similarly novels prepared their audience for a politically appropriate and expedient perception of the Jews both prior to and during the Second World War. Malcolm J. Turnbull examining the image of the Jews in detective fiction states that negative images and stereotypes of the Jew "were in the mindsets of a number of influential precursors of the Golden Age, it is also indisputable that they were reinvigorated and multiplied alarmingly during the interwar years, parallel with the intensification of Jew-dislike manifested themselves elsewhere in British popular culture, notably as racist caricatures in light periodicals such as *London Opinion* and *Punch*; on radio, stage and music hall; in non-crime fiction, comic books and picture postcards; even occasionally in the movies."[27] Such unchecked negative portrayal in British popular fiction (in addition to other European languages) no doubt played an important part in the tragic consequences that the Jews suffered in Europe.[28]

Spy novels and political thrillers are particularly useful for authors to ostensibly define and malign the enemy of the day and boost support for whatever political perspective seems to be in vogue, with a view to influencing both public and political opinion, and they have been doing this for quite some time. In "Introduction: Fictions of History," Wesley K. Wark points out that "hacks like William Le Queux and E. Phillips Oppenheim produced spy fiction in profusion."[29] They were popular in spite of the fact that they lacked any real talent for writing novels. Le Queux had "no talent as a writer of spy novels, detective novels, love romances, or anything else. His plotting is execrable, his characters are buffoons, and his style is tedious to the extreme."[30] The irony is that he was one of the few writers to have had an impact on "events and public morality" as well as "a broad impact on the twentieth century."[31] According to I. F. Clarke, in *Voices Prophesying War 1763–1984*, Le

Queux played a part in the *"making* of the First World War."[32] Clarke writes: "There can be no doubt that the authors of many tales of future warfare shared in the responsibility for the catastrophe that overtook Europe. Men like Danrit, Le Queux, and August Nieman helped raise the temperature of international disputes."[33] Le Queux's warning in his novel *The Secret Service* (1896) of a German invasion was being taken seriously as early as 1900 by Britain's Naval Intelligence Department which translated a novel by a French naval officer entitled *La Guerre*

L'Angleterre for circulation to British officers.[34] He also wrote *The Invasion of 1910* (1906) and *The Spies of the Kaiser* (1909). Le Queux "convincingly claimed that Britain was full of German agents." This was "supported by Lord Northcliffe's popular newspaper, the *Daily Mail*, which warned that German waiters and barbers were agents of the Kaiser."[35] Another publication, *Weekly News,* ran a "spy-spotting" competition.[36] The impact of these novels and media stories, "led to thousands of reports filed at police stations about suspected acts of espi-

Le Queux, The Invasion of 1910

onage."[37] Le Queux's "scare novels set off panic" about German espionage activities that led the British government to establish "a secret service to ward off the (*fictional*) threat."[38] He was "a pioneer of the faction industry, deliberately blurring the line between fiction and fact."[39] According to Marc Cerasini, the tone of Le Queux's fiction had "a strong impact on readers before the Great War. The tone of his fiction no doubt influenced popular opinion in Britain and helped to lead public acceptance of the First World War."[40] Another novel about a possible German invasion which helped shape public opinion and was taken seriously by the authorities was Ereskine Childers's *The Riddle of the Sands* (1903), a war prophecy novel which, despite its "awkward plotting" and other weaknesses "appealed to a wide spectrum of British society; yachtsmen, detective story readers and politicians … politicians and military strategists were particularly interested, yet were puzzled as to who Childers was and how he had arrived at such a strangely precise knowledge of the

German coastline."[41] E. Phillips Oppenheim, who "wrote lousy plots, wooden characters, clichéd dialogue, and bogus descriptions" produced "a whole cartload of spy novels" (116 of them). In the novels he wrote before America's decision to join the First World War, he adds "out and out flattery [of the Americans] in order to move public opinion in the U.S. toward the camp of the Allies."[42]

In a monumental, investigative and detailed work Frances Saunders stresses the fact that many intellectuals and thinkers whose works and ideas "acquired an international audience" and popularity in the 1950s and 1960s where actually "second-raters, ephemeral publicists, whose works were doomed to the basements of second-hand bookstores." Their appeal was only enhanced by the support of the CIA's cultural consortium.[43] A very recent example of low standards is the "popularity" of the *Left Behind Series* of Evangelical novels. They were inspired by an Evangelist and badly written by a second-rate writer. They are bland, underwhelming, pedestrian, dull, prosaic and humdrum yet continue to have overwhelming popularity, made even more popular through the en masse distribution of copies to American soldiers in Iraq and Afghanistan.[44] Also produced have been *Kids Series* and *Military Series* of the work. They are sold on CD-ROM,

The Left Behind Series

as graphic-novel editions, and as videos. The series has been spectacularly successful, by 2005 selling over 62 million copies having "outstripped the popular *DaVinci Code*."[45] The 12th and final title published in 2004 entitled *Glorious Reappearing* sold two million copies prior to publication in March 2005, reaching no. 2 on *The New York Times* list.[46] On 24th May 2004, *Newsweek* magazine published a powerful picture of a GI in Iraq reading a hard copy of *Glorious Appearing*.

In part of my presentation given at the "Citizenship, Security and Democracy" conference (2006) I dealt with the possible impact of the French novel *The Camp of Saints* (1978) by Jean Raspail on Turkey's bid to join the European Union and argued that fiction, old and new, does have an impact. I pointed out that popular fiction is enforcing old stereotypes and creating new ones. Thomas Harris' *Black Sunday*[47] illustrates this further. The novel showcases terrorists who use an American agent to detonate a bomb in an observation balloon over a stadium during a Super Bowl match, intending to cause the death of more than 100,000 people. The book, already a best seller by the mid-seventies, was made into a blockbuster film directed by John Frankenheimer, with a cast that included Robert Shaw, Bruce Dern and Marthe Keller. All well and good, but during the second Gulf war, Sarah Helm, writing for *The Independent*, reported from Washington on January 26, 1991:

> Fears are now focused on the Super Bowl game in Tampa, Florida, climax of the American football season. There will be stringent security, but ticket sales for the game are said to be holding up. As part of the largest ever anti-terrorist security operation within the US, the Federal Aviation Authority has banned aircraft from flying within half a mile of the stadium .... A total of 22 law enforcement agencies are coordinating security and anti-terrorist surveillance at the stadium.[48]

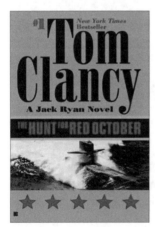

Tom Clancy, *The Hunt for Red October*

As earlier novelists in the late nineteenth and early twentieth centuries had an influence on public opinion and played a part in shaping events, more recently Tom Clancy's *The Hunt for Red October* (described by President Ronald Reagan as "the perfect yarn") marked an important psychological shift from a pervading "fiction of defeat and cynicism," which dominated military films and popular fiction, after the defeat in Vietnam. Published the same year that President Reagan was re-elected, it marked the beginning of a new trend in returning to "traditional values ... of personal heroism, honor, and self-sacrifice."[49] Cerasini sees Clancy's hero Jack Ryan, as a champion embracing civilisational responsibility. We may find a strong echo of this mentality (which had to be embraced no matter what the cost) in Rudyard Kipling's *The White Man's Burden*. Cerasini believes that Clancy's novels, as well as those of Patrick Robinson, Dale Brown and many others paved "the way for Operation Desert Shield, then Desert Storm. The shift in public opinion regarding the use of the military can be traced in part to the popularity of the techno-thriller genre, which educated us about the weapons, the strategies, and the very nature of modern warfare."[50]

In *The Hunt for Red October* Clancy dealt with an important period of Soviet-American relations concerning "vital issues" which the American electorate had to decide on.[51] His fiction engaged the reader and as seen in the first pages of *The Hunt for Red October* he managed to get his readers "off the fence" to choose sides.[52] The popularity of Clancy and his fiction is, according to Cerasini, partly the result of his ability to reverse a trend in popular fiction of "bashing the military-industrial complex," and instead, to portray his country and its political, military, and intelligence systems in a positive way, by presenting "male role-models in his fiction," which ran "counter to the fashion in popular literature for the past twenty or so years."[53] Clancy sees the United States as "a beacon and a leader in the decades and perhaps centuries to come, as a force for justice in an unjust world."[54] If this vision is to materialise – according to Cerasini – American citizens must allow and support their government "to take a painful stand, and perhaps fight another war like the one fought in Iraq [1991]."[55] However, Cerasini is quick to add that, "we must not forget that all Americans are potential soldiers, that we are a nation of citizen-soldiers, and, in principle, do not make war without the will and consent of the people of the United States."[56] Of course, influencing and manipulating public opinion is always needed before any major conflict. R. W. Johnson seems to echo Greenburg's views when he concludes his article, "A Suitable Enemy for Crusaders," rather acidly by stating that "in the West, at least, modern wars cannot be fought without popular backing."[57] The power of Clancy's fiction (and of many other authors and thousands of fiction titles) and the breadth of its *influence* on the public has indeed helped in making possible three wars in the late twentieth and early twenty-first centuries, and the spread of Islamophobia.

It is interesting to note that in the American cultural war against Communism, the Psychological Warfare Division commissioned the translation and publication of "general books" and novels through commercial publishers. They realised, as Grant Hugo mentioned above, the power of such material to affect public opinion and consent. Such books are "more accepted than government-sponsored publications, because they do not have the taint of propaganda."[58]

The "Predictive Novel," The "Prophetic Novel," and The "Anticipatory Novel"

There are many examples of novels that not only seem to influence political opinion, as discussed, but also appear remarkably to predict political/military events. Although it would be enormously difficult to establish whether events taking shape could be the result of having consulted novels for inspiration, and even more difficult to speculate as to who would possibly do so, nevertheless it is indisputable that certain incidents of a militaristic/political nature seem to find a counterpart in a fictionalised setting, sometimes in quite a spectacular fashion. In *Black Storm* (2002)[59] for instance, Poyer talks of an American invasion of Iraq and a marine-army-navy team mission to Iraq a few days before the invasion to find and neutralise Saddam's weapons of mass destruction. The team manages to find such weapons under a main hospital (The Medical City) in the centre of Baghdad. *The Times* reported in June 2003 that "following repeated claims that hospitals were being used to hide chemical and biological weapons" hospitals became the first sites searched immediately after the war. According to *The Times* thirty British troops including special forces and bomb-disposal experts, as well as civilian experts went to the Bittar Hospital and informed its astonished director that "they knew there was an underground chemical weapons laboratory" and demanded to search the hospital. The search found neither laboratory nor weapons.[60] It is extraordinary that the novel was published prior to Colin Powell's claims made at the United Nations that a "secret biological laboratory" was concealed in a hospital in central Baghdad, a claim echoed by Downing Street a month later. Coincidence? It's not the only one.

One of the most stunning examples of this effect is the sensational best seller of the seventies, *The Crash of 79*[61] by Paul Erdman. The general plot is well known: Iran – under the Shah – attacks and occupies the oil fields of southern Iraq, the Gulf and Saudi Arabia. Passages from the novel are remarkably reminiscent of the two Gulf wars that were to follow in real life:

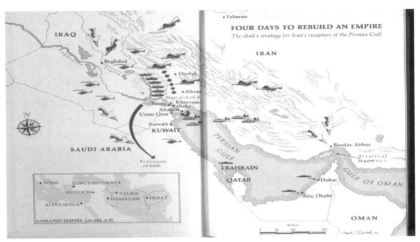

Paul Erdman, The Crash of 79 – Inside Map

The scene that followed on the beaches of the Persian Gulf, just to the east of Abadan, was a spectacle that no participant ever forgot. At 11:05, the wild howl of hundreds of these Hovercraft engines began to fill the air, producing an incredible torrent of sound. Then, slowly, the mechanical monsters began to rise, as the air pressure built up within the skirts beneath the vehicles. Then, in columns of five, they began to move off the beaches and onto the shallow waters of the Persian Gulf, creating cloud after cloud of swirling mist ...

Only two hours later, they began opening up their ramps on firm ground to the rear of the Iraqi forces. At the same time the main body of Iranian panzers, which had been grouped between Dezful and Ahvaz, began a frontal assault from the east .... American military personnel were arriving in the capital of Saudi Arabia at the rate of three thousand men per hour. It was thought that they could stabilize the entire area within a few days.[62]

Although the four-day war depicted in *The Crash of 79* was different in many ways from the two Gulf wars, there is still a striking similarity. The two maps provided on the book's inside front and back covers could easily have been of the Iraqi forces attacking Iran in 1980, were the direction of the arrows to be changed from west to east. Other details are reminiscent of the 1990 conflict.[63]

This was not the only novel to predict the first Gulf War. Robert Lawrence Holt's *Good Friday*[64] first published in the USA in 1987, seven years after the first Gulf War and three years before the second also

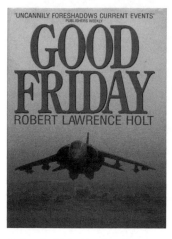

'UNCANNILY FORESHADOWS CURRENT EVENTS'
PUBLISHERS WEEKLY

GOOD FRIDAY

ROBERT LAWRENCE HOLT

Robert L. Holt, Good Friday

features an extraordinary plot development. The opening section of the novel is a riveting read, and for more than just its storyline; one need only replace the words "Iran/Iranians" with "Iraq/Iraqis" to describe almost to a remarkable degree events that occurred on August 2, 1990:

> After the pointless slaughter of 1.2 million soldiers (a fifth of whom were under 14- to 16-year old boys of Khomeini's Revolutionary Guards) in a twelve-year war of attrition with Iran, the army of Iraq abandons their strategic port of Basra in disorganised retreat northward.

> Two weeks later, the Iranians invade the oil-rich state of Kuwait; and by mid-April, the Iranian army is massed along the Kuwait/Saudi Arabia border … their southern advance temporarily halted by an influenza epidemic.

> To oppose the 300,000-man Iranian army in Kuwait, the Saudis have moved 45,000 men (three-quarters of their ground forces) to their northern border. The Saudi army is reinforced by the Peninsular Shield – 9,000 men in a loosely-organised band of military units from neighbouring Persian Gulf states.[65]

Among other thrillers related to the Gulf and which appeared prior to the second Gulf War are: *Gulf*[66] and *The Gulf*.[67] The latter depicts a devastating American attack on the island of Abu Musa in reaction to a "ferocious aggression" which had sunk a US destroyer. A reviewer in the *Ocala Star-Banner* wrote: "Today's headlines are frighteningly close to the fiction in this tale."[68] In *Stalking Horse*[69] the SAS and Delta Force endeavor – with brilliant success – to neutralise Saddam's "deadly terror options" before they are deployed against the allies. In Frederick Forsyth's *The Fist of God*,[70] an SAS major – who can pass for an Arab – ventures behind Iraqi lines to seek Saddam's secret nuclear weapon and destroy it before it rains death on "hundreds of thousands" of British and American soldiers. This secret weapon is code-named Qubth-ut-Allah [sic] or "the fist of Allah."[71] Far more prophetically still, Gordon Thomas's *Godless Icon*,[72] which was given to the publisher on 1st August

1990, (just one day before Iraq invaded Kuwait) describes an Iraqi invasion of Kuwait and bloody conflict in the Gulf. Reviewer Frances Hardy talked to Gordon Thomas, whom she described as "the author with the psychic touch." Under the eye-catching title, "This Man's Novels Really Do Come True," Hardy stresses that Thomas' predictions – like Iraq's invasion of Kuwait – are "not vague, mealy-mouthed prognostications, but big, bold global ones that have an unsettling capacity for coming true;" she refuses to accept the views of cynics who may see this as "an astute reading of Middle Eastern politics by a writer who had spent 40 years as a foreign correspondent."[73] Again, in Dale Brown's *Shadows of Steel* a surgical stealth campaign to silence Iran's modern weapons is the only option left for the US.

Whether viewed as coincidence or conspiracy, the emergence of the "prophetic/predictive novel" is a development that cannot be ignored. Furthermore, the exercise is not without value for it urges deeper exploration into the complex relationship that oscillates between fiction and fact, or in the words of McCormick and Fletcher, "facts beget fiction and fiction begets fact."[74] There are indications that contemporary thrillers are doing exactly the reverse. Novelists seem to be able now-a-days to suggest action and events which bring about a tragic reality.

The predictive nature of novels can also be seen in the works of William Le Queux, E. Phillips Oppenheim and Erskine Childers, as also in the fiction of Graham Greene described by Masters in *Literary Agents* as "The Abrasive Spy."[75] In *The Quiet American* (1955) he "accurately anticipated the American intention to intervene on a massive scale in Vietnam."[76] The novelist attributed this "clairvoyance" to his personal experience and the knowledge he had gained during long stays in the country in the early 1950s.[77] Smyth also notices that in *Our Man in Havana* (1958) Greene "exhibited such a power of *anticipating actuality* ... as apparently to transcend informed inference and attain veritable *second sight*."[78] Only within four years of its publication the Cuban crisis took place and "life appeared to imitate art."

Masters, *Literary Agents*

Fiction and Politicians

The popularity of the genre in the United States is not limited to the "working" classes but included the middle class and the educated.[79] The same is true of Europe. There has always existed a somewhat incestuous relationship between novelists, politicians, and the intelligence services. This is not a challenge to the conventions of modern authorship for the issue has long been established, but it does throw into question the role of authors and sheds light onto the inspiration behind some of the more political/militaristic elements of plotlines. Popular fiction is extremely popular with various strata of society and various age groups but what may not be widely known is that it also forms avid reading for politicians. Politicians and decision makers across the Atlantic are keen readers of popular fiction. Grant Hugo points out that "Baldwin reveled in the works of Buchan; two of his successors in the office of Prime Minister paid public tribute to Agatha Christie on her jubilee as a writer; President Kennedy was one of Ian Fleming's faithful readers; and many less illustrious politicians have been happy to confess to interviewers their addiction to so innocent and popular a form of relaxation."[80] Richard Helms, the former CIA director very much liked Ian Fleming's novels. It is a known fact that President Ronald Reagan was an admirer of Tom Clancy, who we are told, lectured Pentagon and CIA staff. He was so close to the White House at the time that he was "regarded by the media as a sort of de facto spokesman for the Reagan administration." President Bill Clinton is not only an avid reader of popular fiction but "devours thrillers and modern detective stories" and has recommended Walter Mosley's novel, *His Devil in a Blue Dress*.[81] Some politicians have written novels during or after their political careers. Among them Douglas Hurd, the former British Foreign Secretary, Edwina Curry, former Conservative MP, Ian Smith, former Conservative Party leader and Lord Jeffery Archer, former Deputy Chairman of the Conservative Party. President Jimmy Carter published his first novel, *The Hornet's Nest* in 2003, and Congressman Peter T. King published *Vale of Tears* also in 2003. Senator Gary Hart published four novels, two of which were under the pseudonym John Blackthorn. His novel *The Double Man* (1984) was co-authored with former Senator and Secretary of Defense William Cohen. It may be relevant and very interesting to note that Richard Clarke, who served as National Coordinator for Security and

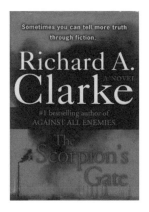

Richard A. Clarke
The Scorpion's Gate

Counterterrorism for both Presidents Clinton and Bush, added the following to the cover of his first novel *The Scorpion's Gate* written after his resignation: "Sometimes you can tell more truth through fiction."[82]

Fiction and Intelligence Services
Many authors have written some tantalizing facts about well-documented, even well-publicised links between many fiction writers on both sides of the Atlantic with the secret services showing that novelists and authors have always been employed by services all over the world in a variety of capacities. McCormick and Fletcher state that there is a long list of novelists who "have actually been involved at some time or other in intelligence work."[83] They suggest the number – in the United States – is now growing. They also stress the point that "intelligence services in recent times have actually used novelists to work into their books either facts or suggestions which they feel might help their own cause."[84] They add:

> "Factional" is a horrible word, but how else can one describe the increasing number of spy stories which, according to Jonathan Green's *Newspeak: A Dictionary of Jargon*, can be described as works of "fiction that is taken with only minimal alterations from events that actually happened?" It is partly because [of] the factional spy novel that Intelligence services all over the world eagerly study spy fiction as new books come out if only to see whether they have been compromised in some way, or if there are any worthwhile facts to be picked up.[85]

However, this is not new. There has always been a link between literature and the arts with intelligence services. It is a well-known fact that Daniel Defoe worked as a secret agent and a book sensationally claimed that even William Shakespeare was involved with the "secret services" of the day, and may have been assassinated because of this involvement.[86] Geoffrey Chaucer was involved with the secret services and was sent on a mission to discover state secrets in Flanders in the 1370s.[87] So was Christopher Marlowe.[88] Daniel Defoe was sent as an undercover agent to Scotland to "ensure that the Scottish parliament voted for union with England."[89]

Many contemporary popular fiction writers appear to belong to a tradition in which such authors have come not only from political and diplomatic careers or journalism but from the military, air force, navy and secret services. Such information is not disguised but sometimes advertised (no doubt for commercial reasons) on the dust jackets of fiction titles.

Masters gives an interesting insight into the subject, and shows that before, during, and after the First and Second World Wars a host of novelists worked for or were connected with the secret services. These include John Buchan, the "skilled propagandist" who was made Director of Intelligence in the First World War (and later Governor General of Canada), Somerset Maugham (who served as agent of the SIS in Switzerland, and chief agent in Russia), Compton Mackenzie, Malcolm Muggeridge Graham Greene (SIS) and later MI6, David Mure, Ian Fleming (who was chief assistant of the Naval Intelligence Division), Tom Driberg, John Bingham, and Dennis Wheatley.[90] Other novelists also worked for the Secret Service including William Le Queux, and Ted Allebeury. David Cornwell (writing under the pseudonym John le Carre) was recruited into MI5.[91] These and other writers were recruited because of their fertile imagination and sharp and questioning minds.[92] The very introduction to Masters's book was written by the thriller writer Len Deighton:

> I confess to not knowing much more about the British Secret Services than is contained in this book. But it tells us quite a lot. If its former members offer us the truth here – and it is difficult to believe that all of them are entirely wrong – Britain's security systems provide an abundance of material for plays, films and books for many years to come. You shudder? But read on. Here are characters no writer could invent, situations that even television producers would find too broad.[93]

The case of the American novelist Howard Hunt, who wrote more than forty novels under various pseudonyms and was, in Earle Davis' words, "a lifetime American agent, a spy, a member of OSS and then later the CIA and the White House Political Dirty Tricks Agency,"[94] is well documented. He has produced more than 40 novels which were as

bad as many written by Le Queux and
Oppenheim. At the suggestion of a friend, and
the approval and support of Richard Helms,
Howard wrote (under the pseudonym David
St. John) the Peter Ward series as "an
American counterpart to the James Bond
series." Helms felt that this would help the
image of the CIA through "a popular all-
American hero who would give them the
clean-up image of the intrepid lion heart who
always serves the nation's interest."[95] In addition, the American novelists Ib Jorgen

*American Novelist
Howard Hunt*

Melchior and Edward Weismiller were involved with the intelligence
service during the Second World War.[96] In the USSR, the KGB also
employed authors and novelists to "improve the image of the USSR" and
popularise "the KGB and GRU officers as noble heroes" who protect
their country. Andrei Gulyashki, a Bulgarian novelist invented a Soviet
hero with the aim of destroying James Bond.[97] Many others, like Joe
Maggio, Victor Marchetti and David Atlee Phillips were career officers
in the CIA.[98] One of the latest contributors to the genre is Stella
Rimington, former Director-General of MI5. Her first novel *At Risk* was
published in 2004 followed by *Secret Asset* in 2006.

Conclusion

Given the size of the industry and its global reach, not to mention the
almost cult status of some of its biggest names, it is indeed legitimate to
look at how popular taste evolves or is shaped by popular fiction; and,
furthermore, to what extent it is genuinely or spontaneously "popular,"
or rather foisted, in this consumerist age, on the social leviathan from
above. A sensational TV documentary revealed that modern art itself
was a "CIA weapon" as art and more generally culture became part of
the Cold War arsenal even as early as 1947.[99] From the American perspective the aim was to demonstrate that "the US was devoted to
freedom of expression" and was more progressive and forward-looking
than socialist art critics and theorists made it seem. This largely covert –
but heavily financed – campaign succeeded in making Abstract
Expressionism the dominant art movement of the post-war years giving

it high visibility in popular and specialist publications, banks, airports, city halls, great galleries and boardrooms almost all over the world.[100] In a monumental work David Caute explored the "cultural war" fought between the Soviet Union and the West in literature, theatre and the arts. He detailed the cultural "battles" fought in theatre, film, classical and popular music, ballet, painting, sculpture, and cultural exhibition and examined extensively and skillfully books and manuscripts in several languages to illustrate the depth of this cultural propaganda.[101] He also gives examples of its impact. Caute stresses that this war has no precedent or parallel noticing that "despite the intensity of religious and cultural animosity during the holy wars and *jihads* of earlier centuries, the Crusades, the Moorish invasions of Spain, the Thirty Years War, all of them were conducted by armed conquest."[102]

Saunders explores this "cultural war" in astonishing detail in *Who Paid the Piper?* She takes the reader through a list of names, organizations, and publishers who were part of a consortium started in 1947 to "nudge the intelligentsia of western Europe away from its lingering fascination with Marxism and Communism towards a view more accommodating of 'the American way'."[103]

The centerpiece of this campaign was the Congress for Cultural Freedom, run by the CIA from 1950–1967 to use psychological cultural propaganda in "a battle for men's minds" deploying as their weapons books, novels, journals, conferences, seminars, art exhibitions, concerts and awards. Saunders notes that:

> Whether they liked it or not, whether they knew it or not, there were few writers, poets, artists, historians, scientists or critics in post-war Europe whose names were not in some way linked to this covert enterprise. Unchallenged, undetected for over twenty years, America's spying establishment operated a sophisticated, substantially endowed cultural front in the West, *for* the West, in the name of freedom of expression.[104]

In "Waging the War of Ideas: Why There Are No Shortcuts," John Blundell summarises the "strategic insights" of F. A. Hayek. One of these is this:

> Over the long run, it is a battle of ideas, and it is the intellectual – the journalist, novelist, filmmaker, and so on, who translates and transmits the ideas of

the scholars to the broader public – who is critically important. He is the filter who decides what we hear, when we hear it, and how we hear it. [105]

No doubt some popular fiction authors can congratulate themselves on a job well done if they have taught their readers not only to accept the prevailing worldview but also to imagine their illusion of knowledge to be of substance by making fiction appear as fact. Without hard evidence people are convinced of the veracity of ideas, which the novelist in effect has romanticised into existence, giving shape to fears and prejudices.

The harmonious melting of perceived political truths with fiction is an irresistible combination, and many novelists have used this to persistently give a negative image of Islam and Muslims. Using smoke and mirrors to feign fictional events as factual possibilities, and to project Muslims as lying hotheads with an axe to grind, writers have taught us that our motives are always right and just, and that our position by definition always correct. They have also defined political discourse and turned it into a ludicrous game of power play and heroic posturing, our good guys outwitting your fanatics. It may be crass and simplistic, but it is effective.

REFERENCES

Alldritt, Keith, *The Poet as Spy: The Life and Wild Times of Basil Bunting* (London: Aurum Press, 1998).

Beeston, Richard, "Hospital Search Fails to Find WMDs," *The Times* (9th June, 2003).

Blundell, John, "Waging the War of Ideas: Why There Are No Shortcuts" (The Heritage Foundation, n.d.), Monograph 254.

Burrowes, John, *Gulf: At Last the Real Story of Arabia as it Truly is in the Eighties* (Edinburgh: Mainstream Publishing, 1988).

Caute, David, *The Dancer Defects: The Struggle for Cultural Supremacy During the Cold War* (Oxford: Oxford University Press, 2003).

Clarke, Richard, *The Scorpion's Gate* (New York: G.P. Putnam's Sons, 2005).

Colla, Elliot's Response, in Letters to the Editor, *ISIM Newsletter* (Spring, 2005).

Colla, Elliot, "A Culture of Righteousness and Martyrdom," *ISIM Newsletter* (June, 2004).

Crowdy, Terry, *The Enemy Within: A History of Espionage* (Oxford: Osprey Publishing, 2006).

Davies, Earl, "Howard Hunt and the Peter Ward-CIA Novels," *Kansas Quarterly* (Fall, 1978), X.

Easterman, Daniel, "The New Anti-Semitism," in *New Jerusalems: Reflections on Islam, Fundamentalism and the Rushdie Affair* (London: Grafton, 1992).

Erdman, Paul E., *The Crash of 79* (London: Secker & Warburg, 1976).

Fallaci, Oriana, *Inshalla* (London: Chatto and Windus, 1992).

Greenburg, Martin H., ed., *The Tom Clancy Companion* (London: Fontana, 1992).

Hamilton, Alex, "Top Hundred Chart of 1993 Paperback Fastsellers," in *Writers' and Artists Yearbook 1995* (London: A. & C. Black).

Holt, Robert Lawrence, *Good Friday* (London: W.H. Allen, 1988).

Hugo, Grant, "The Political Influence of the Thriller," *Contemporary Review* (December, 1972).

Magill, Frank N., ed., *Critical Survey of Long Fiction: English Language Services* (Englewood, NJ: Salem Press, 1983).

Masters, Anthony, *Literary Agents: The Novelist as Spy* (Oxford: Basil Blackwell, 1987).

McCormick, Donald and Katy Fletcher, *Spy Fiction: A Connoisseur's Guide* (Oxford: Facts On File, 1990).

Nourallah, Riad, "Sorcerers, Straight Swords, and Scimitars: The Arab-Islamic East in Modern Fantasies of Magic and Conflict," *The International Journal of Islamic and Arabic Studies,* Indiana University (1990).

Panek, LeRoy L., *The Special Branch: The British Spy Novel 1890–1980* (Bowling Green, Ohio: Bowling Green University Popular Press, 1981).

Philips, Graham and Martin Keatman, *The Shakespeare Conspiracy* (London: Century, 1994).

Pierce, William Luther, *The Turner Diaries* (USA: National Vanguard Books), 1978.

Poyer, David, *Black Storm* (New York: St. Martin's Press, 2002).

_____, *The Gulf* (New York: Saint Martin's, 1990).

Riggs, David, *The World of Christopher Marlowe* (London: Faber and Faber, 2004).

Shaheen, Jack G., *The TV Arab* (Bowling Green, Ohio: State University Popular Press, 1984).

Simon, Reeva, *The Middle East in Crime Fiction: Mysteries, Spy Novels and Thrillers 1916 to the 1980's* (New York: Lilian Barber, 1989)

Stoner Saunders, Frances, *Who Paid the Piper?: The CIA and the Cultural Cold War* (London: Granta Books, 1999).

Turnbull, Malcolm J., *Victims or Villains: Jewish Images in Classic English Detective Fiction* (Bowling Green, OH: State University Popular Press, 1998).

Wark, Wesley K., ed., *Spy Fiction, Spy Films and Real Intelligence* (London: Frank Cass, 1991).

ELMIRA MURATOVA

Crimean Tatar Revival: National Identity and Islam

Introduction

THE CRIMEAN TATARS PRESENT a particularly fascinating example of ethnic cleansing in the twentieth century. They were not only removed en masse and in toto from their homeland to a far-off land where they had no connections; they were then after more than four decades allowed to return. A people who during recent centuries experienced annexation, oppression and even deportation has returned to its homeland and is reviving its national culture with immense patience. Despite numerous problems and considerable provocation during this process, the Crimean Tatars intend to reestablish their right to be seen as an indigenous Crimean nation through the use of legal democratic methods.

National identity and Islam which form the main components of national identification, played a very important role during the period of deportation, helping to prevent the assimilation and disappearance of the Crimean Tatars. Now they are also key components in the revival process. The Tatars returned to the Crimea with a strong sense of national identity that has become even more clearly defined during the revival process. In the case of Islam, the process of its revival started from scratch, because almost all symbols of Islamic culture in the Crimea had been destroyed by the previous regime. Only the Crimean Tatars' faith and the religious traditions that they had preserved came to the Crimea with its indigenous inhabitants.

There is a degree of interest from Ukrainian scholars in the Crimean Tatar revival. Numerous publications and conferences have been devoted to the process of their rehabilitation and integration into Ukrainian society. Today most reasonable people in the Ukraine recognise that without a resolution for the Crimean Tatars' problems, peace and normal development in the Crimea are impossible. Western scholars have evinced some interest in the process too.

The main purpose of this paper is to present a brief overview of the process of the Crimean Tatar revival, concentrating on the role that national identity and Islam are playing in it. I will first provide a brief survey of the chief milestones in Crimean Tatar history. I will then present the key points in the process of national revival: the creation and functioning of national organisations, the main problems in the repatriation process, and the ethnic situation in the Crimea. Finally, I will concentrate on the process of Islamic revival in modern-day Crimea.

The Historical Legacy

Before beginning any discussion of the process of national revival among the Crimean Tatars, it is important to consider the nation's past. In order to be able to understand fully the context of the modern revival, it is essential to be aware of the key points in Crimean Tatar history.

The Crimean Tatar nation was formed on the territory of what is now the Crimean Autonomous Republic (in modern-day Ukraine) in the early 15th century. This process went side by side with the process of state building in the course of which various local ethnic groups (Cumans, Khazars, Pechenegs, for example) and newly arrived (Mongols and Tatars) were integrated into the Crimean Khanate under the Gerei dynasty. After a lengthy process of ethno-genesis, the Crimean Tatars, a Turkic-speaking people, whose religion became Islam, had appeared. It is noteworthy that the Crimean Khanate was only independent for a few decades and in 1475 the Gerei dynasty accepted the Ottoman Empire's protectorate. From that time on all political, economical, and religious processes in the Crimea were directly connected with the politics of the Ottoman Empire in the region. The Crimea became an outpost of Turkish policy in Eastern Europe and numerous wars with their Slav neighbors formed one of the main activities of the Crimean Tatars. At the same time, in the 16–17th centuries the Crimea became the centre of Muslim culture in the region, and a huge number of mosques, mausoleums, madrasahs, as well as Islamic elementary schools (*mektebes*) were set up. Thus, according to some scholars, by the end of the 18th century there were around 1600 mosques, 25 madrasahs and many *mektebes* active in the Crimea.[1] The whole of life in the Crimean Khanate was regulated according to Islamic Shariʿah law.

As the Ottoman Empire's power was declining by the 18th century, the position of all its satellites also weakened. The fate of the Crimean Tatars was especially dramatic. In 1783 the Russian Empire annexed the Crimean Khanate and declared it part of its own territory. Many Crimean Tatars who did not want to live in a country ruled by an infidel Empress decided to emigrate to Turkey. This resulted in the first and the biggest wave of Crimean Tatar emigration. Many villages were abandoned and mosques, madrasahs, and *mektebes* were closed as a result. Those Tatars who were left were forced to submit to Russian rule. All administration in the Crimea, including the new Spiritual Administration of Crimean Muslims (*Tavricheskoe Magometanskoe Dukhovnoe Pravlenie*), was firmly under the state control.

The second wave of Tatar emigration began in 1853 when the Crimean War which set the Russian Empire against England, France, and Turkey, broke out. The Crimean Tatars protested against their forced involvement in the war on the Russian side. Furthermore, both armies destroyed Tatar villages, requisitioned their animals, and so on. The third wave of emigration began in 1918 after the October Revolution and the establishment of an atheist government. Many Tatars just fled the Crimea, however they might. Many of them died of diseases while waiting to escape by ship from seaports in the Crimea.

Because of all these waves of emigration, the total number of Tatars in the Crimean Autonomous Republic decreased considerably. If, by the middle of the 19th century, Tatars constituted about fifty per cent of the Crimean population, by the early 1940s they formed only about twenty-five per cent. The decline in the population influenced the economic and cultural life of the peninsula. Many mosques were closed and were constantly being destroyed. For example, by 1914 there were only 729 mosques left in the Crimea.[2]

In the 1930s the Soviet government started the final process of destroying Muslim culture in the Crimea. By 1940 there were no active mosques at all in the peninsula; many of them were closed on the pretext of being in poor condition and turned into clubs, grocery stores, schools, and so on. On 18 May 1944 the whole Muslim population of the Crimea (about 200,000 people) was deported from its homeland and settled in the Central Asian republics. After that, all symbols of Crimean Tatars' presence in the Crimea were eradicated. The Soviet government justified this terrible act by claiming that the Crimean Tatars had been collaborating with the Nazis during the Second World War. Almost half the nation died during deportation and in the first months of resettlement. The Tatars were settled in special places and for the first few years had various restrictions placed upon them, for instance, on their movements. Only in 1956 did the government rescind the accusation of treachery, but they were still prevented from returning to the Crimea. Some amelioration occurred in the 1980s during the 'perestroika' period. Because of the liberalisation of the regime, the Tatars began returning to their homeland and this process became a genuine mass movement during the first years after the collapse of the USSR.

The Crimean Tatar National Revival

Between the late 1980s and 2006 more than a half of all Crimean Tatars returned to their homeland. According to official statistics, in 2005 there were about a quarter of a million Tatars in the Crimea. The most active period in the repatriation process occurred in the early 1990s; thereafter it declined year on year. If, between 1989 and 1992 about 35–40,000 Crimean Tatars returned each year, in 1997 the total was only 5,300 Tatars (in 1998 – 3,400, in 1999 – 2,800, in 2000 – 2,200, in 2001 – 2,000, in 2002 – 1,000).[3] Hence, according to various sources, almost 100,000 Crimean Tatars still remain in the places to which they were deported (80,000 in Uzbekistan, 15,000 in Russia, and 5,000 in Tajikistan and Kyrgyzstan).[4]

All the Crimean Tatars who came to the Crimea possessed the idea that their homeland lay there, the place where they and their parents were born and where they were planning to revive national statehood and culture. Thus, the Tatars came to the Crimea with a strong sense of national identity and there it was simply defined and developed.

In 1991 during the first *Kurultai* (national congress) of the Crimean Tatars the representative body of the nation, the Medzhlis was created. The leaders of the Medzhlis declared this organisation 'a national Crimean Tatar government.' Although this status was not officially recognised, for many years the Medzhlis remained the sole representative organisation at state level as well as in the international arena. The head of the Medzhlis was a former Soviet dissident, Mustafa Dzhemilev. At the first *Kurultai* the Crimean Tatars also issued a 'Declaration of National Sovereignty' in which an orientation towards national statehood was openly declared.

From the early 1990s on, the Medzhlis tried to construct a vertical system of power to connect all Crimean Tatars from the bottom up, one which could then be used as a convenient tool for mobilising people for political activity of various kinds. From the inception of their activity in the peninsula Tatar leaders have pledged their support for the idea of Ukrainian national sovereignty and independence, and for many years the Tatars have been almost the main loyal pro-Ukrainian force in Russian-dominated Crimea.

From the early 1990s, Crimean Tatar leaders have demanded representation in the administration at both republican and local levels appropriate to their numbers. But numerous problems have meant their representation is less than they would wish. In May 1999, on the 45th anniversary of the Crimean Tatars' deportation, a Council of Crimean Tatar Representatives was created under the aegis of the President of Ukraine. It mainly consists of the members of the Medzhlis, who have drafted numerous laws and other projects which, when adopted, will improve the situation of the Crimean Tatars. But bureaucratic delays and the confused situation among the political elites in Ukraine mean that the Council has not been able to achieve any tangible results.

The Main Difficulties and Problems in the Repatriation Process

The Crimean Tatars have faced numerous socio-economic, political, and cultural problems during the process of repatriation. These include problems with housing, employment, the revival of the language, and others. Almost half the people (120,000 people) have nowhere to live; 22,000 of them rent, while 14,000 live in hostels. The settlements where the Crimean Tatars dominate numerically, where people have already built or are still building houses, have problems with the electricity supply (75 percent of the places), water (27 percent), gas (more than 90 percent), as well as problems with roads and sewage.

The other main problem is unemployment. According to official statistics, only 56 percent of Crimean Tatars have permanent jobs.

Although in the places to where they were deported Tatars mainly lived in towns, 55 percent of them today draw their income from agriculture. Only about 20 percent work in industry and construction while another 5 percent work in markets. Many Tatars, even those with higher education, have been forced to seek jobs at the food and clothes markets. According to statistics, Tatars constitute about 70 percent of all traders in the food markets and 30 percent in the clothes markets.[5]

There is also a problem with land. About 75 percent of all Crimean Tatars live today in rural areas, but according to the legislature only 18 percent have been able to acquire any private land.[6] During the process of privatisation following the collapse of the Soviet Union the Tatars, who had come to the Crimea only a few years before, many of whom were not members of the collective farms in the peninsula, were excluded from land distribution. Numerous demonstrations demanding a share of the land failed to resolve the problem, and served only to complicate relations with other ethnic groups.

In the political sphere, the Crimean Tatars demand official recognition of the *Kurultai* and Medzhlis as primary representative bodies. They further demand that they be assigned the special status of an indigenous people, that drafts of laws – 'On the renewal of rights and freedoms for deported Crimean Tatars, national minorities and people deported for reasons of their ethnicity' and 'On the status of the Crimean Tatar nation' which have been drawn up – be adopted. If these laws are passed, the Tatars will be able to receive financial compensation for deportation and defend their economic and political rights. Among other problems are those of inadequate representation in senior positions within the local administration as well as the recognition of the Crimean Tatar language as the second state language of the Crimea.

Other problematic spheres such as language, culture, and religion exist in modern Crimea. Because of their fifty years of deportation, the Crimean Tatar language has been excluded from the sphere of education and learning. Now it is basically only spoken at home and unfortunately, not by all families. Tatar leaders constantly insist on resolving this problem, seeing language as one of the main factors that may prevent assimilation. By 2004 their efforts had resulted in the opening of twelve secondary schools where instruction is in the Crimean Tatar language. Two Crimean universities (Taurida National V. Vernadsky University and the Crimean Engineering Pedagogical University) have departments teaching degrees in Crimean Tatar language and literature, with a combined annual enrolment of about 80 students.

It is essential to remark that over the last 16 years there have been some achievements in resolving the Crimean Tatars' problems. The Ukrainian government pays about 40 million *gryvnas* (the national currency) annually to help the Tatars build homes and help them resolve their other socio-economic difficulties (through financial support for students, for national newspapers, and so on). Although this money is too little (some experts claim that the whole process of repatriation, adaptation, and integration of the Crimean Tatars requires around 2 billion dollars) it does help improve the situation. There is also some financial help from international organisations and certain Muslim countries, such as Turkey, Saudi Arabia, the United Arab Emirates, and so on.

The Ethnic Situation in the Crimea

There are three main ethnic groups in modern Crimea: Russians (about 57 percent), Ukrainians (about 25 percent), and Crimean Tatars (about 13 percent). From the very beginning of their return, Tatars were and still are a minority in the peninsula. They are an ethnic minority, a Turkic nation surrounded by Slavs as well as a religious one, being Muslims in a region where the vast majority of the population is Orthodox. Hence, we have an interesting situation where a nation that was dominant in the Crimea in the past is now just a minority in its own homeland. The Crimean Tatars who created a state that was influential at that time, the Crimean Khanate, have now returned and are concerned about defending their right to be in their own home.

There is real historical debate about the origin of the Crimean Tatars. A popular theory produced by Russian and then Soviet historians holds that the Tatars are not native to the Crimea. According to this view, the Tatars came as invaders during the Mongol invasion of the thirteenth century. Hence, they are not indigenous and that is why, according to this extreme point of view, they do not have the right to return to the Crimea after deportation nor demand anything. Even if they have this right, according to a more liberal view, their status in the Crimea should not differ from that of other ethnic groups. The main argument against this view is that Crimean Tatars do not have a homeland anywhere in the world except Crimea, unlike other ethnic groups such as the Russians, Ukrainians, or Armenians.

As a result, relations among different ethnic groups in the Crimea are very complex. Many Slavic (mainly Russian) people have a hostile attitude towards the Crimean Tatars. During many years of Soviet propaganda, the image of Tatars as enemies who helped the Nazis during the war, a people who are hostile to outsiders, uneducated and backward has been fostered. And even today after the collapse of the Soviet system, this stereotype still influences many people. The situation is complicated by the fact that the Tatars are strongly oriented towards the West, while the Slavic population is mainly connected and oriented to Russia. According to sociological surveys conducted by Crimean scholars among students at secondary schools, the gap in understanding members of different ethnic groups is very wide. For example, the Slavs living in the peninsula expressed a high level of xenophobia toward all deported people.[7] This is not only sad but dangerous. It evidently results from an education and upbringing which are not oriented towards the building of a tolerant society.

The Revival of Islam in the Crimea

When the Crimean Tatars began returning to the peninsula, there was nothing to show that the Crimea had once been a centre of Muslim culture in Eastern Europe. Mosques had been razed to the ground or else used for inappropriate purposes; Muslim cemeteries too had been destroyed and cities and streets renamed. After 16 years of the Islamic revival in the Crimea some progress can be observed. The quantitative indicators of the process – the number of Muslim communities, mosques and clergy are steadily growing. At the same time, contradictions between quantity and quality in the process still remain.

Muslim Communities

In other parts of the world, an Islamic revival begins with the creation of a Muslim community. The same scenario has also been happening in the Crimea. By the end of 2006 there were 361 Muslim communities in the Crimea. The vast majority (324) was under the jurisdiction of the Spiritual Administration of Crimean Muslims (*Dukhovnoe Upravlenie Musul'man Kryma*), the DUMK, with its office in Simferopol, while one recognised the authority of another Spiritual Administration based in Kiev. Apart from these, there were more than thirty autonomous communities in the Crimea.

Figure 1. Graph illustrating the numerical rise in Muslim communities

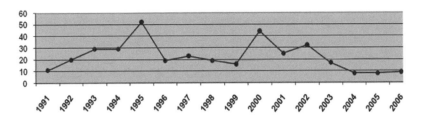

The rise in the number of Muslim communities constitutes a dynamic process which began in the late 1980s, reached a peak in 1995 and after a brief decline was reactivated in 1999.

The dynamics of this process correlates to the personalities of the individual Muftis of the DUMK. It was possible to form these communities on a mass scale during the time of the first mufti, Seitdzhelil Ibragimov (1991–95), who at the time was the only Crimean Tatar who had received an Islamic education (he had graduated from the *Mir-Arab* madrasah in Bukhara). Then a slight slowing down of the process coincided with the time of the second mufti, Nuri Mustafaev (1995–99). The second growth spurt occurred in the time of the third mufti Emir-Ali Ablaev (1999–). It would appear that, leaving aside other objective reasons, the personal actions of each mufti must have influenced this process in some respect.

What is remarkable is that a considerable proportion of Muslim communities created between 2000 and 2006 were almost entirely autonomous from the DUMK. Such communities appeared because of the disputes between the DUMK which supports the revival of Islam 'traditional' to the Crimean Tatars, and those Crimean Tatars who have their own views on what kind of Islam should be revived in the Crimea.

Judging by the number of Muslims in the Crimea, it would appear that the rise in the number of Muslim communities is particularly intense. For example, it is twice as intensive as in the Russian republic of Tatarstan.

At the same time it is necessary to emphasise that Muslim communities in modern Crimea do not act as they once did, for instance during the Crimean Khanate. Today they are more dependant economically and politically (on the DUMK and Medzhlis) and their self-regulatory function does not work well. Apart from this, in some places Muslim communities exist only on paper.

Mosques in the Crimea

Between the early 1990s and 2006 about 124 mosques opened in the Crimea; of these 76 were built from scratch while others were reconstructed. Other than these, about 150 buildings throughout the Crimea were adopted as Muslim prayer spaces. The process of mosque construction started in 1991 when Turkish representatives laid the foundation stone of the main mosque in Simferopol, *Kebir Dzhami*. The first new mosques opened in 1995.

During the first period of Islamic revival in the Crimea almost all the new mosques were built by Turkish sponsors – some sixteen new mosques in total. From 1997 on, Arab sponsors also started supporting the Tatars in this process. By 2006, 45 mosques had been built by organisations and private sponsors from different Arab countries (Saudi Arabia, United Arab Emirates, and Kuwait). Another twelve mosques were built by Ukrainians including some Crimean Tatars, and another three were built by members of the Crimean Tatar Diaspora in the West.

Figure 2. Sponsors of new mosques in the Crimea

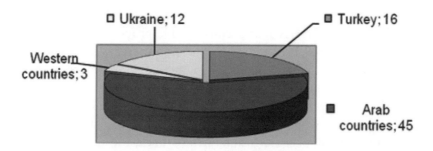

The Crimean Tatars started building mosques with their own funds quite late, in the early years of this millennium. It is understandable; in the 1990s people were busy dealing with other socio-economic problems. What is more, even today when the economic situation of many Crimean Tatars has certainly improved, it is still not widespread.

The total number of mosques in today's Crimea is, of course, much below what it was in the khanate period. At the same time, we should not perhaps compare the current situation with the historic one for a number of objective reasons. Of these the most significant is that there was a different level of religiosity among Crimean Tatars in the past and hence the number of mosques required to serve the people also differed. According to a sociological survey conducted in 2000, only 12.2 percent of respondents attend mosque everyday or every week; 4.3 percent once a month and 42.4 percent sporadically, mainly on Muslim holidays. Hence, 41.1 percent of respondents never go to a mosque.[8] This data is supported by observations that many mosques in modern-day Crimea are empty most of the time.

Islamic Education

From the early 1990s, there was a real problem in the Crimea with finding Muslim clergy. Muslim communities were being rapidly formed, but there was almost a total absence of educated imams in them. There are two main ways to receive an Islamic education in the Crimea today. The first is 'external,' receiving an education at Muslim universities in different Arab countries or in theological departments in Turkey. This option was deemed unproductive by Crimean Tatar national and religious leaders, because only a few of the students sent abroad ever returned, and those who did had been 'infected' by various 'dangerous' ideologies. The leaders, therefore, brought in another way of acquiring an Islamic education. With the support of official and private Turkish organisations, four madrasahs have been set up in the Crimea.

These madrasahs offer a 2–3 year programme. On graduation students normally receive a diploma that qualifies them as imams. Madrasahs in the Crimea mostly follow the same syllabus as in Turkey, but with an additional subject, the Crimean Tatar language. Students at Crimean madrasahs are generally a little older than in Turkey. The biggest madrasah in *Azovskoe* village has been functioning since 1998.

It has a three year course that is absolutely free for students, and has separate departments for boys and girls.

Apart from the madrasahs, there is the Hafez School in Simferopol that concentrates on teaching students to learn the Qur'an, as well as other Qur'anic and Friday schools that offer basic Arabic and the basics of Islam to anyone who wishes to attend.

It must be emphasised that despite the existence of madrasahs, there is still a shortage of educated imams in the Crimea. The vast majority of active imams are over thirty, people who as a rule do not have any religious education, because they were of school age in the Soviet period when there was only one madrasah (in Bukhara) for the whole country, and thus, unsurprisingly, the competition for places was ferocious. Thus, they basically studied Islam on their own. This category of imams constitutes about 75 percent of the total. The remaining 25 percent, who are under thirty, includes a large number of graduates of Crimean madrasahs and other religious institutions in Muslim countries.

Pilgrimage

In the last fifteen years, the Crimean Tatars have been able to perform Hajj to Makkah. By 2006 the pilgrimage had been organised six times with overall more than 400 people taking part. There are some features of Hajj specific to the Crimean Tatars. Firstly, only once (in 2006) did the Crimean Tatars finance their Hajj themselves. The other five times it was paid for by the Saudi government.

Secondly, in contrast to other post-Soviet regions, the Crimean people first went on pilgrimage only in the second half of the 1990s. Only in 1997 did the first twenty Crimean Tatars along with other Ukrainians visit Saudi Arabia. The explanation is that Arab organisations only came to the Crimea in the second half of the 1990s.

Thirdly, the Hajj was organised primarily not by the official Islamic body, the DUMK, but by private charitable organisations. While in 1999–2000 the DUMK was somehow connected with this process, in 2002–03 it was completely excluded from it.

Fourthly, organisation of Hajj became politicised. Members of the DUMK and Medzhlis tried to select only those who were loyal to them for Hajj. Arguments between the Medzhlis and the DUMK on the one hand and charities on the other provoked the Saudi government into canceling the invitation to the Hajj in 2001.

Thus according to the indicators listed above (communities, mosques, Islamic education, and pilgrimage) the process of Islamic revival in the Crimea is proceeding in a dynamic fashion. The number of communities and mosques is rapidly increasing. At the same time, this does not indicate a growth in religious feeling among the people. In this particular case, quantity definitely prevails over quality.

The Medzhlis and Islam

From the very beginning, the Medzhlis took an active part in the process of Islamic revival. Between 1991 and 2006, Medzhlis leaders participated in more than 100 meetings where they discussed the religious problems of Crimean Muslims.[9] Their activity in this sphere peaked in 1998 and then slowed. In this particular year, the Medzhlis was trying to resolve the problems connected with the activities of the Muslim Party of Ukraine (*Partiia Musul'man Ukrainy*) which first appeared right before the parliamentary elections and was opposed to the Medzhlis. Other than this, with the support of various Islamic organisations, the Medzhlis tried to organise an international Islamic conference on the Crimean Tatars.

Figure 3. The frequency of Medzhlis meetings devoted to the problems of Crimean Muslims

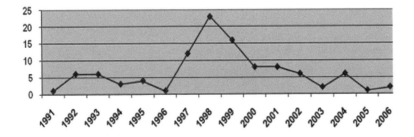

Using the figure above, we can highlight three periods of Medzhlis involvement in Islamic revival in the Crimea. The first (1991–1996) may be characterised as a period of great enthusiasm. Crimean Tatar leaders were highly optimistic about Islamic revival and were convinced of the strength of Islamic solidarity on the part of other Muslim states. The second (1997–2000) was the peak of Medzhlis involvement. In these three years, the topic of Islamic revival made up fifty per cent of the Medzhlis leaders' contacts. And, finally, the third period (2001–2006) is characterised by the slowing down of communication with Muslim leaders. Enthusiasm was replaced by scepticism and pragmatism. Medzhlis leaders undertook several initiatives, aimed at 'saving' the Crimean Muslim community from Islamic ideologies that they viewed as "non-traditional" for the Crimean Tatars.

Objective data reveal the Medzhlis' interest in Islam and the large part it has played in the process of Islamic revival. At the same time, some scholars criticise the Medzhlis for its direct control over the DUMK and the whole revival process. Some stress that the role of the Medzhlis is largely negative, because it uses Islam for political purposes; hence, Islam is just a symbol in its nationalist project.

About 75 percent of all the meetings held by the Medzhlis that were about Islam were with foreign Islamic organisations and Ukrainian charities funded from abroad. For example, the Medzhlis has had contacts with Muslim countries such as Turkey, Saudi Arabia, United Arab Emirates, Kuwait, Libya and Iran. Apart from this, Islamic revival has been supported by international Islamic organisations such as the Islamic Bank of Development, the World Islamic League and the World

Figure 4. Meeting between foreign Islamic countries and the Medzhlis

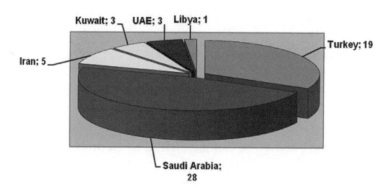

Kuwait; 3   UAE; 3   Libya; 1

Iran; 5

Turkey; 19

Saudi Arabia; 28

Association of Islamic Youth. The contribution of all these countries and organisations in Islamic revival in the Crimea varies as can be seen from the chart below detailing their contacts with Medzhlis leaders.

The significant figures in the Islamic revival in the Crimea are thus Saudi Arabia (28 meetings), Turkey (19), Iran (5), Kuwait (3), United Arab Emirates (3) and Libya (1).

Contacts between the Medzhlis and international Islamic centres take a number of specific forms. The *first* aspect is related to the religious education and training of Muslim clergy from the Crimea in educational institutions in Muslim countries. Crimean Tatars go off to study in Turkey, Saudi Arabia, Iran, Libya and elsewhere. The *second* involves the humanitarian work of charities in the Crimea. Islamic organisations are constructing new and restoring old mosques, helping orphans and the poor. Some organisations dig wells or construct roads and medical buildings for the Crimean Tatars. The *third* is the cultural and educational work of Islamic organisations in the Crimea. They open Qur'anic and Friday schools to teach Qur'an and Arabic and organise conferences and seminars. For example, for several years now Turkish organisations have been conducting conferences celebrating the birthday of the Prophet Muhammad.

Despite the active support of Islamic countries and organisations in the Islamic revival, many scholars stress that their role is ambivalent. On the one hand, they help in all the areas mentioned above, and on the other, they have divided the Crimean Tatars into followers of different Islamic teachings. Crimean Tatar leaders have claimed that foreign missionaries have imported ideas that contradict what is traditional for Crimean Islam. On the one hand, they are right, because over the centuries the Crimean Tatars practised an Islam that differs from that practised by, for example, Muslims in the Middle East. On the other hand, many national leaders are in fact mythologising the notion of 'traditional' Islam which they identify as a unique Crimean 'form' of Islam.

The Chronology of Islamic Revival

The process of Islamic revival in the Crimea has a specific chronology in which three main periods can be discerned. The first period (1989–95) should be seen as a *period of institutionalisation* of Islam in the Crimea. It may be characterised by phenomena such as:

- The development of Muslim communities;
- The formation of administrative Muslim bodies: the DUMK and the Council of Imams;
- The opening of the first educational institutions (madrasahs) and revival of Muslim clergy.

The second period (1996–2000) constitutes a *period of the politicising* of Islam in the Crimea. This is characterised by the following features:
- The establishment of control over the DUMK by the Medzhlis and drawing it into political activity;
- The use of Islam as a mobilisation tool for political purposes by the Medzhlis;
- The maneuvering between different religious organisations and directions by the Medzhlis.

The third period (from 2000) may be identified as the *period of realism,* because of the Medzhlis' and DUMK's consciousness of what kind of Islam they want to revive in the Crimea and how they wish to do this. The main features of this period include:
- The revision by the Medzhlis of its policy of politicising Islam and radicalisation;
- Defining the priorities in Islam's development in the Crimea, the orientation towards "traditional" vs. "foreign" Islam;
- The decrease in relations with international Islamic organisations, and the policy of selective contacts.

Conclusion

Throughout the process of deportation, a sense of national identity and Islam both played very important roles in saving the Crimean Tatars as a nation. Although Crimean Tatars had lost their homeland, their history, the chance of an education in their own language and a feeling of pride in belonging to a distinctive nation, they still preserved their identity. Although the environment in the Central Asian republics was among fellow Muslims who spoke a related Turkic language, the people returned home with a strong self-identification as Crimean Tatars.

Furthermore, the Crimean Tatars preserved their religion despite an oppressively atheist regime. They practised it at home and handed it down from generation to generation. They therefore arrived in the Crimea as representatives of a Muslim religion and civilisation. In deportation national identity and Islam were very closely connected. For Crimean Tatars it was impossible to be a Tatar and not be a Muslim at the same time. Of course, there were some deviations from this rule – some Tatars did become atheists – but they were not numerous. The vast majority identified themselves as Crimean Tatars and Muslims at the same time and both identifications were interconnected and carried equal significance.

After deportation, once the process of national revival was under way, national identity and Islam acquired a slightly different meaning. Now Crimean Tatars have begun to question themselves and others, asking what is more important: to be a Tatar or a Muslim? This question became relevant because of the appearance of different schools of Islam in the Crimea. Many Crimean Tatars have become supporters of "traditional" Islam (with its many borrowings from the nation's pre-Islamic past), while others insist on adopting 'true' Islam (without any later ethnic accretions). Hence, today national identity and Islam still unite many Crimean Tatars but may, in some cases, also divide them.

REFERENCES

Aleksandrov, I., *O musul'manskom dukhovenstve i upravlenii dukhovnymi delami musul'man v Krymu posle ego prisoedineniia k Rossii* [On the Muslim clergy and the management of Muslim affairs in the Crimea after its incorporation into Russia] (Simferopol: Tipographiia Tavricheskogo gubernskogo zemstva, 1914).

Aradzhioni, M., Issledovanie sovremennogo urovnia tolerantnosti naseleniia poluostrova i istoricheskogo opyta mezhetnicheskikh i mezhkonfessio al'nykh otnoshenii v Krymu (po materialam issledovanii, 2001–2004 gg.) [Research into the current level of tolerance among the population of the peninsula and the historical experience of interethnic and interfaith relations in the Crimea (based on the materials of 2001–2004)]. In *Problemy integratsii krymskikh repatriantov v ukrainskoe obschestvo* [The problems of integrating Crimean repatriates into Ukrainian soc-iety] (Kiev: Svitogliad).

Avamileva, E., "Nekotorye aspekty zemel'noi reformy v Krymu" [Some aspects of land reform in the Crimea]. In *Problemy integratsii krymskikh repatriantov v ukrainskoe obschestvo* [The problems of integrating Crimean repatriates into Ukrainian society] (Kiev: Svitogliad, 2004).

Grigor'iants, Vladimir, *O nekotorykh osobennostiakh protsessa vozrozhdeniia isla-ma v Krymu 1989–2001* [On some features of the Islamic revival in the Crimea, 1989–2001] (Simferopol: Krymskii arkhiv, 2002).

Dzhanguzhin, Rustem, *Islam v politicheskoi zhizni Ukrainy* [Islam in Ukrainian political life] (*Tsentral'naia Aziia i Kavkaz,* 2001), vol. 2.

Kiryushko, Nikolai, *Islam u zhitti kryms'kikh tatar* [Islam in the Crimean Tatars' life]. *Liudina i svit* [The individual and the world], 2001, vol. 1.

Kratkaia khronika deiatel'nosti Medzhlisa krymskotatarskogo naroda, iiul' 1991–iiun' 1996 [Short chronicle of Crimean Tatar Medzhlis activity, July 1991–June 1996] (Simferopol: Odzhak, 1996).

Kratkaia khronika deiatel'nosti Medzhlisa krymskotatarskogo naroda, ianvar'-oktiabr' 2001 [Short chronicle of Crimean Tatar Medzhlis activity, January–October, 2001] (Simferopol: Odzhak, 2001).

Krichinskii, A., *Ocherki russkoi politiki na okrainakh. K istorii religioznykh prites-nenii krymskikh tatar* [Studies in Russian policy on the borders. On the history of religious pressure on the Crimean Tatars] (Baku: Izdanie soiuza musul'manskoi trudovoi intelligentsii [Publication of Muslim working intelligentsia union], 1919), Chapter 1.

Voronin, V., Realizatsiia zakhodiv derzhavy shodo integratsii v ukrains'ke suspil'st-vo deportovanykh kryms'kykh tatar i osib inshykh natsional'nostei: sychasnii stan i perspectyvy [The realisation of state initiatives towards deported Crimean Tatars and other nationalities concerning their integration into Ukrainian socie-ty: the current situation and outlook]. In *Problemy integratsii krymskikh repatriantov v ukrainskoe obschestvo* [The problems of integrating Crimean repatriates into Ukrainian society] (Kiev: Svitogliad, 2004).

Uehling, Greta Lynn, *Beyond Memory: The Crimean Tatars' Deportation and Return* (New York-Basingstoke: Palgrave Macmillan, 2004).

MOHAMMAD SIDDIQUE SEDDON

Global Citizenry Ancient and Modern: British Yemenis and Translocal Tribalism

Introduction

WHILST IT IS RELATIVELY EASY to study and understand many aspects of religious and cultural identity within their traditional cultural space, the processes of migration and settlement in a new social domain transform the established constructions of identities. Notions of communal religious identity and ideas about what actually constitutes 'Muslimness' have led to a number of different if not dichotomous interpretations amongst Yemeni Muslim community members in Britain. Another equally perplexing identity question within the diaspora British Yemeni community is what constitutes being a Yemeni when one is located beyond the traditional cultural space and geographical boundaries? Again, identity constructions are normally facilitated through social institutions as a primary means of reifying religious and cultural distinctiveness. But, unlike public institutions that incorporate and propagate religious expression and identity, manifestations of Yemeni cultural identity are less visible in the public space. Instead, it is the private and intimate domains – the family, home, relatives, friends, food, dress, music, language, etc – that represent and signify aspects of 'Yemeniness,' or Yemeni culture.

This paper will explore some of the important facets of British Yemeni identity constructions that nurture and develop a sense of cultural belonging within the diaspora community. By examining their notions of diaspora Yemeniness, we can perhaps understand how the community maintains and establishes its sense of distinctiveness or difference and what specific practises aid the construction of cultural identity and how it develops any new or hybrid identities within the context of contemporary Britain.

MOHAMMAD SIDDIQUE SEDDON

What is a Cultural Identity?

According to Stuart Hall, migration reparticularises people and cultures in relation to one another and their places of settlement. In addition to large scale migrations of people from their original place of settlement in both the twentieth and twenty-first centuries, the added phenomenon of globalisation has reconstructed the relationship between the 'local' and the 'global' in terms of meaning and attachment to a particular place. Migrated communities to Britain, like the Yemenis, have a global dimension to their traditional culture through a number of new formations of identity facilitated by globalisation. The systems of shared meanings and identity markers, what Peter Berger describes as 'human products' by which a community defines itself – in other words its culture – is now more easily transported from its traditional geographic space.

This has occurred through the means of modernisation and the development of global technologies: the postal system, television, satellite TV, telephone, email, internet and other easier means of travel. For example, one can visit any Yemeni home in Britain and observe how satellite TV helps to transport one directly to Sana'a – twenty-four hours a day, seven days a week. And, whilst global technology may have hegemonised modern-Western culture over the rest of the world's civilisations, conversely, under the shade of Western globalism, there have mushroomed new transnational forms of traditional 'local' cultures facilitated by the same technologies.

The term culture includes embodied ideas and beliefs that help us to interpret and make sense of the world. Culture also includes social practises that are regulated and organised by those shared meanings. Sharing the same pool of meanings naturally produces a sense of belonging to a culture and forms a common bond and community identity with others. For the individual, having a sense of position within a set of shared meanings provides ideas about 'who are we' and 'where we belong' – a sense of our own identity. Berger believes that culture remains 'real' in the sense of subjective plausibility only when or as it is confirmed in relation to the individual and the society. He agrees with Marx in that man's world only becomes an 'objective reality' by 'reification.' Culture and society are therefore understood only within themselves and their particular environment, and Berger asserts that man forgets that the world he lives in has been produced by himself. More importantly, for Berger, culture and society can only function through 'meaning': humans infuse their own meanings into reality by necessity and the individual attaches subjective meaning to all actions. As such, mankind understands its actions as intentional and as having a direct purpose within society.[1] Therefore, it can be said that culture is one of the principle means by which identities are constructed, maintained and/or transformed.

Cultures are usually thought to be stable or fixed in their meanings and practises and are established through settled communities in a particular place over a period of time. To think of oneself as 'Yemeni,' for example, would inevitably locate one within those specific sets of meanings that have a history and continuity and, because all cultures pre-date the individual, they provide a stable frame of reference. This frame of reference or 'tradition' connects the current mode of existence to a historical or ancestral past. Historical connections through tradition give culture a distinctive coherence and a specific form over time, making it internally homogeneous to those who identify with a culture, share a cultural identity and forge a cultural belonging through membership. The 'marking-off' of cultures through strong bounded formations like tribal membership increases the sense of community (us) and difference (others) amongst those who belong to a particular culture.

Because cultures are distinguished from each other through a sense of belonging and difference, it is not surprising that the impact of globalisation is seen as a de-stabling influence on cultures and cultural identity. With the acceleration of flows of goods, people, ideas, images and meanings, globalisation has stretched social relations beyond the geo-cultural states of time and space. More specifically, globalisation has cast a shadow over the Muslim 'micro-worlds' – the syncretic and 'localised' multi-expressions of Islam. This is not to say that these acculturated forms of Islam are aberrations; rather, in the blinding light of globalisation, they present themselves comparatively as anachronistic and somewhat introspective.[2] Further, the hegemonic nature of global Western consumerism with its modern tropes and universal motifs (McDonalds, Nike, Starbucks, Coca-Cola, Levis, etc.), has seductively imposed itself on traditional cultures. The unsettling effects of the 'new global cultural industries'[3] are that pre-modern cultures are often caught between the desire for the material rewards of modernity and the nostalgia of stability and traditional coherence that are no longer present in a fast-moving and constantly changing modern world.

Kevin Robbins has articulated the unsettling impacts of globalisation on culture, stating:

> Globalisation is profoundly transforming our apprehension of the world: it is provoking a new experience of orientation and disorientation, new senses of placed and placeless identity. The global-local nexus is associated with new relations between space and place, fixity and mobility, centre and periphery, 'real' and 'virtual' space, 'inside' and 'outside,' frontier and territory.[4]

Whilst traditional culture in the Yemen may be experiencing a process of splintering and fragmentation under the intense and relentless influences of global consumerism, Yemeni emigrants and settlers in new displaced communities, such as Britain, can tap into the Yemen through global communication networks.

It is through all of these modern technologies that diaspora Yemenis maintain their sense of identity and belonging to the Yemen whereas in the nascent stages of community formation, it was Arab cafés that provided the primary means of 'linking-up' with news and events back home. The new technological linkages between the 'global' and 'local' have inculcated a heightened sense of 'Yemeniness' amongst Yemenis abroad, creating in some cases a hybrid form of cultural identity within the diaspora communities. Yet, as previously stated, Yemen – 'the homeland'– is fast transforming from the often imagined, romanticised and idealised country left behind by economic exilic sojourners some fifty years ago. Admittedly, there are some forms of traditional culture of the Yemenis in Britain that have been eroded or obscured in their significance within their new geo-cultural environment. However, a 'virtual' Yemen is always at hand, either via the electronic tap of global technology or through maintained cultural institutions and networks such as the 'chew' (a *qāt* chewing session).

Religion is a powerful bearer of shared meanings about the sacred, and it carries a great deal of symbolic meaning with regards to authority and 'belonging-ness.' Like culture, religion can also provide an identity marker of difference and otherness because customs and traditions are the distinctive ways in which 'things are done' within a particular culture or faith community. The way people talk, eat, dress, celebrate and commemorate their rites of passage, represent or preserve the narratives of their people or tribe, are all systems of meaning which maintain the collective memory and historical record of the member group. Hall asserts that:

> Shared meaning systems can develop between people who live in different places – across time and space ... the most recent forms of globalisation, where, for example, transnational migrants maintain important linkages between place of origin and place of settlement.[5]

In this respect, the significance of 'place' in cultural systems of meaning is an important component, and despite a new sense of 'place' within a global context, Hall maintains that it is still 'common to *think* [sic] of cultures as if they depended on the stable interaction of the same people, doing the same sorts of things ... in the same geographical location.'[6] But in a global age it may no longer be necessary to associate culture literally with 'place' and perhaps 'place' is now simply a symbolic guarantee of cultural belonging, establishing 'virtual' boundaries around a specific culture marking it off from others. As we can observe, it is quite possible for many cultures to maintain their identity beyond the confines of their historic 'place.' However, there is no doubt that physical settlement, continuity of occupation and an established 'way of life' emanating from and rooted within a particular location and physical environment provide powerful frames for conceptualising culture. Further, social relations through tribal bonds, kinship and intermarriages, facilitate the development and shaping of cultural identity.

Strongly bonded ideas of culture through meaning systems are underpinned by the historical settlement of people formulating cultural identity through a historical unbroken common genealogy, kinship, residence and descent which, in the context of a strong well-bounded cultural identity, is a way of defining ethnicity. That is, the shared activities and meaning systems located in one place that are underpinned by human bonds of kinship and blood ties. The evidence of this shared meaning can sometimes be 'read' into certain shared physical features and characteristics of a population. Hall says this is evident where people share not only a culture but also an *ethnos*, a belongingness or binding to a certain group or place. Here, the sense of cultural identity is very well defined or strongly bounded and although ethnicity is historically constructed, rather like cultural identity, it is unified between its social groups on so many levels that over a long period of time it appears as though membership or belonging is transmitted or imprinted by nature.

Ethnicity then appears to transcend the experience of what we call history and culture. When located in a particular 'place' and based on historical origins of 'kith and kin,' cultural identity becomes based on 'blood and soil.'[7] In the specifics of Yemeni identity, where tribal belonging is largely the primary cultural identity, the idea of 'belonging' to a 'place' is signified by the use of the excluding term, *muwallad*. Although the term literally means, 'born of,' it is actually used to denote one who is born of emigrant origin, i.e., someone born outside the Yemen, usually of a 'local' mother.

So it would appear that 'place' locates and fixes 'systems of meaning' (culture) and it functions in helping to stabilise and anchor cultural patterns and identities beyond purely historical interpretations and understandings. Further, when we recognise a culture we perceive or imagine it to have a place or setting and this is how we give cultures a background or a frame of reference by which we can understand a particular culture. For example, we might 'think of England,' through an imagined idyllic rural setting complete with thatched cottages, rose gardens and cricket on the green. This could be one way of perceiving or framing 'Englishness.' Likewise, 'thinking of the Yemen' may conjure images of the desert, a blinding sun with parched landscape and mysterious nomadic travellers.

However, these stereotypes of national representations and identities based on 'place' and culture are what Edward Said describes as 'landscapes of the mind' and 'imaginary geographies.'[8] What Said means here is that cultural identities are ascribed an imagined 'home' in which the characteristics of the identity in question are fixed. These locations may be real or purely conceived within the imagination of the inquisitor. The linkage between cultural identity and placement within a particular landscape constructs powerful associations of a 'place' as a 'home' – a location which not only reflects a specific cultural identity but binds that identity to the landscape. Therefore, if cultural identity can be strongly associated with a place through historical, genealogical and ethnic bonds, a real sense of belonging through culture and place is established, securing and familiarising identity.

On a micro scale, cultural identity is more strongly bound through marital ties, blood relations and familiarity, but at the macro-level, on the scale of national cultures, the sense of identity and belonging becomes an abstraction. This is because we can never 'actually' know or meet all the people who belong to our nation or national community. At this level identity becomes more like an idea and Benedict Anderson has articulated this abstract notion of national belonging when he describes national cultures as 'imagined communities.' In this context cultural identity is represented through 'an idea or narrative of the nation' sustained via different cultural systems which give it meaning. Anderson also argues that nations differ from each other largely because of the different ways in which they are imagined which represents what sorts of people belong and do not belong to it. National cultural identity, community and belonging relies, therefore, on the imagined or conceptualised meanings that are associated with it coupled with the sense of community and belonging with others that is internalised.[9]

Perhaps this is why Enoch Powell wrote 'the life of nations no less than that of men is [sic] lived largely in the imagination.'[10] Ironically, Powell's quote serves to example Said's notions of 'landscapes of the mind' and the importance of mythical and invented traditions, stories, customs and ceremonies which help to construct a definition of the nation, spanning time and place. These invisible bonds of cultural identity give us an imagined origin, a location from where we came and to which we belong or that which we call home.

Yemeni Notions of 'Britishness'
The development of British national identity suggests a homogeneity that might be culturally realised through aspects of 'Britishness.' However, the problematic quest for a British identity can only truly be realised as a historical political construction, and the creation of a British national identity would have certainly not existed before the eighteenth century. 'Great Britain' was born out of the Scottish Union Act, which was concluded in 1708, by which English hegemony was firmly established over the British mainland.[11] In the historical and developed sense of 'English-Britishness,' British-born Yemenis respondents seem more aware of being excluded and less integrated into 'Britishness.' Beyond the simple political definitions and the restrictive forms of 'Englishness'

they constantly confront, the exclusion they face because of their ethnicity and race almost forces them into an identity of difference.

It is perhaps because of the resistance to English hegemony that new religious and ethnic minorities fair much better amongst the 'Celtic fringe' than their counterparts in the English metropolis. There is likely to be more empathy to minority sub-groups among the Welsh, Scots and Irish because of their own history and experiences of colonisation by the English.[12] Yet, despite the colonial imposition, the political terms 'British' and 'Britain' might still seem somewhat artificial to both the diverse inhabitants who comprise the present population of the UK and to many foreigners who still often refer to the 'British' people as 'English.' For a few Yemenis 'being British' can never fully be realised and so their ideas about who they are, and more importantly who their children are has appeared to have been framed by their experiences of exclusion. The problem of established representations of new Britons as 'perpetuated others' continues to hinder all processes of social inclusion particularly when, as Hall states:

> Our picture of them is defined primarily by their 'otherness' – their minority relationship to something vaguely identified as the majority, their cultural difference from European norms, their non-whiteness, their 'marking' by ethnicity, religion and 'race.'[13]

British Yemenis have formed a community that is distinctly marked, both culturally and religiously but it is not particularly separatist or exclusive. Whilst many of their cultural traditions and religious practises have been preserved, degrees and forms of attachment are fluid and constantly negotiated both between genders and across generations. Similarly, both Yemeni traditions and Muslim practises co-exist with new forms of identity and cultural manifestations that maintain 'Yemeniness' and include 'Britishness.' But, these hybrid identities are often painfully forged through the intra-community dynamics of preserving tradition and identity and also against the wider social tensions of assimilation and social exclusion. In the British Yemeni context, their specific cultural traditions are removed from the Judeo-Christian, classical Western traditions and, in addition, past colonisation by the west, particularly Britain, has marginalised and disrupted the traditional and stable aspects of their religion and culture. Furthermore, the unsettling processes of migration and settlement in the UK have added to the destabilisation of their traditions and culture. Ashis Nandy has described European postcolonial communities like the Yemenis of Eccles as 'intimate enemies,' a phrase that reflects both the historical relationship as colonised subjects and present situation as 'perpetuated others' of new migrant communities and the West.[14] Hall has insightfully described the predicament of postcolonial communities in Britain and Europe as:

> [Having] dwelled for many years, and long before migration, in the double or triple time of colonisation, and now occupy[ing] the multiple-frames in between or 'third' spaces – the homes-away-from-homes of the post-colonial metropolis.[15]

I would suggest that the construction of a British Yemeni identity is an ongoing process of negotiation. That is, through a process of appropriation and adaptation of certain elements of the dominant culture into the developing and acculturated forms of the minority or subjugated culture, 'Britishness' is both deterritorialised and fused into an interactive hybrid identity. A visible manifestation of this social phenomenon was observed at a Yemeni wedding I attended in Manchester where the groom wore a grey English-style morning suit complete with stiff collar, silk cravat and silver-buttoned waistcoat. His traditional English wedding apparel contrasted with his marriage celebration where he danced his Yemeni-tribal dance and then reclined on cushions to chew *qāt* in a huge *maqil* held honour of his wedding. The males from the bride's family chose to wear traditional Yemeni *shawāl* (headdress) and *fowṭah* (sarong) complete with a *jambiyyah* (ceremonial dagger) which was waved around as part of the dance ritual. Here, the Yemeni traditional dress contrasted with the occasional fluent smatterings of English in a broad Liverpudlian accent. To complete the multicultural hybrid experience guests were served with neither traditional Yemeni dishes nor English, but instead, ubiquitous chicken and lamb curry dishes with *briyani* and *naan* supplied by the local Bengali restaurant.

Yet beyond the lived realities of new identity formations for the Yemeni community of Britain, representing the multi-faceted and complex experiences of minority new Britons through the current discourses of difference may at best be only half the story, particularly when their presence is a constant (if not uncomfortable) reminder of our imperial past. The trajectories of 'difference' and 'otherness' of religious and ethnic minorities in Britain are well studied but their pathways into new inclusive forms of British cultural experiences and expressions are severely blocked by markers of difference.[16] Only by redefining and re-imagining notions of 'Britishness' and even 'Englishness' can we 'de-colonise' and then 'globalise' our sense of national identity in order to realistically reflect the contemporary realities.

A revolutionary approach towards the inclusion, preservation and representation of 'other cultures' in their new diasporic forms, need not be at the expense of our national sense of cultural heritage. The production of contemporary hybrid forms of cultural expression, through the arts has combined both a traditional and preserved past and new cross-cultural, transgressive and innovative expressions. For example, the cutting-edge and *avant-garde* musical forms, whether Afro-Caribbean *raga*, North African *rai*, or South Asian *bhangra,* have no 'heritage' or 'archive' and need no authority to permit or sanction their modern (or even, post-modern) creative explorations. Making a cultural claim on 'Englishness' is an important progression in an evolving British-Yemeni identity.

The responses to the current dilemmas of national identity revisit, if not replicate, the polemical discourses of 'difference' and 'other' developed through Orientalism. By presenting some aspects of British Muslim identity as conflicting and problematic, the suggestion is that a synthesis with their developing British cultural identity is impossible. The assumptions that integration into a British national identity is not possible, presents a discourse of difference that is largely representative of outdated ideas of otherness located in Orientalism, and extensively critiqued and deconstructed in postcolonial studies.[17] Leela Gandhi has described this divisive form of representation as 'procedures whereby the convenient Othering and exoticisation of ethnicity merely confirms and stabilises the hegemonic [and exclusive] notion of "Englishness."'[18] In the historical process of othering, the study of the Orient through the discourse of Orientalism has previously helped Europeans define themselves in terms of what they are *not* as well as providing a monolithic construct by which the East is both comprehended and imagined.

But, this faulted process of othering presents itself as little more than an inverted form of self-definition and identity reification because in its final analysis, the self simply becomes everything the other is not. In the context of the identity politics of minority Muslim communities in Britain, the migration and settlement of postcolonial and Commonwealth communities has been used to ignite racist fears of being dominated or 'overrun' by the beliefs and cultures of new religious and ethnic others. Given that the largest minority groups amongst Britain's new communities are Muslims, one might conclude that Islam therefore, represents the biggest threat to national identity and the 'British way of life.' A visible manifestation of this common ungrounded fear is increasingly expressed through the phenomenon of 'Islamophobia.' However, despite an alarming increase in the fear of the Muslim other, politically being British has no relation to either religion or race but historically notions of Britishness have been closely associated with both. Hence, the popular misconception is that being British is synonymous with being 'white and Christian,' therefore, racially and religiously exclusive.

British Muslim Identity
So visible is the presence of new Muslim communities in Britain that they have prompted Tim Winter to note that, 'the arrival and demonstrable sustainability of a large Muslim presence in these islands is the most significant single event in our religious history since the Reformation.'[19] In 1997, whilst on a state visit to Pakistan, the Queen offered an interesting possibility for the diverse communities of Muslims in Britain when she commented on their national and religious characteristics, stating, 'a distinctive new identity that of British Muslim, has emerged. I find that healthy and welcome.'[20] However, despite the optimism of the British monarch regarding the inclusion of her Muslim subjects into the wider British national identity, the details of how and why this new hybrid identity is actually constructed suggest a complex backdrop of negative perceptions about British Muslimness as an identity of 'unbelonging,' evolved through a 'culture of resistance' in contestation with the hegemonic British Identity.[21] And whilst still engaged in the on-going process of negotiating a national identity, new British communities of 'other' religious and ethnic origins are also caught in the current political crisis that is challenging our already precarious notions of a British identity.

In exploring the challenges of 'multiple identities' amongst British Muslims many social scientists portray the increased acculturated Britishness, an increasing identity experience, as being in considerable contention to perceived traditional Muslim and ethnic identities. David Nicolls has alluded to the dangers of representing minority communities as perpetual others, stating:

> The structural-functionalist theories, with their concept of groups or institutions which are 'dysfunctional' to the social system and the notion of ethnic minorities laying 'outside the system,' have definite totalitarian implications. It is only a short step in the same direction to recommend that these dysfunctional groups should be eliminated or that these extra-systemic minorities should be deported.[22]

In addition, as this research and others conducted on specific Muslim communities in Britain illustrate, the monolithic perception and projection of Muslims in Britain and the West needs to be constantly addressed in order to recognise the particularities of changing diasporic communities that defy clichés and common stereotypes. The emerging, yet still contested, British Muslim identity endorsed by the present monarch perhaps has more to do with the generational paradigm shifts – from migrant settlers opting for the citizenship of the received country where their native-born offspring are already part of the social fabric as active contributors to the developing multicultural public spheres – than any political or legal recognition in British law.[23]

In this process of new identity construction the traditional concepts and values of parents, their ideas and expressions of Yemeni identity, may lose their significance in the experiences of acculturation, social interactivity and day-to-day life in Britain of second and third-generation Yemeni children. This paradigm shift is present among the generations of British Yemenis largely because the young are interacting in a completely different way with the wider society than their migrant parents. And, in contrast to their parents, young British-born Yemenis have to negotiate multiple identity choices as a result of their differing social circumstances. Here, identity constructions are formed to facilitate both contrasting identities, often 'bridging' the inherited traditional world of their parents and their own experiences as contributing social actors. The resultant hybrid or hyphenated identities reflect the multiplicity of their identity experiences, British-Arabs, British-Yemenis and British-Muslims. In these multi-identity formations the young need not conflict in being 'Yemeni,' 'Muslim' or 'British,' rather they can exist under the wider umbrella of British identity that includes varied forms of being British.[24] These hybrid forms of identities, therefore, do not require Yemenis to reject their ethnic, religious and national identity. Further, because religion and religious communities are among the oldest forms of transnational movements that are not confined to the nation-state territorial boundaries, the emergence of a British Muslim identity conforms to both the 'local' and 'global' paradigms. In this new hyphenated identity construction British-born respondents are able to tailor the cultural and religious facets of 'who they are' in order to accommodate their own social realities. In other words, the universal validity of Islam as a divinely revealed religion with its own way of life and belief system, and its localised assemblages of organised social structures and institutions that are geo-culturally specific accommodate a fusion of facets of British (cultural) and Islamic (religious) identities – 'British Muslimness.'[25]

Whilst the British Yemeni community, compared with other Muslim communities in Britain and the West, has experienced a certain degree of cultural displacement as a result of the migration and settlement processes, these experiences have been counter-balanced by the establishment of religious and cultural practises and institutions that both maintain traditional aspects of communal identity and facilitate new expressions of self-identity. Simultaneously, the new forms of identity manifest amongst second and third-generations often display a distinct facet of acculturated "Britishness." These hybrid identities still exhibit a degree of cultural distinctiveness but are specifically located within the emerging cosmopolitan spaces of the urban metropolis. Noha Nasser argues that the multicultural inner-city spaces of Western cities have become metaphors not only of urban forms with distinct cultural identities, but also metaphors for the Occident and the Orient.[26] She further asserts that it is becoming increasingly difficult to comprehend the emergence of multicultural locales in British cities without any recourse to an understanding of the colonial legacy that has precipitated the processes of decolonisation and migration.[27]

In the specific context of the Yemeni community, research indicates that a regional or local identity is more pronounced and assimilated than any notions of 'belonging' to a British national identity. The Yemeni sense of regional identity in Eccles is locally specific and even conforms to local indigenous resistance to imposed national or European geo-political identities. The evolution of regional and localised hybrid identities displayed by minority Muslim communities in Britain has also been observed by Nadeem Malik in his study of how Muslim communities identify themselves both locally as British Muslims and globally as members of the universal family of Islam. Malik raises many questions concerning the connection between legal recognition of British Muslims as a social minority and the concept of citizenship or what he calls the 'citizen link.' He concludes that as British Muslim communities slowly became noticed and despite the 'bouts of oppression and prejudice' they suffered, 'they did not seek to dominate the host community politically or militarily, they simply wanted to live in a different place according to their own customs, values and beliefs.'[28] Referring to the process of acculturation experienced by pioneering first-generation Muslim settlers in Britain's industrialised urban sprawls he wryly comments, 'their palates had not quite adapted to Yorkshire Pudding and mushy peas, not every day at least!'[29] Contesting the famous maxim attributed to Saint Ambrose, 'When in Rome, do as the Romans do,' Malik has questioned where the boundaries of citizenship and belonging lie by challenging the rationale of the assimilationist argument against the reality of a historical background of strongly bonded regional British identities in addition to new British identities as a postcolonial phenomenon. He asks rhetorically, 'do we extend the phrase "when in London, do as the 'Cockneys' do," or, "when in Birmingham, do as the 'Brummies' do?"' answering 'obviously, most rational people would argue against any such suggestion.'[30]

But regional identity amongst minority communities of new Britons is less contested than the inclusion into a British national identity as Barry Carr's study of the acculturation of Yemenis and Bangladeshis into notions of a north-eastern regional 'Geordie' identity shows. Carr's research traces the identity shifts of first-generation migrant parents and second and third-generation British-born progeny noticing that once the children of the Arab and South Asian communities opened their mouths to speak they made their bid for regional identity.[31] However, whilst a local identity may be less contested and easier to negotiate than a British national one, Carr also admits that as the traditions and values of a region are eroded, racism may become a more dominant force, excluding 'new immigrants' and their children from developing regional 'Geordie,' 'Mancunian,' 'Brummie' or 'Cockney' identities.[32]

The Urban Village: Translocal Tribalism

Whilst the *qabīlah* (tribe) plays a primary role in both the identity construction and social interactions of Yemenis in their country of origin, tribal belonging and identity of the Yemenis of Britain has a greater degree of invisibility. This is largely because the pre-modern social structures of tribal societies are not factors in the social order of modern industrial Western societies and, therefore, the tribe as a facet of self-identity is somewhat redundant outside the context of Yemeni society and culture. But, for first-generation migrants the tribe still remains the major facet of self-identity. That is not to say that tribal identity is absent amongst the diaspora Yemeni communities, but rather the usual social constructions of the tribe and tribal identity are tenuous beyond that of the tribal ancestral homeland. Understanding the importance of tribal belonging amongst the community only becomes apparent after an extended period of ethnographic observational research and a field trip to the Yemen. Initially, as a community the British Yemenis appear to be a homogenous ethnic group whose community formation experience is generally one of fusion rather than fission. And, whilst many aspects of their religious and cultural identities are visible and facilitated through social institutions, organisations and strong social networks, tribal identities are part of an 'invisible' intra-dynamic of the community's identity construction and formation. Understanding the importance of tribal belonging as a major facet of the multi-identities that construct notions of 'Yemeniness' is a phenomenon that has exclusive meaning and value only within and amongst the community.

The term 'tribe' is widely used in anthropology but its precise definition and appropriate application is contested amongst anthropologists. Etymologically, the word has its roots in ancient Latin: the Romans used the word *tribua* to mean a political unit, but it was also used to refer to social groups defined by the territory in which they lived or settled.[33] Tribal societies and tribes are categorised in the evolutionary scheme of social types and are usually envisaged as primitive socio-political groups, prevalent in pre-modern societies. This anthropological description of 'the tribe' generally refers to groupings which consist of more than one local community that are united by common cultural characteristics and some form of political leadership or organisation at a supralocal level. Anthropologists assert that wherever a supralocal leadership is well-established then there is a greater development of occupational specialisation in crafts, military and religious activities that facilitate a redistributive economy precipitated and patronised by the emergence of chiefdoms or shaykhdoms. However, modern anthropologists prefer to employ the notion of ethnicity or inter-ethnic relations in order to analyse and interpret issues relating to inter-tribal conflicts, particularly those of African 'tribes' where it is considered that tribal notions in the African continent were largely colonial creations. In the postcolonial debates on African peoples it is thought that tribal ideas were attributed to pre-existing colonised African peoples whose characteristics were then problematised to hinder moves towards independence and self-governance. It is also argued that the creation of tribal divisions and tribal consciousness were largely the creation of the colonial rulers in order to impose hierarchy and supralocal unity upon previously, largely autonomous, local communities where before colonisation a loose and relative sense of ethnic identity existed. Tribal divisions were, it is claimed, extenuated as a means of maintaining colonial rule and administrative control. Later studies of African peoples showed the colonial concept of the 'tribe,' in the African context, perceived as ethnically, linguistically, culturally and politically autonomous and self-conscious units, where gross simplifications and misrepresentations undermined the complex regional inter-ethnic social relations of pre-colonial Africa.[34]

Despite the increasing unpopularity of tribal definitions and classifications of African peoples in modern anthropology discourses, tribal identity is still a major feature of traditional Arabian societies, particularly in the Yemen. Tribal identity as a primary marker of socially constructed identities amongst the Yemeni diaspora communities has been explored in some detail in the studies by Boxberger and Freitag and referred to in more general terms in the works undertaken by Bahr Uddin Dahya, Fred Halliday and Richard Lawless. Most Yemenis view tribal identity in the Yemen as a positive contributory facet of a traditional and conservative society. This is because in the Yemen the central authorities have relatively little impact on society beyond the capital and main cities and beyond these realms the tribes and tribal shaykhs still have a significant role to play.

The migration process and subsequent diaspora communities have reshaped the notions of tribal identity and belonging for emigrant Yemenis which as a consequence have also challenged existing interpretations of tribal identity that have generally viewed tribes as pre-modern and traditionally defined them by the territory in which they lived or settled. Dresch asserts that 'territorial fixity is definitive of collective identities, while families and particular men can move and take their names with them,'[35] confirming that tribal categories and identities are not displaced by migration, although they may be re-ordered due to the geo-cultural proximity to the tribal homeland. His study refers to the historically fluid nature of sub-tribal allegiances which are determined by the outcome of hostilities and disputes between larger tribes and tribal shaykhs. In the process, local historical narratives become assimilated into the collective 'history,' honour, narrative and memory of the supralocal tribe, or tribal confederations.[36]

Putting Yemeni tribal identity into a wider cultural context, Dresch has observed that whilst the modern period of the Yemen is defined by the language of the national context and the preceding period of imamate rule was defined by Zaydi law and religious scripture, the longer tribal period which incorporates both, is defined by the specific way in which the structure of collective equivalence is transformed through time and is altered only in the longer duration. Subsequently, when sub-tribes change their allegiances and form a new 'brotherhood' based on ʿaqd ('agreement' or 'treaty') Dresch comments that:

> What has changed is an identity: an element of one set becomes another, although the sets are still defined in the same terms of territory, of honor and contradistinction as before. Solidarity is a separate question.[37]

Within tribal relations there exists an element of opposition between sections that is solely about guarding one's clan and territory against others. Further, in terms of tribal allegiance, the whole tribe is then in turn opposed to other tribes. However, in times of conflict tribal sections may stand aside from the hostilities and conversely, in times of calm little stress can be placed on the idea of a 'common identity' and tribal belonging becomes scarcely relevant.[38] As a result, tribal identity is maintained through conscious efforts and constructed through events that maintain bondsmen alignments via reified binding agreements. The major form of agreement and obligation being *qabl* ('ancestry') between one tribe and another and migration, regardless of how far from the ancestral homeland, does not usually sever such ancient genealogical bonds.

Lawless has described the Yemen highlands of South West Arabia as an 'ethnic reservoir' from which migration movements have historically extended far beyond its borders.[39] In the modern period migration was facilitated, if not accelerated, by the imposition of Western colonial powers into the region, particularly the British occupation of the port of Aden in 1839. As northern tribesmen filtered their way down towards the Protectorate via the mountain river valleys, the port became not the end, but rather the beginning of the journey, settlement and formation of diaspora tribal Yemeni communities. These tribal communities were to establish themselves in France, Holland, America and Britain as well as adding to the previously well-established communities in East Africa, South East Asia and the Far East. Through the process of 'chain migration' Yemenis were able to facilitate the emigration of their families and tribal bondsmen into the new communities of economic Yemeni migrants globally. In Manchester, for example, it initially took only three Yemenis to forge a community that at its migration peak in the late 1970s numbered over two thousand, a significant number in a town where the total population today numbers only 11,413.[40] Lawless' work has identified a number of tribes from both the southern highlands and the central region (known as, *al-manṭiqah al-wusṭā*), that has members located in the early docklands communities of Britain from the late-nineteenth century. His research shows the official government explanation, that the majority of migrants came from the Hujariyah district of Yemen located south of the provincial capital of Ta'izz on the western border of the Aden Protectorate, was inaccurate. In fact, tribesmen from many regions and areas of the Yemen migrated to Britain through the colonial port. Certainly in the context of the British Yemeni community, the migration and community formation replicates both the 'chain migration' process identified by Anwar (1974) and the 'second wave' migration later observed by Halliday (1992).

In its nascent stages the community developed primarily through tribal connections facilitated by 'chain migration' either from the Yemen or by 'second wave' migration of tribal bondsmen living in the British ports. But as the community expanded tribal tensions were exacerbated in the late 1960s due to the civil war and hostilities between the divided North and South Yemen which brought regional and political allegiances into play within the local politics of the diaspora Yemeni communities. But at the same time, quite often tribal and regional loyalty and belonging ran counter to political convictions. In the shifting Yemeni politics of independence, civil war and reunification struggles, it would appear that tribal identity often provided a stable means of self-identification in a world where geo-political boundaries, traditional theocracies and revolutionary ideologies were in a state of constant flux. Tribal identity and affiliation amongst first-generation migrant Yemenis in Britain remains a very real and tangible facet of their self-identity. Further, tribal identity is reified through the formation of diaspora tribal 'villages' in the industrialised urban spaces of Britain, that has largely been facilitated by the process of 'chain migration' and by transnational, or what I would prefer to describe as 'translocal,' networks and links with the tribal homeland.

However, the notion of 'tribe' remains somewhat abstract for second-generation British-born Yemenis and tribal identity or belonging is only realised through a visit to the ancestral tribal homeland. Many of the young respondents, particularly males, became 'tribesmen' only after a visit to their father's village in the Yemen. In contrast, female notions of tribal belonging and identity were much less pronounced even after visiting the Yemen. The female responses suggested that only an honorary sense of tribal belonging was developed, thereby lending weight to the opinion that patriarchy is the dominant factor in the construction of tribal identity and collective belonging. The experience of patriarchal domination in Yemeni tribal society is perhaps best reflected in the phrase *'min jadd wāḥid'* ('from one forefather') as the maxim of a collective tribal history and narrative. Translocal tribal politics forms part of the intra-community dynamics of the British Yemeni community but tribal disputes and tensions only surface occasionally and may even be virtually 'invisible' to the outsider. For example, the burden of a son's obligation to his parents is a traditional feature of tribal and village life in pre-modern societies. Betsy Hartmann and James Boyce's study of village life in

Bangladesh has observed this patriarchal obligation and they note, 'in return for the love they give to their children, parents expect respect and support during their old age – a reciprocation which is basic to village society.'[41] In addition, it is because daughters leave the family home after marriage that the responsibility of care for parents ultimately falls on the son. The need to conform to the collective conventions, even though one may be far beyond the cultural space and geographical place of ones ancestral homeland, is essentially self-imposed. And so, through the strongly-bonded links and tribal allegiances nurtured in both the tribal village or homeland and the 'urban village' of the diasporic tribal bondsmen, a unique dimension of tribal identity and belonging based on traditional notions of honor, shame, rights, blood and customs, has produced a new form of transnational identity. This is a phenomenon I would describe as 'translocal tribalism.'

For migrant diaspora communities the nature and relationship between space and place has a direct interplay between the terms 'local' and 'global.' For example, the universal or global dimensions of Muslim identity – the sense of belonging to the Ummah, have direct implications in the construction of an identity that transcends both time and space. Theologically, belonging to the Ummah has both genealogical and chronological 'links' to Adam as the first man and Prophet according to the Qur'anic narrative. It is through Adam, the *ummatic* Patriarch that the historical communities of believers are spiritually connected, beyond time and space via the monotheistic Prophets. The religious and political notions of 'belonging' according to the Islamic *Weltanschauung* extend beyond the well-defined and restrictive notions of belonging based on the experiences and ideas developed from the creation of the modern nation-state.

The British Yemeni community displays aspects of its Muslim 'universalism' which extend beyond their ideas of 'Yemeniness' based on their cultural, historical, tribal and political expressions of identity. In this way they are able to formulate notions of 'brotherhood' with other tribal bondsmen and non-Yemenis that are facilitated by both theological justifications and religious conviction. Through the process of migration it could also be argued that 'Yemeniness' has been globalised and the presence of diaspora Yemeni communities in America, Europe, Africa, South Asia and the Far East gives some credence to claims of a 'local' culture

becoming global. Conversely, the understanding of local as being something small and parochial or particular to a specific space and place –
defined in opposition to the 'global' – need not be merely confined to
space but is perhaps more relative to size.

'Global' dimensions of 'Yemeniness' are obviously based on 'local'
constructions of identity, culture, language, traditions, customs and
tribe. In this context Yemeni identity would be defined through a local
character yet transported and manifest in a wider global setting. This
translocal form of 'Yemeniness' is a product of defining a specific identity
in the wider global context of (and against) all others. Obviously, for
Yemenis in the diaspora the impact and influence of the Other cannot be
denied as a process to varying degrees of acculturation and integration.
Equally, it may also be argued that the pervading hegemonic nature of
Western civilisation, through previous colonisation the recent phenomenon of globalisation, is beginning to impact and erode 'local' cultures.
Alarmingly, this intrusive aspect of globalisation might mean that eventually there would be no distinctiveness or local character, place or
culture remaining within the globalised world. However, from the point
of view of the 'local' and the 'global,' they may not necessarily be terms
existing in counterdistinction. In fact, in a very real way – particularly in
the construction of 'Yemeniness' as a distinctive identity – the 'local' and
the 'global' constitute each other. This is perhaps best exemplified in
the tribal identity as a translocal phenomenon amongst the Yemeni
community in Britain.

Conclusion

To be a Yemeni, in both the traditional geo-cultural place of the Yemen
and within the new diaspora communities, is a specific identity that, in
contrast to the universalism of a religious (Muslim) identity, is both culturally distinctive and socially different. But, whilst Islam as a world
religion can embrace the global or *ummatic* dimensions of communal
identity that are also often heightened by modern global technologies,
specific cultural identities would appear to be distinctly 'local,' if not
somewhat syncretic or even anachronistic. However, as the phenomenon of globalisation appears to propagate dominant and hegemonic
cultures, 'local' cultures are equally able to reach out via global technologies beyond the confines of traditional space and place. As a result,

minority faith communities like the British Yemeni community are able to transcend the apparent limitations of what might be considered to be their parochial tribal customs and culture, particularly when located within a new and completely different cultural and social environment. The resilience of the religious and cultural facets of Yemeni identity raises some interesting questions relating to both the perceptions and expectations of the social integration and assimilation of minority faith communities into the wider identity constructions, notions and definitions of 'Britishness' in the modern multicultural and religiously pluralistic Britain.

REFERENCES

Ameli, Saied, R., Manzur Elahi, and Arzu Merali, *British Muslims' Expectations of the Government – Social Discrimination: Across the Muslim Divide* (Wembley: The Islamic Human Rights Commission, 2004).

Ameli, Saied, and Arzu Merali, *British Muslims' Expectations of the Government – Dual Citizenship: British, Islamic or Both? Obligation, Recognition, Respect and Belonging* (Wembley: The Islamic Human Rights Commission, 2004).

Anderson, Benedict, *Imagined Communities: Reflections on the origins and spread of Nationalism* (London: Verso, 1983).

Ansari, Khizar Humayun in *Muslim Identity in the 21ˢᵗ Century: Challenges of Modernity*, eds. Bahmanpour M. S. and H. Bashir (London: Book Extra, 2000).

Anwar, Muhammad and Qadir Bakhsh, *British Muslims and State Policies* (Warwick: Centre for Research in Ethnic Relations, 2003).

Araeen, Rasheed, Cubitt Sean, and Ziauddin Sardar, eds., *The Third Text Reader on Art, Culture and Theory* (London: Continuum, 2002).

Bahmanpour, M. S. and H. Bashir, eds., *Muslim Identity in the 21ˢᵗ Century: Challenges of Modernity* (London: Book Extra, 2000).

Colls, Robert and Bill Lancaster, eds., *Geordies: Roots of Regionalism* (Edinburgh: Edinburgh University Press, 1992).

Dresch, Paul, *Tribes, Government and History in Yemen* (Oxford: Oxford University Press, 1993).

Evans, Mohammed, *Islam in Wales* (Cardiff: Pawb for S4C, 2003).

Fryer, Peter, *Staying Power: A History of Black People in Britain* (London: Pluto Press, 1984).

Gandhi, Leela, *Postcolonial Theory: A Critical Introduction* (Edinburgh: Edinburgh University Press, 1998).

Hall, Stuart, "Whose Heritage? Unsettling 'The Heritage,' Re-imagining the Post-Nation," in *The Third Text Reader on Art, Culture and Theory*, ed. Rashid Araeen, Sean Cubitt, and Ziauddin Sardar (New Zealand: Continuum International Publishing Group, 2002).

Hall, Stuart, "New Cultures for Old," in *A Place in The World?* Edited by Doreen Massey and Jess Pat (Oxford: Oxford University Press, 1995).

Hartmann, Betsy and James Boyce, *A Quiet Violence: View from a Bangladesh Village* (London: Zed Press, 1983).

Hunter, Shireen, ed., *Islam, Europe's Second Religion: The New Social, Cultural and Political Landscape* (Westport, Connecticut: Praeger, 2002).

Kucukcan, Talip, "The Making of Turkish-Muslim Diaspora in Britain: Religious Collective Identity in a Multicultural Public Sphere," *Journal of Muslim Minority Affairs* (October, 2004), vol. 24, no. 2.

Langford, Paul, "The Eighteenth Century," in *The Oxford Popular History of Britain*, ed. Kenneth O. Morgan (Oxford: Oxford University Press, 1998).

Lawless, Richard I, *From Ta'izz to Tyneside: An Arab Community in the North-East of England during the Early Twentieth Century* (Exeter: University of Exeter Press, 1995).

Mann, Bashir, *The New Scots: The Story of Asians in Scotland* (Edinburgh: John Donald Publishers, 1992).

Massey, Doreen and Pat Jess, eds. *A Place in The World?* (Oxford: Oxford University Press, 1999).

Morgan, Kenneth O., ed., *The Oxford Popular History of Britain* (Oxford: Oxford University Press, 1998).

Nandy, Ashis, *The Intimate Enemy* (Oxford: Oxford University Press, 1983).

Nasser, Noha, "Expressions of Muslim Identity in Architecture and Urbanism in Birmingham, UK," *Islam and Christian-Muslim Relations* (January, 2005), vol. 16, no. 1.

Nichols, David, *Deity and Domination: Images of God and State in the Nineteenth and Twentieth Centuries*. Reprint. (London: Routledge, 2001).

Powell, Enoch, *Freedom and Reality* (Farnham: Elliot Right Way Books, 1969).

Ramadan, Tariq, "Europeanisation of Islam or Islamisation of Europe," in *Islam, Europe's Second Religion: The New Social, Cultural and Political landscape*, ed. Shireen Hunter (Westport, Connecticut: Praeger, 2002).

Robbins, Kevin, "Tradition and translation: national culture in its global context," in *Enterprise and Heritage: Crosscurrents of National Culture*, eds. J. Corner and S. Harvey (London: Routledge, 1991).

Said, Edward, "Narrative and Geography," *New Left Review* (March–April, 1990), no. 180.

Seddon, Mohammad Siddique, "'Some thoughts on the Formation of British Muslim Identity' – A Response to T. J. Winter," *Encounters: Journal of Inter-Cultural Perspectives* (September, 2002), vol. 8, no 2.

_____ et al., eds. *British Muslims: Loyalty and Belonging* (Markfield: The Citizen Organising Foundation and The Islamic Foundation, 2003).

_____ et al., eds., *British Muslims Between Assimilation and Segregation: Historical, Legal and Social Realities* (Markfield: The Islamic Foundation, 2004).

Seymour-Smith, Charlotte, *Macmillan Dictionary of Anthropology* (London: The Macmillan Press, 1986).

Winter, Tim, 'Some thoughts on the formation of British Muslim identity,' *Encounters: Journal of Inter-Cultural Perspectives* (March, 2002), vol. 8, no. 1.

Wuthnow, Robert, James Davidson Hunter, Albert Bergesen, and Edith Kerzweil, eds. *Cultural Analysis: The Work of Peter L. Berger, Mary Douglas, Michel Foucault and Jurgen Habermas* (Boston: Routledge & Kegan Paul, 1984).

US–UK 'War on Terror': Implications to Security

CHARLES E. BUTTERWORTH

Blinkered Politics: The US Approach to Arabs and Muslims

Introduction

THE EVENTS OF SEPTEMBER 11, 2001, say George W. Bush and his followers, justify all-out war against terrorism and transforming select regimes in the Middle East. Equally spurious are the reasons offered for the ill-conceived invasion of Iraq, cruel treatment of persons seized abroad and imprisoned secretly, infringement of constitutional rights to privacy for US citizens, refusal to allow foreign nationals with unorthodox political views entry to the US, and, currently, support of Israel's vicious, inhumane, and criminal assaults upon the civilians of Gaza and Lebanon. Americans killed in battle since 9/11 now surpass the victims of that day, and the toll of Iraqi civilians is perhaps 100 times as large. To all this, the American public is astonishingly compliant. Why are such unjust policies so readily endorsed? More important, how might those affected help turn them around? To answer these two questions is my goal here.[1]

A Refusal to Accept Responsibility

For official Washington, the World Trade Center attacks show hatred for the American way of life and freedom, not disagreement over US policy and its blind support for Israel in oppressing Palestinians and usurping their land. Thus Mayor Rudy Giuliani could pretend publicly to reject a $10 million gift from a benefactor who dared raise that issue at the award ceremony – even while banking the gift privately. Israel and its policies may not be criticized in the US, not in public fora nor in university classrooms.

CHARLES E. BUTTERWORTH

Elected officials who dare censure Israel find sources of funding evaporate as they face election challenges from opponents backed by the all-powerful AIPAC (American Israel Public Affairs Committee). Professors deemed unfavorable to Israel are attacked on a web-site then pursued by e-mails to university officials demanding that the culprits be fired.[2] Congress is now debating a bill to require "balance" in courses concerning the Middle East, that is, mandated representation of the Israeli point of view. Not academic freedom, nor the spirit of inquiry, but a pressure group's sense of what is needed to protect Israel is supposed to guide the syllabi of future university courses. Moreover, Jewish pressure groups are already preparing to counter expected criticism on university campuses over Israel's attacks upon Lebanon – the goal is pro-Israeli propaganda, not analysis of the conflict between Israel and its Arab neighbours.[3]

The same censorship is to be found with respect to the media. There is no Robert Fisk of American journalism, and the clear, objective voice of the *Christian Science Monitor* hardly compensates for the biased reporting of the *New York Times* and the *Washington Post*. Most daunting are the articles of the editorial page staff and columnists of these newspapers with their bias against Arabs and Muslims. Moshe Yaalon, retired lieutenant general of the Israeli Defense Forces and IDF chief of staff from 2002–05, now a "distinguished military fellow" at the Washington Institute for Near East Policy, was not challenged when he falsely contended in the *Washington Post* that Israel had committed no war crimes against the Lebanese or Palestinians.[4] Such lies and distortions find no counter in the American press, and so US citizens hew willy-nilly to the dominant pro-Israeli line without ever pausing to ask how that position serves the US national interest. Ironically, for a balanced account of such issues, one must turn to the Israeli press.[5]

Freedom of discussion is so limited in the US that an article critical of the Israeli lobby and its influence upon American foreign policy could be published only in the *London Review of Books*. I refer, of course, to the famous Mearsheimer and Walt article,[6] reaction to which and subsequent attempts to silence even its foreign and internet appearance only proved the very point they were trying to make. Yet the issues raised by the article cut to the very core of current US foreign policy.

116

These days it is not even possible for foreigners suspected of opinions critical to the US or its Israeli allies to enter the US. Some instances actually make the news: Professor Tariq Ramadan's revoked visa and Sir Zaki Badawi's refused entry to the US despite his status as an advisor to Queen Elizabeth and invitation to give a prominent address to the UN. Far too many others receive no attention – to wit, the handcuffing, harsh interrogation, and eventual refused entry to some 80 Iranian academics and intellectuals who arrived with visas on US soil in mid-August to participate in a conference on improving US-Iranian relations.

In sum, a new mentality pervades all aspects of life in the US. Americans – or at least those who shape opinion in the US – are intent upon using America's super-power status to achieve a new world order, one that accords special place to Israel in the Middle East and seeks to impose a particular version of democracy upon Arabs and Muslims. "Particular," for it rejects the will of the people if they dare vote for religious parties. And it is a version that can accommodate non-democratic rulers deemed useful for the US. According to this imperialist mentality, not Muslim and Arab resistance to indiscriminate American support for Israel and its subjugation of Palestinians plus occupation of their territory in defiance of UN resolutions, nor resentment over the US invasion and destruction of Iraq, but envy for American freedom is at the root of current problems.[7]

Don Quixote to the Rescue

Don Quixote's vivid imagination pales in comparison to that of George W. Bush and his neo-conservative fellow knights. Full of pride over the demise of a Communist regime, they rush to the conclusion that they have defeated Communism and declare a new war on terrorism. But the enemy is not an idea. Nor are those accused – Hamas and Hizballah – the real terrorists.

A well-fed, comfortably sheltered, financially sufficient, and generally complacent individual has difficulty imagining why anyone would sacrifice life or limb to harm others. But one struggling to nourish self and family, forced to live in a hovel, without prospect of employment, insulted and harassed day after day along with parents and children by foreign usurpers intent on driving him or her from ancestral lands, and void of hope that politics as usual will put an end to such misery – such a person may well conclude that to die so as to harm the oppressor is worthwhile. Sadly, although there are no smart bombs and maybe no smart bombers, there are all too many who "smart" from despair.

More must be said. If terrorism consists in aggression against innocent civilians, then bombing, shelling, and assassinating the same by state action is as much terrorism as the act of any suicide bomber. For a guerilla to fire a rocket against civilians is no more an act of terrorism than for a soldier to shell civilians on a beach or in their homes. Pre-emptive war, targeted killings, collective punishment, and destruction of civilian infrastructure are not part of self-defense. They are illegal acts condemned by international treaties. Israel has long engaged in such actions, but raised them to criminal levels in Gaza and Lebanon since June 2006. In the midst of it all, George W. Bush vaunted the new order he was helping usher in and eagerly furnished Israel with weapons to decimate civilians. While cluster bombs may not qualify as weapons of mass destruction, they are nonetheless horribly inhumane.

These reflections justify terrorism by the oppressed no more than by the oppressor. Both are to be condemned. But apartheid walls and violence intent upon extirpating all suspected of such acts will not achieve security. It will come about only by a just righting of deep-rooted, decades-old wrongs – one that includes a real stake in society for the dispossessed and disenfranchised.

According to Condoleeza Rice, the goal of US foreign policy is to fight terrorism by spreading freedom and democracy.[8] In practice, however, it consists in subjecting – by persuasion or coercion – all others to the will of the US. This follows from the erroneous and excessive reaction of George W. Bush and his advisors to the events of 9/11 and their decision to wage war against an idea – terrorism – rather than against the individuals who have declared their opposition to US policies. Along the way, the US has come to rely unduly upon Israel and to model its actions in Iraq on those Israel follows with Palestinians – even to the manner in which those detained in Abu Ghraib prison were treated. Relying too much on the fallacy that Israel is the sole democracy in the Middle East, the US has accepted Israel's notion that the sole path to success there is the subjugation of all other nations – especially Syria and Iran. This policy, called deterrence by those in Israel who espouse total war against their neighbours, deserves another name: unjust, foolish aggression.[9]

The tales of knight errantry that have put such strange notions into the head of our Don Quixote come from the insidious writings and whisperings of many who have gained the ear of those in power and of the public: Bernard Lewis, Steven Emerson, Daniel Pipes, Richard Perle, Charles Krauthammer, and William Kristol. They are not members of a cabal, much less of a conspiracy. But they share in opinions about promoting a strong Israel and successfully advance them in ways that demand serious attention. The same holds for lesser figures occupying positions of power at various levels throughout the US government and in the offices of think-tanks and the media: Paul Wolfowitz, Elliot Abrams, Douglas Feith, Abram Shulsky, Hillel Fradkin, and others. Their voices drown out the sober thinking of Patrick Buchanan and push reporters such as Anders Strindberg to the sidelines.[10] Because of their prestige and power, the US public has never given serious attention to the one proposal that might resolve the impasse in the Middle East, the Abdullah Peace Plan of 2002. As Prince Turki al-Faisal noted in a speech that received all too little attention, it is "the most comprehensive peace plan" offered to date to Israel, namely, "the end of hostility and normalization of relations in return for total Israeli withdrawal from Arab occupied territories, including Jerusalem."[11] Ariel Sharon's response to the plan was the destruction of Jenin, and George W. Bush seems as unaware of this plan as of other matters counter to his unique vision for a new Middle East.

A Return to the Right Path

In sum, US foreign policy today consists in determination to reshape the world in its image by whatever means available.[12] It invades, controls, and threatens other nations at will by its might. To sustain its military forces, it eludes previously honored contracts and returns troops to danger zones over and over without regard for their preparedness or well-being. In retaliation for the deaths of a small number of people, not all of whom were American citizens, it has struck out blindly against myriads of citizens of other countries or abetted its chief ally in such acts. It demonstrates thereby the extent to which it prizes American lives over others. Dispassionate examination of that policy reveals it to be based on two false premises. First, that might makes right – obviating the need to question what is just.[13] The second is untenable racism. The same can be said of Israeli foreign policy. Neither is likely to change soon, but it is important to identify the flaws in both and suggest how the opinions supporting them might be refuted or altered.

Of immediate importance is providing an accurate portrait of Islam and explaining why it is perfectly reasonable for Muslims or any other fair-minded persons to criticize US and Israeli policies as they relate to both. However foolishly erroneous a term it is, "Islamic fascism" was not coined by George W. Bush. Public policy institutes and universities are all too happy to invite would-be specialists to hold forth on Islam and speculate on why it alone among the Abrahamic faiths incites to violence.[14] Yet there is no paucity of well-qualified spokespersons who can provide clear, honest analysis of this and other phenomena having to do with Islam. Muslim social scientists and humanists need to work together so that such a message comes to the fore. To begin with, they must reach beyond parochial organizations and publications to speak to the world in which they live, in the terms used by professional analysts, to explain themselves as Muslims and their faith in all of its aspects.

Much has been and is being done, to be sure. Praises must be heaped upon CAIR (Council on American-Islamic Relations), FAIR (Forum against Islamophobia and Racism), IIIT (International Institute of Islamic Thought), the Minaret of Freedom, and CSID (Center for the Study of Islam and Democracy), as well as many others, for their tireless efforts in explaining and defending Islam and Muslims in their respective communities. Through them much has been accomplished. But more is needed.

Permit me, nonetheless, a minor rebuke: for an organization as powerful and wide-reaching as AMSS to hold its annual conference on the same weekend as that of the prestigious American Political Science Association is counter-productive. The political scientists attending AMSS have a more pressing duty, namely, contributing to the proceedings of the APSA. The same holds with respect to annual meetings of other professional organizations. The voices of those able to present a correct picture of Islam and of Muslims will be heard only when qualified scholars, who are intimately familiar with Islam, participate actively in such fora.

Clear, dispassionate studies of Islam and of the political, economic, and social problems faced by Muslims around the world are also needed. They must be published in newspapers, journals, and books distributed to non-Muslim as well as Muslim audiences. No longer can anyone opposed to lies and bias stand apart from the wider Western world, especially not as long as Muslims continue to be part of it. Now an intelligent exposition of the faith and practice as well as of the political aspirations of Muslims as Muslims is all-important.

At the same time, Arabs – Muslim as well as Christian – must begin to promote their many achievements. Arab culture in all its richness and breadth must be brought to the attention of those who have been ignorant of it heretofore.

The opinions about Islam, Muslims, and Arabs that now hold sway have been formed slowly and affected by many events – most unforeseen. But the dangers of allowing those opinions to continue to dominate without challenge affect the world and ourselves more than ever before. That is why it is time to put scruples aside, to accept mingling intellectually and socially with those whose ideas and habits are repugnant, and to enter the fray as scholars, opinion-makers, and concerned fellow-citizens.

At the moment, it is not clear what the future will bring in the way of a modus vivendi. A melting-pot society that seeks to do away with the different opinions and habits with which we were raised no longer seems possible or even desirable. Yet it is not clear how we might live as members of separate communities or *milal* and still come together as fellow citizens in pursuit of common interests. Finding a way out of our current dilemma, a path to mutual understanding, security of life and limb, and some degree of human bliss will not be easy.

Clearly, George W. Bush – but also all of us – have much to learn from that astute and ever irreverent political sage from Baltimore, H. L. Mencken. We, as well as those who so threaten our lives, must come to appreciate the wisdom of his observation that "for every complex problem there is a simple solution ... and it is wrong."

REFERENCES

Blumenfeld, Laura, "In Israel, a Divisive Struggle Over Targeted Killing," in *The Washington Post* (August 27, 2006), A1 and A12–13.
Esposito, John L, "It's the Policy, Stupid: Political Islam and US Foreign Policy," in *Harvard International Review*, http://hir.harvard.edu/articles/1453/.
Halevi, Yossi Klein, "Israel's Broken Heart: Final Rekoning," in *The New Republic Online* (August 15, 2006).

Hart, Alan, "The Beginning of the End of the Zionist State of Israel?" Speech delivered at the International Institute of Strategic Studies, August 10, 2006, http://mparent7777.livejournal.com/11313638.html.

Hass, Amira, "Nasrallah Didn't Mean To," in *Haaretz* (August 17, 2006).

Kramer, Martin, "A Wise Guy at College Park," *Campus Watch*, February 25, 2003, www.campus-watch.org/article/id/557.

Mearsheimer, John J. and Walt, Stephen M., "The Israeli Lobby and U.S. Foreign Policy," in Harvard University, John F. Kennedy School of Government, Faculty Research Working Paper Series (March, 2006) RWP 06–011.

Mearsheimer, John J. and Walt, Stephen M., "The Israeli Lobby and U.S. Foreign Policy," (New York: Farrar, Straus and Giroux, 2007).

Nasr, Vali, "After Lebanon, there's Iran," in *Christian Science Monitor* (August 9, 2006).

Porter, Henry, "Comment: The Land of the Free – But Free Speech is a Rare Commodity," in *The Observer* (August 13, 2006).

Rice, Condoleeza, "A Path to Lasting Peace," in *The Washington Post* (August 16, 2006).

Rosenblatt, Gary, "Campus Groups Brace For Anti-Israel Campaign," in *The Jewish Week* (August 11, 2006).

Scheuer, Michael, et al., "9/11/06, Five Years on: A Symposium," in *The National Interest* (September/October, 2006), no. 85.

Strindberg, Anders, "Hizbullah's attacks stem from Israeli incursions into Lebanon," in *Christian Science Monitor* (August 1, 2006).

Thucydides, *Thucydides: The Peloponnesian War, the Thomas Hobbes Translation*, ed. Grene, David. Intro. Bertrand de Jouvenel (Ann Arbor, MI: University of Michigan Press, 1959).

Wurmser, Meyrav, *National Review Online (NRO)* (August 2006).

TAHIR ABBAS

British Islamic Culture After 7/7:
Ethnicity, Politics and Radicalisation

Introduction

THIS PAPER IS A DISCUSSION OF THE experiences of British Muslim communities in light of the events of 7/7. The social, economic and political positions of British Muslims have been important public policy, and popular academic and discourse considerations since the focus on the Rushdie Affair of 1989, the general rise of Islamophobia and the publication of the Runnymede Trust report in 1997. The events of 9/11 and the impact of anti-terror legislation upon Muslim communities, the subsequent discussion of questions in relation to multiculturalism in society and the experience of Islamic political radicalisation since 7/7 have led to the current research. After introducing the British Muslim communities, I focus on multiculturalism and Islamophobia in Britain. A discussion of the problem of the radicalisation of young Muslims is followed by a focus on anti-terrorism legislation and its impact on civil liberties. The example of the 'foiled terror plot' of 10 August 2006 is a discussion of the intersection of the interest on radicalisation and its impact on multiculturalism in a climate of intense Islamophobia. In conclusion, I believe that the many different parameters of Islamophobia are increasingly converging, further problematising already disadvantaged and disaffected religious minority groups.

Muslims in Britain

There has been a Muslim presence in Britain since the beginning of the nineteenth century when Muslim seamen and traders from the Middle East began settling around the major British ports. Muslims from the British Raj also came to England to study or engage in commerce.[1] The major growth of the Muslim population however dates from the postwar immigration of Pakistanis, Bangladeshis and Indians to fill specific labour demands in certain declining industrial cities in the South East, the Midlands and the North. In the 1970s, Arab communities began to settle in London, through gains made in sending economies. Since the late 1970s, a steady follow of Muslim political dissidents and economic migrants has entered and successfully settled in Britain. In the 1990s, there has been an intake of Eastern European and Middle Eastern Muslim refugees from such places as Bosnia and Kosovo, to Afghanistan, Somalia and Iraq.[2]

Although it is understood that there are conceptual overlaps, British discourse on racialised minorities has transformed from 'colour' in the 1950s and 1960s, 'race' in the 1960s, 1970s and 1980s, 'ethnicity' in the 1990s, to 'religion' in the present climate. Here, Islam has had the greatest profile. British popular discourse has shifted from seeing minorities as a homogenous entity, to discerning differences within and between 'Blacks' and Asians, and then within South Asians, to differences between Indians, Pakistanis and Bangladeshis and then between Muslims, Hindus and Sikhs. Religion has emerged as a major social signifier. In Britain, the burgeoning interest in religion has come from both awareness within the ethnic minority population of Islam and from its heightened international profile. In 1951, the British Muslim population was approximately 21,000. By 2001, it had grown to 1.6 million. Two out of three Muslims in Britain are of South Asian origin, with around half of all British Muslims of Pakistani ethnicity.[3]

Muslim communities have remained concentrated in the inner city areas of older towns and cities in the North, the Midlands and in the South. It is an indicator of how they have not benefited from the levels of mobility enjoyed by other migrant communities, and of their inability to move out from areas facing high levels of social tension and economic deprivation through direct discrimination, racial hostility and cultural preference.[4] Birmingham is typical of many of the challenges faced by Muslims across the country. Approximately one in seven of the city's inhabitants are Muslim and their unemployment rate is three times that of the overall city levels. The experience of Birmingham's Muslims brings into focus the fact that economic opportunities have tended to bypass Muslim communities, even when other communities have prospered.

While other cities with large Muslim populations, such as Bradford, are in economic decline, Birmingham's economic performance has been good, despite the decline of its manufacturing and engineering sectors. The city has undergone successful regeneration and this has begun to attract a thriving retail service and commercial sector. Nevertheless, these opportunities have largely evaded most Muslims and may have even given rise to some of the barriers which they face. While the indigenous population has moved out of inner city Birmingham through 'white flight,' South Asian Muslims have failed to move beyond the inner city areas to which they originally migrated. Subsequently, these areas have become further disadvantaged with new employment created elsewhere.[5]

Multiculturalism and Islamophobia in Britain

In Britain, since the 1960s, governments have shaped policy and practise in relation to ethnic minority groups based on various strategies of anti-immigration and anti-discrimination legislation, on the one hand, with a programme of assimilation, integration and latterly multiculturalism, on the other.[6] However, the underlying assumption concerning the inevitable assimilation of immigrant groups permeates policy and practise. In relation to British Muslims, this has not occurred to the extent envisaged. This is partly due to the impact of racism on people and group potential to integrate into the economy and larger society but also because of a lack of appreciation of the extent to which ethnic minority communities have come to rely on group class and ethnic resources to mobilise what little economic and social development they can achieve. In effect, Muslims often have had little choice but to retreat into their communities. Even before the events of September 11, 'loyalty' to a cultural-national identity was being asked of British Muslims. The Rushdie Affair placed the concerns of British South Asian Muslims firmly on the political and social map,[7] with issues of civic engagement, blasphemy laws, multicultural philosophy, the nature and orientation of certain religio-cultural norms and values and socio-economic exclusion and marginalisation dominating rhetoric, policy and practise throughout the 1990s. Combined with matters in relation to cultural hybridisation and the recognition of minority religions, the experience of and dominant attitudes towards British Muslims throughout the 1990s were reflective of the entire range of insensitive debates and discussions in this field.[8]

In Britain, assimilation began, in part, as a policy to persuade indigenous white groups that the arrival of immigrant groups would not mean the loss of the social, cultural and political identity and of the importance of maintaining the *status quo*. But in the current climate matters are made more complex because the nation-state has developed into a culturally heterogeneous entity, constantly in a state of flux as result of population movements that are combinations of ethno-religious tensions and the internationalisation of capital and labour. Nations now have to manage the needs and aspirations of diverse immigrant populations as well as more established ethnic minority citizens. Any attempts to make multiculturalism work in the British case has been fraught with ambiguities, inconsistencies, challenges and political leanings, all affected by present politics and collective memory. The New Labour experiment has had both successes and failures – but, then, as a result of September 11 and the northern 'riots,' public policy focus has been on domestic security, the war against international terrorism and making 'communities cohesive.'

Issues in relation to the experience of British Muslims allow the debates in multiculturalism to be conceptualised in their fullest form. Given the ways in which multiculturalism is viewed, understood, accepted and applied, it is clear that no other group provides greatest exposure on its effectiveness than British Muslims. Indeed, there were both external and internal forces affecting the positions of British Muslims before September 11. Externally, after September 11 the international agenda dominates domestic politics, there is a tightening of security and anti-terrorist measures and there are citizenship tests for new immigrants. Important to consider too are the disturbances in the North in 2001, as government reaction to them has direct and lingering implications for British South Asian Muslims. Internally, young British Muslims are increasingly found to be in the precarious position of having to choose their loyalties, being impacted by externally-driven radical Islamic politics, on the one hand, and developments to British multicultural citizenship at home, on the other. There is a contestation between the forces of radicalisation, secularisation and liberalization, impacting the lives of young British Muslims. In the post-September 11 climate, British Muslims are at the centre of questions in relation to what it means to be British or English. The basis of this rests with issues on the global agenda as well as local area concerns in relation to 'community cohesion,' citizenship, and multicultural political philosophy.[9]

There is certainly a problem in trying to make comparisons of the British with the Canadian and Australian case. Although both have had to come to terms with the history of how they treated the indigenous aboriginals, they are not as affected by the complex ethnic and cultural relations of a postcolonial society found in Britain. As such, there are different starting points for different nation-states as they attempt to manage their diverse populations. In relation to the British case, there are two areas of concern. First, where the policy of cultural integration is strongly assimilatory, there is a moral dilemma as well as the potential for resistance, with the likelihood of stereotyping and stigmatising immigrant populations who are thought to be unwilling to adapt. Conversely, if the policy is pluralist there is every eventuality of it being seen as an obstacle to 'integration' or a threat to 'our common culture.' Second, if the policies in relation to the 'political or public culture' are accommodationist stressing a political character, ethnocentric or nationalist reactions are enforced. If, however, they are 'ethno-nationalist and assimilationist they create "fundamentalisms" on both sides.'

Youth, Muslims and Radicalisation

Patterns among ethnic minority communities, where groups are also Muslim, are remarkably similar across Western Europe in relation to immigration, settlement and the current malaise in relation to radicalism. Post-war immigrant groups who mostly came searching for improved economic opportunities have found their children growing up in societies which exhibit prejudice, discrimination and racism towards minority Muslim communities. Local education for the young is limited, for much the same reasons as in Britain; that is, poor schools in poor neighbourhoods and children often having less educated parents. It affects the likelihood of securing effective higher education or labour market entry. It also prevents individuals and communities from participating as 'good' citizens in society. There are also inter-generational tensions as a result of language, culture and attitudes towards majority communities. Invariably, as the process of adaptation begins to evolve in subsequent generations of migrant communities, an adjustment to majority society occurs. At times there is resistance as in the case of a few Muslims who see integration as a negative feature in their life in liberal secular nation-states regarded by some as somewhat antithetical to the life of 'a good Muslim.' For others integration has been a positive effort but once people are negatively impacted on by the system a sense of dislocation and alienation, perceived or real, affects the consciousness. It encourages some to seek to resolve 'Muslim issues,' home and abroad. These individuals are often targeted by radical interest groups which may result in their carrying out acts of violence which invariably involves the annihilation of the self and other Muslims. For some commentators, the incessant interest and focus by the state and the media on 'militant jihadi' activity in Britain potentially perpetuates the problem. Certainly, there is a feeling among many that British and US Foreign policy has an impact on the perceptions of already much maligned and disenfranchised young Muslim males who feel they have no voice.[10]

There are earlier periods in this so called radicalisation of Islam, particularly in the twentieth century. It is through the Salafi ('early Islam') writings of Muslim ideologues, such as Sayyid Qutb, Hassan al-Banna's *Ikhwān al-Muslimīn*, Maulana Abu'l A'la Maududi in the 1930s, 1940s or 1950s, actions of the Palestinian Liberation Organisation and its wings, the Popular Front for the Liberation of Palestine and Fateh in the 1960s and 1970s, or Libyans, Iraqis, Iranians or the Lebanese, such as, Hamas or Hezbollah in the 1980s. A perceptible pattern is found where Muslims in Islamic lands have opposed the dominant interests of major capitalistic states vying for a 'new world order.' The overall response has come about over the last two hundred years as Islam and Muslims have had to counter the imperial and colonial onslaught, often supported by US and British interventions in the Middle East and the Muslim world in regards to important economic concerns or to fight the Third World War – the cold war against the 'red enemy.'[11]

Before the events of 9/11, the Rushdie Affair of 1989 highlighted to the world that there were issues pertaining to the South Asian Muslim community regarded as relatively innocuous until then. Pictures of the 'book burnings in Bradford' reverberated around the globe and the media reaction to it was particularly negative, home and abroad.[12] The collapse of the Soviet Empire in 1991 and troubles in far off Muslim lands firmly placed Islam and Muslims in the immediate sphere of media attention and political concern. After 9/11 and certainly after 7/7, a whole host of factors have negatively impacted on British Muslims. These include increased anti-terrorist measures, increased policing powers, and racial and ethnic profiling in the criminal justice system. An apparent unassimilability of Muslims, with a focus on community cohesion and widening cultural and economic and social positions has also existed alongside the apparent and increasing 'jihadi salafi' radicalisation of young Muslims. Gender issues are important to explore as it is often men who are more likely to be embroiled. Young Muslim women have demonstrated a better ability to deal with the theological, political and social pressures placed on their identities as British and Muslim. Certainly, it is reasonably well confirmed that Muslim women outperform their male counterparts in higher education and, where possible, are better able to negotiate issues of ethnicity, identity and religious minority status.[13]

The Decline of Civil Liberties

In Britain, the Human Rights Act of 1998 guarantees the right to life, freedom from torture, freedom from slavery and forced labour, the right to liberty and security, right to a fair trial, right to privacy, freedom of conscience, freedom of expression, freedom of assembly and association, and the right to marry and have a family. They are also the freedoms that protect the individual from arbitrary government interference which peculiarly include freedom of speech, freedom of assembly, and trial by jury – usually created and protected by a constitution. As a result of local, national and international events, namely the disturbances in the North in 2001 and the war 'on terror' as a reaction to the event of September 11, policy has sought to place the concerns majority groups have in relation to Muslim groups at the heart of practise. The community cohesion reports and the official Home Office's response to the northern disturbances seemed to many on the community level to be a blame-the-victim pathology. As such, it seeks to placate the current policies of multiculturalism and ensures that the focus remains firmly on the British South Asian Muslim communities themselves. At the same time, in the aftermath of September 11, the Anti-terrorism, Crime and Security Act of 2001 was rushed through Parliament. It gave powers to hold without charge foreign nationals suspected to be involved in terrorism. In order to do this, it meant 'opting out' of article 5 of the European Convention on Human Rights, allowing for this 'in time of war or other public emergency threatening the life of the nation.' Britain was the only nation to take this route.

Pressure mounted to alter the way in which this legislation seemingly affected Muslim groups, and in December 2004 the Law Lords ruled 8–1 on the All-Party Human Rights Commission support to repeal the internment powers in the legislation. It did so when the Court of Appeal, under Lord Woolf, reversed the decision of the Special Immigration Appeals Commission ruling that detention without trial was compatible with British and international law. Lord Hoffman said, 'the real threat of this life of the nation, in the sense of a people in accordance with its traditional laws and political values, comes not from terrorism but from laws such as these.' Rather than immediately repealing the act, it was suggested by the Home Office that 'control orders' would be adopted – a non-custodial response, applicable to both foreign *and* British subjects, without charge and for an indefinite period if it was suspected that an individual was involved in domestic or international terrorism. Measures included electronic tagging, curfews, a ban on the use of the internet, and 'house arrest' (although this term was not used by the incumbent Home Secretary, Charles Clarke, MP). Although some minor concessions were made, it was still felt necessary to derogate from the European Convention on Human Rights. If anything, the government has more powers than ever to hold people without charge, a function of the current climate of fear generated by politicians and the media, the constitutional crisis raised by the Law Lords judgement and the availability of technology in relation to constraining.[14] The erosion of the principle of *habeas corpus* severely undermines the civil liberties that have made this nation great in the eyes of the many. The justification provided is that a trial would be damaging to the interests of the security services as it would expose their secret wire-tapping operations.

The continued racist profiling of asylum seekers and migrants is yet another feature experienced by new Muslim groups, shown too in New Labour's attempts to evade the 1951 UN convention on refugees. The somewhat blanketed targeting of young Muslims under stop and search laws continues unabated, exacerbated by comments made by Hazel Blears MP, the minister responsible for counter-terrorism, who said in March 2005 that Muslims will have to accept as a "reality" that they will be stopped and searched by the police more often than the rest of the public. Since the original terror laws were passed in 2001, around 900 people have been arrested. As of 30 September 2005, although half have been released without charge, around 350 have been charged under anti-terror and other legislation. But, only 17 have been convicted for terrorist offences; 3 Islamists and 7 Irish.[15] The Institute of Race Relations states that the arrests under the anti-terrorist laws have attracted widespread media coverage while convictions of non-Muslims in court have not been widely reported. Most people are left with the impression that the criminal justice system is successfully prosecuting Muslim terrorists in Britain. Up until 7 July 2005, large numbers of innocent Muslims were being arrested, questioned and released.[16] In the post 7/7 period, it seems very likely this pattern will remain, if not intensify, particularly given that three of the four perpetrators of the suicide bombings in London were young British-born Pakistanis.

Government policy in the area of race relations and multiculturalism tends to be one of 'integration with cultural tolerance,' but the striking feature of the structural experience of British Muslims, new and old, is the economic and social positions they possess. It is, indeed, difficult to generate a position of cultural and social integration from a weak economic and social base. The recent development to anti-terrorist legislation, the ways in which young British Muslims have been overly targeted by stop-and-search, the debates in relation to multiculturalism and the integration of Muslim minorities serve to provide a multi-pronged attack on the civil liberties of Muslims in this country. The general election in 2005 has seen New Labour's majority plummet, and partly based on the Muslim vote dramatically switching, for example in Bethnal Green and Bow (and given also that in fact more people voted for the Conservatives in England than New Labour). Rather than seeking to empower individuals and groups who seek to integrate successfully into a racially, culturally and religiously tolerant society, the view from government tends to focus on anti-terrorism. It does so at the acute expense of civil liberties and particularly in relation to Muslims in Britain who remain trapped in poor localities facing direct and indirection cultural and religious racism. What recent events leading up to July 7 have served to illustrate is the continued rhetoric of a benign multiculturalism that is soft on inequality but hard on identity and culture. Furthermore, neo-Orientalist considerations in relation to Islam continue to perpetuate negative political and media discourses. There is no attempt to disentangle the broad category of British Islam which contains class, cultural, ethnic and even theological nuances.

'10/8': Politico-Media Manufactured Event or a Threat to 'Our Ways'?

The recent 'foiled terrorist plot' of 10 August 2006 has revealed an interesting set of observations in relation to the developing nature of Islamophobia in Britain. Within hours of the arrests, high profile policing figures were airing concerns in relation to the 'biggest terrorist event since 9/11' and 'death and destruction on an unprecedented scale.' As the day unfolded, details emerged that over twenty arrests had been made, largely relating to British Pakistanis, but with a number of 'converts' also among them. Countless passengers suffered in long queues, with mothers made to taste their baby's bottled milk to assure the aviation authorities of its legitimacy. This was a nonsensical approach, as chemicals used to make liquid bombs do not harm people if they are taken in limited quantities; rather they need to be mixed together to cause the devastating effects. By the next day, a healthy dose of scepticism began to emerge from the communities in which these so-called suicide bombers emerged. As one began to talk with professionals on the ground and on the university campus, it became further apparent that a great many were of this view, confirmed by the many bloggers, letters in newspapers and opinion columns that one could read on the matter. A media manufactured attempt to be inquisitor, jury and judge ultimately resulted in people becoming suspicious of such negative institutionalised voices. The actions of Forest Gate and the untruths in relation to the brutal mowing down of Jean Charles de Menezes are too recent a set of events in the memory for many. Having had time to reflect, interpret the events and reporting on it, it is clear we are back at where we started, if not worse off, even if the many who were arrested are released without charge. The nation is under the grip of rampant Islamophobia. And it is a media-driven phenomenon that is supported by a wider geo-political campaign to undermine, destabilise and effectively remove Islam's ever-growing presence. Islam is simply a threat to a new world order.

What has been quite remarkable is how Muslim elites and commentators went on the offensive so quickly. After 7/7, Muslims felt a double whammy: as Britons, many were frightened by the terrible acts of indiscriminate violence; as Muslims, communities did not have the confidence of leaders to take on the establishment. A year on, leaders are stronger, wiser and more articulate, and they have come to appreciate that a great many people in this great country are with them too. Inevitably, there has been a backlash as Muslim criticism in relation to such matters is often dismissed out of hand, another quite specific feature of Islamophobia. Indeed, six Muslim parliamentarians and twenty-eight leading organisations published an open letter to Prime Minister Tony Blair two days after the 'foiled plot.' It spoke of the role of foreign policy and how it was furthering the causes of militant suicide cults. However, they found themselves quickly ostracised as a result.

A particular question in relation to '10/8' and the events before it is, 'why Pakistanis?' Why are other South Asian groups who arrived to and settled in this country at the same time not implicated in such acts of terror? The answer is not entirely about ethnicity; rather is it more to do with factors such as social class and community cohesion. Clearly, when we speak of young Muslims who are involved or suspected of being involved in terrorist attacks, a great many do emerge from poor neighbourhoods, including 'reverts.' But, a number do not. However, what these sets of people share are characteristics in relation to the limited opportunities to engage with others in particular spheres, and not being able to feel a certain sense of belonging. There is a lacking in cultural awareness, an under-appreciation of the position of Britain in relation to, for example, the rest of Western Europe, and most do not have the confidence to take part in mainstream politics. Notions of cultural and social capital are implicit concepts behind the ideas of community cohesion but alienation, disaffection, disenfranchisement and isolation are functions of both poorer and richer Muslims, and enough to lead either into radicalisation, although clearly the latter are perhaps less susceptible.

In effect, the nation-state has failed Muslims at many different levels. In October 2005, as the Home Office appointed working groups detailed their recommendations and suggestions in how to tackle extremism; however, only a small number have since been taken forward, many with limited long-term benefits. Indeed, there has been a wholesale failure on the part of the state to implement the vast majority of the recommendations of the working groups. Internationally, how foreign policy influences the perceptions of already severely disaffected groups is dismissed, if not entirely negated. Nationally, we are continuing to witness a shift to new right politics and an unadulterated sympathy with a US-driven neo-conservative political and economic agenda. Locally, there is limited inward investment in the areas in which South Asian Muslims are concentrated. Poor education and high unemployment continue to influence life chances in starkly negative ways. These circumstances are further compounded by the rural origins of first-generation migrants, who have largely organised community and political culture around clan-based kinship networks, where opportunities for the subsequent generations to break out do not always exist. Local Muslim leadership is weak, including its capacity and the vision it has for the future. Inter-generational tensions are not being resolved, particularly in relation to patriarchy. And, for the most part, mosques and imams have failed their communities, not in how the young are thought to have become radicalised; in fact, quite the opposite. It is rather in how they have been removed from the direct religious edification of Muslims, who have subsequently gone on to form their own study circles, use the internet for their information, and utilise modes of communication familiar to them, i.e., the English language. Here, the already disposed are particularly vulnerable to negative influences from outside when all else has failed them inside.

Conclusion: After 7/7

Witnessing the events of the last three decades, from the Iranian Revolution of 1979 onwards, the Muslim world has been in turmoil while Muslim minorities in the Western world have faced economic, social, political and cultural marginalisation. It is these harsh experiences that characterise the study of British Muslims in the social sciences. In the current climate, it is quite apparent we now need to refer to the notion of 'British Muslim communities,' not 'Muslim communities.' Many South Asian Muslims trapped in poor economic conditions are far removed from a growing body of high-income, well-integrated savvy class of professional Muslims, often living and working in the South. As part of this analysis, what is also clear is that the debates in relation to integration and multiculturalism have been sidelined by a focus on religious minorities and their supposedly 'alien ways.' What we are also witnessing is the formalisation of the discussion on multiculturalism away from a concentration on equality and diversity to one which emphasises culture and *values*. It becomes obvious enough that this sentiment refers to Muslims. How long we are to endure this phenomenon is yet to be determined.

The British state has determined a range of responses to the events of 7 July but the call for an official inquiry is one essential concern that has fallen on deaf ears. This is exacerbated by the fact that the state completely dismisses any link between home-grown terrorism and foreign policy, particularly in relation to activities in Muslim lands. Indeed, the FCO, as part of its engaging the Muslim world programme, routinely sends scholars, academics, community leaders and high-ranking members of influential civil society organisations across the Muslim world to elaborate on the nature of the British Muslim experience. In specific attempts to directly tackle extremism, the state has orchestrated the setting up of MINAB (Mosques and Imams National Advisory Board). Formally launched at the end of June 2006, this body consists of members from the Al-Khoei Foundation, Muslim Council of Britain, Muslim Association of Britain and the British Muslim Forum. It is a tremendous step in the right direction.[17] First, it spells wide Muslim ownership of such an important set of issues. Second, it shows the importance of Muslims building consensus with other Muslims – something which has been significantly lacking up until recently. What happens now in terms of delivery will be important to explore.

In the final analysis, with the state making its moves through the empowerment and incorporation of a burgeoning professional and, more importantly, a moderate middle class of Muslims, there have been some gains particularly in how this process has positively engaged young people and Muslim women. At the level of the community, which is differentiated by ethnicity, culture, social class, region and sect, a number of Muslim civil society and community organisations are working together, and these projects are delivering some valuable outcomes. As developments emerge in the light of concerted efforts to confront the problems of extremism, what will remain important are issues that exist at the heart of the problem. For most Muslims in Britain, there is pernicious socio-economic exclusion. As structural pre-conditions emerge to permit education, jobs and housing opportunities, only then will groups value their presence in society, becoming engaged citizens in the framework of an ever-evolving national politico-cultural paradigm. At the level of the nation-state, popular discourses have been focusing on culturally-essentialist notions of 'the Muslim' – for example, based on the perceived problems of 'arranged marriages,' 'cultural relativism' and 'self-styled' segregation. It is a blame-the-victim pathology that is subliminally inculcated within the majority society. In a hostile local, national and international climate, susceptible young Muslim men are easily targeted by radical Islamism, directly or indirectly. The violent radical Islamist ideology appeals because of its political and theological context, however improperly legitimised. It is also fuelled by perceptions in relation to the actions of certain nation-states and their approaches to foreign policy as well as how they go about effectively integrating Muslim minorities at home. The 2004 Madrid and 2005 London bombings, and the continued threat to Britain, perceived or real, are testimony to this. As the state continues its legal, social and cultural assault on Muslims, with its attempts to ever-strengthen draconian anti-terror legislation at home while fighting Muslim 'insurgents' abroad, many more young Muslim men are being radicalised. Unless there are greater efforts to tackle the structural issues and politico-ideological constructs in relation to Muslims, the potential threat of violent Islamic political radicalism and its impact on how Muslim minorities experience and help to determine a viable multicultural *and* multi-religious society will remain in the near future.

REFERENCES

Abbas, Tahir, "Recent developments to British multicultural theory, policy and practise: the case of British Muslims," *Citizenship Studies* (2005), vol. 9, no. 3.
_____ *Muslims in Birmingham, UK*. Background paper for the University of Oxford: Centre on Migration Policy and Society, 2006.
Anwar, Muhammad, Patrick Roach and Ranjit Sondhi, eds., *From Legislation to Integration? Race Relations in Britain from Integration to Legislation* (London: Palgrave, 1999).
Dreyfuss, Robert, *Devil's Game: How the United States Helped Unleash Fundamentalist Islam* (New York: Metropolitan Books, 2005).
Institute of Race Relations, *Arrests Under Anti-Terrorist Legislation Since 11 September 2001* (London: Institute of Race Relations, 2005).
Matar, Nabil, *Islam in Britain, 1558–1685* (Cambridge: Cambridge University Press, 1998).

Nielsen, Jorgen, *Muslims in Western Europe*, 3ʳᵈ edn., (Edinburgh: Edinburgh University Press, 2005).

Macey, Marie, "Islamic Political Radicalism in Britain: Muslim Men in Bradford," in *Islam Political Radicalism: A European Perspective,* ed. Tahir Abbas (Edinburgh: Edinburgh University Press, 2007).

Modood, Tariq, "British Asian Muslims and the Rushdie Affair," *Political Quarterly* (1990), vol. 61, no. 2.

_____ *Multicultural Politics: Racism, Ethnicity and Muslims in Britain* (Edinburgh: Edinburgh University Press, 2005).

Modood, Tariq et al., *Ethnic Minorities in Britain: Diversity and Disadvantage – The Fourth National Survey of Ethnic Minorities* (London: Policy Studies Institute, 1997).

Modood, Tariq, "Anti-Essentialism, Multiculturalism and the 'Recognition' of Religious Groups," *The Journal of Political Philosophy* (1998), vol. 6, no. 4.

Mosques and National Advisory Board, *Best Practise Guide for Mosques and Islamic Centres* (London: MINAB, 2006).

Nellis, Mike and Richard North, "Electronic Monitoring and the Creation of Control Orders for Terrorist Suspects in Britain." Unpublished paper, University of Birmingham, 2005.

Peach, Ceri, "Muslims in the UK," in *Muslim Britain: Communities under Pressure,* ed. Tahir Abbas (London: Zed, 2005).

Rai, Milan, *7/7: The London Bombings, Islam and the Iraq War* (London: Pluto Press, 2006).

Sanghera, Gurchathen and Thapar-Björkert, Suruchi, "'Because I am Pakistani ... and I am Muslim ... I am Political' – Gendering Political Radicalism: Young Masculinities and Femininities in Bradford," in *Islam Political Radicalism: A European Perspective,* ed. Tahir Abbas (Edinburgh: Edinburgh University Press, 2007).

Travis, Alan, "Community relations hit by terror laws, says MPs," *The Guardian* (6 April, 2005).

Werbner, P., "Divided Loyalties, Empowered Citizenship? Muslims in Britain," *Citizenship Studies* (2000), vol. 4, no. 3.

Alternatives to Violence

IMAD AD-DEAN AHMAD

Alternatives to Violence in Muslim History: Parallels to American Cases and Prospects for Future Applications

Introduction

ALTHOUGH ISLAM IS NOT A RELIGION of pacifism, by which I mean that warfare is not entirely prohibited, nonetheless, it is a peaceful religion. Its objective is to achieve a state of peace and security for both the Muslims and for those non-Muslims under its protection. Furthermore, warfare is governed by strict rules of what today would be considered "just war theory." The objective of this paper is to demonstrate that the tactics and strategies of nonviolence are part of the Muslim tradition. In particular, I wish to look at the examples of nonviolent activism in the Muslim tradition, and note along the way how they relate to the basic teachings and how they compare to nonviolent resistance in America.

Before beginning, it is important to emphasise that nonviolence is an active tactic and strategy of resistance and is not a manifestation of pacifism. Practitioners of nonviolence may or may not be pacifists, and Muslims are not pacifists. Nonviolence may be resorted to because one feels that military force is immoral or because one feels it is less effective than nonviolence in a particular situation. Finally, it must be remembered that nonviolence is often accompanied by violence either because other factions in a coalition reject nonviolence or because its practitioners engage in violent as well as nonviolent tactics. The most famous cases of nonviolent resistance were accompanied violence: violent resistance to the British in India coincided with Gandhi's nonviolent movement; the American civil rights movement was accompanied by violent urban riots; and alongside the nonviolent protesters against American involvement in Vietnam was the "Weatherman" terrorist organisation.

The modes of nonviolent action are many. They include flight, boycotts, strikes, and disobedience to civil authority. The practise of flight goes back at least to the time of Moses, and the story of Moses is as much part of Muslim tradition as it is of the Jewish tradition. But flight is so central to Muslim history that the Muslim calendar is dated from the flight of the Prophet Muhammad from Makkah to Madinah, the hijrah. Boycotts are an ancient practise in the Arab tradition, even among the non-Muslims. Indeed, the polytheistic Quraysh boycotted the Muslim community in Makkah for years although that boycott was ultimately unsuccessful. Strikes are a modern phenomenon as the modern modes of production have enormously magnified their effectiveness. Meanwhile, the asymmetry of power between the owners and management of big business, on the one hand, and the numerous employees, on the other hand, have given unique importance to the tactic in the area of labour relations.

Noncooperation is an ancient tactic, not always driven by socially conscious motives. It comes easily to the Arab people as an individual act given the decentralised, even individualistic, nature of desert life. Throughout the history of Islam, there have been many examples of individual civil disobedience. Americans know the concept through the example and teachings of Henry David Thoreau. Thoreau most clearly articulated the moral imperative for noncooperation in his essay on civil disobedience.[1] The New England transcendentalist's arguments often echo Islamic fundamentals. Thoreau wants right and wrong to be determined not by the majority, but by conscience.

> By the Soul, and the proportion and order given to it; And its enlightenment as to its wrong and its right; Truly he succeeds that purifies it, and he fails that corrupts it![2]

An inordinate respect for the laws of man he says leads to warfare and slavery:

> I do not hesitate to say, that those who call themselves Abolitionists should at once effectually withdraw their support, both in person and property, from the government of Massachusetts, and not wait till they constitute a majority of one, before they suffer the right to prevail through them. I think that it is enough if they have God on their side, without waiting for that other one.

Moreover, any man more right than his neighbors constitutes a majority of one already.[3]

The idea that the individual is directly responsible to the Almighty is inherent in the *Shahādah*, or declaration of the faith, "There is no god but God." The demands of leaders to do evil are of no weight in the Qur'an and the hadith.

> And they would say: "Our Lord! We obeyed our chiefs and our great ones, and they misled us as to the (right) path. Our Lord! Give them double Penalty and curse them with a very great Curse!"[4] ...Saith the last about the first: "Our Lord! It is these that misled us: so give them a double penalty in the Fire." He will say: "Doubled for all": but this Ye do not understand.[5]

Individual disobedience to commands to do evil is a natural consequence of the Muslim teaching of direct responsibility to God. Abū Bakr, in his inaugural address, told the assembled people that they had no duty to obey him if he gave a wrongful order, but rather had a duty to correct him. Examples include the founders of the Sunni schools who were imprisoned and/or tortured for their refusal to cooperate with the authorities and the Shia, who historically denied the legitimacy of wrongful rule.

Organised civil disobedience is a tactic normally associated with the modern era, and most of its modern practitioners trace their influence back to Mahatma Gandhi. Yet the first act of organised mass civil disobedience in history of which I am aware was conceived and directed by the Prophet Muhammad. He had a vision in which he led the people on the lesser pilgrimage to Makkah at a time when the city was still in the hands of his enemies. He told the people to put on the pilgrim garb and to come with him unarmed into the city in violation of the expressed will and intention of the authorities in power. The Muslims did not allow their disciplined nonviolence to be broken by the provocations of the Quraysh. This demonstration of the power of active nonviolent resistance resulted in the Treaty of Hudaybiyyah, referred to in the Qur'an as a "Manifest Victory."[6]

> It is He Who sent down tranquility into the hearts of the Believers, that they may add faith to their faith; for to Allah belong the Forces of the heavens and the earth; and Allah is full of Knowledge and Wisdom.[7]

Indian Independence

The modern world knows this style of mass resistance through the work of Mohandas Gandhi. While Gandhi's familiarity with Islam and his admiration for Muhammad are no secret,[8] a direct influence of Muslim tradition on his techniques has yet to be demonstrated. Nonetheless, it is known that the Muslim Indian activist Abdul Ghaffar Khan began his own work at about the same time that Gandhi returned to India (1914). He had been arrested by the British in 1919 for his role in a political rally and in 1929 he founded the Khudai Khidmatgar (Servants of God) whose members "pledged to refrain from violence and [to] devote two hours a day to social work."[9] On April 13 of the following year they performed the single most remarkable example of active nonviolent resistance to the British occupation.

In March of 1930 the mass disobedience campaign had begun with Gandhi's famous march to the sea. In April, when Khan's group followed up with an educational campaign in nonviolent resistance, the British arrested Khan and the other leaders. On April 23 a nonviolent protest of the arrests was about to disperse when the British cracked down on Khan's group with "a barbarity that they did not often inflict on other adherents of nonviolence in India."[10] Gene Sharp, the prominent student of nonviolent resistance, describes the scene:

> When those in front fell down wounded by the shots, those behind came forward with their breasts bared and exposed themselves to the fire, so much so that some people got as many as twenty-one bullet wounds in their bodies, and all the people stood their ground without getting into a panic .... The Anglo-Indian paper of Lahore, which represents the official view, itself wrote to the effect that the people came forward one after another to face the firing and when they fell wounded they were dragged back and others came forward to be shot at. This state of things continued from 11 till 5 o'clock in the evening. When the number of corpses became too many, the ambulance cars of the government took them away.
>
> The carnage stopped only because a regiment of Indian soldiers finally refused to continue firing on the unarmed protesters, an impertinence for which they were severely punished.[11]

Nonviolence scholar Joan V. Bondurant writes that the religious basis of the Khudai Khidmatgar was more obvious than that of the All-India

Congress because the former "pledged themselves to nonviolence not only as a policy, but as a creed, a way of life."[12] Khan insisted that his techniques were taken directly from Islam and the Sunnah of the Prophet and claimed he had "left speechless" a Pashtun who had disputed his claim of a nonviolent core in Islam.

The Iranian Revolution

On June 5, 1963 Iranian authorities repressed nonviolent demonstrations opposing an American military loan and the Shah's reform programme by arresting the Ayatollah Khomeini and throwing some students to their death from a roof of Madrasa Faydiyya.[13] Thousands died in the ensuing mass demonstrations.[14] On the twelfth anniversary of the event on the Iranian calendar, students gathered for prayers at the Madrasa Faydiyya "to recite 20,000 blessings (*ṣalawāt*) upon the defenders of Islam (Khomeini) and *laʿnah* (curses) upon the enemies of Islam (the Shah), keeping count on their prayer beads."[15] Like the American civil rights demonstrators, they were met with tear gas and water canon.[16]

Employing the symbolism of Shia theology, the Iranian Revolution transformed the "Karbala paradigm, shifting from a passive witnessing of weeping for Husayn and waiting for the twelfth Imam to an active witnessing of fighting and working for the overthrow of tyranny.... Shi'ite preaching had been honed into a highly effective technique for maintaining a high level of consciousness about the injustice of the Pahlavi regime and for coordinating demonstrations.[17] The revolution of 1977–79 was a successful and mainly nonviolent resistance 'fought entirely in the Islamic idiom.'"[18] (There were some violent acts by the resistance, but the most of the violence was perpetrated by the regime against the demonstrators.

The wave of resistance began with illegal poetry readings at Arymehr University.[19] Later, when women who chose to wear the chador attempting to register for class at the University of Tehran were turned away, other women who normally wore Western dress engaged in active disobedience by showing up in chadors.[20] In July 1977 the newly formed "Group for Free Books and Free Thought" had published in journals in exile "detailed cases of writers who had been tortured and whose works had been censored."[21] By autumn they openly condemned the Shah's liberalisation programme as a sham.[22]

In August 1977 essentially spontaneous demonstrations by students and rural immigrants erupted in response to rising prices, food shortages, and the government's destruction of unauthorised housing construction.[23] In November 1977, after protestors embarrassingly outnumbered paid supporters of the Shah during his visit to the White House, SAVAK began a severe crackdown on the dissenters in Iran, denouncing them, as "supporters of international terrorism."[24] Instead of being intimidated, the religious leadership, in the person of Ayatullah Shariatmadari, "declared the Shah's government non-Islamic, called for a moratorium on communal prayers, and threatened a funeral march to carry the corpses" to the Shah's palace.[25] At this point virtually every sector of Iranian society had aligned itself against the Shah.

Organised demonstrations began to proliferate in December.[26] In January 1978 a "peaceful demonstration organised by religious students came under attack by the police, killing between forty and two hundred people; martial law was declared in the city."[27] An organisational infrastructure began to emerge centred on the "bazaar guilds, *heyats* (religious sessions), mosques and coffee houses." Mass demonstrations were scheduled on the Shia traditional 40–day mourning patterns and employing the rituals of religious processions.[28]

Both the moderate and radical leaders of the revolution called for peaceful demonstrations, but they did not always remain nonviolent. An initially peaceful demonstration on February 18 "turned violent after an irate police officer shot a teenage student protester." In May Khomeini backed off from his March call for the assassination of the Shah to urge caution. In June Shariatmadari counseled strikers to stay home to avoid death at the hands of the authorities. A burning of a movie theatre in August was blamed on religious fanatics by the Shah, obtaining confessions from five of the ten people arrested, but popular sentiment blame the SAVAK, noting that the film was an Iranian film with social commentary, not one of the foreign films with sexual content that had been targeted by the religious extremists.

At the end of Ramadan demonstrators returned to the streets peacefully handing out flowers to the soldiers,[29] but on September 6 demonstrations were banned. On September 7 hundreds of thousands defied the ban in a peaceful march to Parliament. The next day entered into history as "Black Friday," as thousands of people gathered spontaneously but found themselves marching into a massacre. One soldier refused to fire at the crowd, shooting his commanding officer and them himself, but at least hundreds, perhaps thousands, of demonstrators were killed and the survivors went on a rampage.[30] In the weeks that followed there would be more cases of soldiers siding with the dissidents and rumors of mutinies in the garrisons.[31] Repeatedly in this key period, Ayatollah Khomeini's calls for resistance reflect his appreciation of both the religious basis and the power of nonviolent tactics. For example on November 22 he declared:

> our Imam Hossein ... showed us how the clenched fists of freedom fighters can crush the tanks and the guns of the oppressors, ultimately giving victory to Truth .... If Islam is endangered we should be willing to sacrifice ourselves and save Islam by our blood .... The military government of Iran is illegal, and is condemned by the principles of Islam. It is the duty of all to protest it and to refuse to be a part of it in any way. People should refuse to pay taxes to the government, and all employees of the Iranian oil company should endeavor to stop the flow of oil abroad .... The clergy fulfil their duties to God by disclosing the crimes of the regime more than ever .... I call on the clergy, the students, journalists, workers, peasants, merchants, civil servants and all the tribes to work side by side .... You ... should hold mourning sessions without acquiring the permission of SAVAK or the police ....[32]

The strikes became more sweeping and more effective and the demands more ideological. "5,000 bank clerks, 30,000 oil workers, and 100,000 government employees—coupled their economic demands ... with such sweeping political demands as the abolition of SAVAK, the lifting of martial law, the release of all political prisoners, the return of Khomeini, and the end of tyrannical rule."[33] In Muharram (December) men went into the streets in white sheets symbolising their willingness to be martyred or chanted slogans from the rooftops. Despite BBC reports of 700 deaths, the protests mounted.[34]

The state's attempts to pacify the opposition came too late. Certain bizarre concessions, such as the release of imprisoned guerilla leaders,[35] could have been aimed at increasing the violence. That the Shah's fate was sealed was made clear by the comment of a striking refinery worker that they would only export more oil after they had "exported the Shah and his generals," a threat that undercut Washington's support for the monarch.[36]

Later, when the new Islamic state began to degenerate into authoritarianism, some of the nonviolent tactics employed against the Shah were turned against the new regime. Most notable was the demonstration of Iranian women, in a twist on their earlier demonstrations against the Shah's prohibition of the chador, against calls by conservatives in the new regime for state-enforced chadors.[37]

The First Intifadah

Despite a history of nonviolence in the modern Arab world, including the Palestinian general strike of 1936, the first 39 years of the Palestinian resistance to their occupation by Israel focused on armed resistance, diplomacy, and economic sanctions. The first of these is clearly violent and the second carries the threat of violence behind it. Even the third must be distinguished from the classic nonviolent technique of boycott in that some states employed compulsory sanctions that coerced their citizenry into participation. There were a few Palestinian groups dedicated to nonviolent struggle, but they were small and the best known of them was directed by Mubarak Awad, a Christian inspired by the Quaker tradition.[38] In 1987, however, an indigenous nonviolent movement erupted that was so powerful that it forced the Israelis to enter into a deal with their militant opponents, the Palestine Liberation Organization, in order to end it. This was the first "Intifadah."[39]

When the Arab leaders snubbed the PLO at the November 1987 summit in Amman, it left the residents of the occupied territories embittered. Young people, no longer content to follow the directions of the aging PLO leadership, took to the streets in spontaneous demonstrations often with little boys in the vanguards "firing their slingshots at troops dispatched to disburse them."[40] The first eruption was a reaction to a minor incident in which an army tank-transport killed four Arabs and injured seven others in a traffic accident. As the Israeli response became one of collective punishment, the resistance expanded beyond the youth to include all segments of society.[41]

Initially the movement lacked centralised national leadership and was directed by local "popular committees." In January 1988 Hanna Siniora, editor of *Al-Fajr* issued a call for civil disobedience.[42] Leaflets from a "Unified Command" (UC) mysteriously began to appear.[43] The five tactics most frequently called for in pamphlets #18–39 were (1) strikes,

(2) community support (e.g., aid to victims of the occupation), (3) demonstrations and marches, (4) prayer and (5) fasting. The model of three of the pillars of Islam on tactics (2) zakah, (4) salah, and (5) *sawm* are obvious. Tactics (1) and (3) follow respectively the Prophet's commands to stop evil with your hands if you can and with your tongues if you lack the power with your hands.[44] All are tools of nonviolent resistance.

Among the tactics recommended in the leaflets was one seemingly inspired by Thoreau's dictum that "under a government which imprisons any unjustly, the true place for a just man is also a prison."[45] The leaflets urged "village residents present themselves for arrest at police stations when security forces tried to seize a fellow villager."[46]

Various forms of noncooperation were embraced, including strikes by the merchants.[47] One unique element was the way that Israeli attempt to break the sporadic strikes of shopkeepers by forcing the stores open backfired into making the strikes so systematic that shopkeepers would close stores when the Israelis ordered them open and open them when they ordered them closed.[48] Loathe to admit that the forced closings policy was failing, the Israelis falsely claimed they had abandoned it.[49] As noncooperation became more widespread, Mubarak Awad called for complete noncooperation in every respect,[50] and the Israelis retaliated by illegally deporting him.[51]

Israel treated any resistance, violent or nonviolent, as "incitement and hostile propaganda."[52] Its response was the policy called the "Iron Fist."[53] The consequences were disastrous for Israel for a number of reasons. Israeli officers were concerned about its effects on the Israeli troops.[54] The Israeli public became disillusioned about the nature of the occupation.[55] New Israeli peace groups proliferated[56] and the well established but hitherto cautious Peace Now became emboldened.[57] The Israeli government fell,[58] but the new government only intensified the Iron Fist policies.[59]

The impact on Palestinian society was dramatic and long lasting. On March 6, 1988 all but two of the "Palestinian employees of the Gaza Income and Property Tax division resigned."[60] By March 13 almost half of the Palestinian police in the occupied territories had quit.[61] Not withstanding Israeli claims to the contrary, the mass resignations could not be explained by coercion by the Palestinian leadership.[62] Tax resistance grew to problematic proportions.[63] Thoreau had said, "When the subject has refused allegiance, and the officer has resigned his office, then the revolution is accomplished."[64]

With the closure of the government, traditional civil society institutions returned to fill the void, among them *awni* (mutual help and charity), *atwi* (mediation of disputes by clan members), and *sulha* (extrajudicial arbitration).[65] Necessity bred a reinvigoration of civil society.[66] Policies and programs to free the society from dependence on Israel helped to shake-off the consumerism that inhibited Palestinian development and enable residents to compete with the Israelis in industrial and agricultural production.[67] A major consequence was that splits within the Muslim Brotherhood surrounding the Intifadah precipitated the formation of Hamas,[68] who even claimed to have started the Intifadah.[69] Hamas attempted to stake out a middle position between violence and armed resistance by urging that violence be limited to throwing stones.[70]

Most significant was the impact on the American people's perception of the nature of the Palestinian-Israeli conflict.[71] The enormous American aid that sustains the apartheid state has only been politically palatable because Americans have a skewed perspective on the Israeli occupation, as the American media systematically under-reports Israeli violence and human rights violations while emphasising Palestinian violence.[72] In this case, however, the balance of violence was so badly skewed that the usual propaganda techniques did not work. Even the American public, notorious for its indifference to foreign affairs that do not directly affect their interests, could not accept the claim of moral equivalence between children throwing stones and the most powerful army in the region engaged in beating and shooting unarmed civilians, imprisoning thousands, and bombing Palestinian camps in Lebanon.[73] American sympathy for Israel was further strained in April 1990 when armed settlers took over the St. John's Hospice and all Christian shrines were closed.[74] President Bush had to uncharacteristically express regret over the deaths of 33 Palestinians by Israeli soldiers and settlers in May.[75]

Just as the tide had turned against support for the Vietnam War when television brought the realities of that war into the living rooms of Americans, now, for the first time the mainstream American media were showing video footage that demonstrated that the Israeli occupation resembled the suppression of the civil rights movement in the American South—only more violent.[76] Even American Jews were repulsed.[77] The parallels in the susceptibility of the Israel and the American South to external pressure have been discussed by F. Robert Hunter.[78] I would also draw attention to the parallel effects on public opinion of the violence against student war protesters at Kent State University.

Desperate to put an end to the adverse publicity the Israeli government secretly met with the PLO and agreed to the Oslo accords. Although the Oslo accords themselves were not successful in ending the occupation, they manifested a radical departure from Israel's traditional position. The difference in the response of the American press, public, and administration to the First Intifadah compared to all other Palestinian efforts at liberation (including the Second Intifadah which has been characterised by frequent suicide bombings) attests to the power of nonviolent action to affect the hearts of the unwitting sponsors of state terrorism.

> He has put affection between their hearts: not if you had spent all that is in the earth could you have produced that affection but God has done it: for He is Exalted in might Wise.[79]

Conclusions and Future Possibilities

Both just war and nonviolent actions are Islamically valid methods of social actions. Both also have a significant history in the Muslim tradition. In the modern world, given the nature of high-speed mass communication, nonviolent action is usually preferable both on moral and pragmatic grounds in cases of asymmetrically matched forces.

The utter failure of the violent protests of the European cartoons meant to insult Islam should be a lesson to the Muslim people. They changed the focus of the discussion from the malice, bigotry and bad taste of the publishers to the Muslims' intolerance for freedom of speech. There are many more acceptable and more effective alternative responses. Muslims could have organised mass demonstrations in which they hold signs professing their respect and love for Jesus, and condemning bigotry and hatred. They could have boycotted advertisers in the offending newspapers. The Iranian government tried to engage in a bit of nonviolent retaliation by staging a contest for cartoons mocking the holocaust. While this was nonviolent, it was not effective because it played into the hands of the bigots' premise that modern political struggles are nothing more than ancient religious hatreds. It would have been better for them to have uncovered the holy cows of the offending secularist newspapers and targeted them.

At a seminar on "Nonviolent Sanctions and Cultural Survival" at Harvard in 1994, "Souad R. Dajani analysed the Israeli occupation of the West Bank and the Gaza Strip from a Palestinian perspective, proposing nonviolent civilian resistance as the most practical and strategically sound method for creating an independent Palestinian state in these areas."[80]

The Palestinian resistance is, in fact, mainly a nonviolent resistance. Noah Merrill, coordinator for the American Friends Service Committee's programme in Southeastern New England has nonetheless described it as "invisible" in the mainstream Western media. That invisibility is its weak spot. In Israel it has had some effect. Manifested in the rise of the refusenik movement among Israelis who refuse to be a part of the occupation either because of moral considerations or because they pragmatically understand that the occupation is harmful to Israel. In America, however,

> The Israeli-Palestinian conflict is painted and repainted daily as intractable by definition, with both sides locked into a violent struggle with no winners, only the consistent pain and suffering of two peoples. Palestinians particularly are painted as irrational, violent by nature, prone to corruption, and unwilling to compromise.[81]

Since it is the American financing of the occupation and the apartheid policies that allows them to continue, the challenge to the nonviolent resistance is to pierce the veil dividing the American public opinion from the harsh realities of what they are buying. There are problems of convincing the political leadership of the efficacy of nonviolent resistance, exemplified by the fight against the building of Israeli's "security wall."

> There were martyrs in the struggle against the Wall in Budrus. Nonviolent activists were wounded and killed. But as the struggle concluded, the Israeli Wall had been re-routed, forced back by the strength of the popular committees to the path of the Green Line, leaving the villages' olive groves intact. A politician who had earlier mocked Morrar was convinced: he paid for the

mass printing of signs to be used in the expansion of the campaigns which are ongoing throughout the communities being devastated by the Wall's advance. The signs read: "We Can Do It!"[82]

Merrill argues that Israelis target international activists precisely because these strategies are so successful. The strategies need to be expanded both in the solidity of their employment within the occupied territories and also to the United States where the key support for the occupation and persecution resides, but where the nonviolent resistance remains veiled. While violent resistance is nearly impossible to eliminate its presence can undermine the effectiveness of nonviolence. Even the minimal violence of stone-throwing has been used by the Israelis to justify their response with tanks and automatic weapons.

The practitioners of violence need to understand that their tactics have failed miserably. Not one square inch of Palestinian soil has been liberated by armed resistance. The only Israeli concession to date came as a result of the influence of nonviolence on world opinion threatening Israel's support from America. An admission that nonviolence is more effective than armed resistance is not a declaration of immorality of armed resistance, except to the degree that inefficacy is immoral. With apologies for the violent metaphor, why insist on using the peashooter of armed resistance when we possess the canon of nonviolence?

REFERENCES

Abrahamian, Ervand, *Iran Between Two Revolutions* (Princeton: Princeton University Press, 1982).

Bashiriyeh, Hossein, *The State and Revolution in Iran* (New York: St. Martin's Press, 1984).

Azad, Maulana Abul Kalam, *India Wins Freedom: An Autobiographical Narrative*, with Introduction and Explanatory Notes by Louis Fischer (New York: Longmans, Green, 1960).

Bennett, Brad, "Arab-Muslim Cases of Nonviolent Struggle," in *Arab Nonviolent Political Struggle in the Middle East*, ed. Ralph E. Crow, Philip Grant, and Saad E. Ibrahim (Boulder: L. Rienner Publishers, 1990).

Fischer, Michael M. J., *Iran: From Religious Dispute to Revolution* (Cambridge: Harvard, 1980).

Grant, Philip, "Nonviolent Political struggle in the Occupied Territories," in *Arab Nonviolent Political Struggle in the Middle East*, ed. Ralph E. Crow, Philip Grant, and Saad E. Ibrahim (Boulder: Lynne Rienner, 1990).

http://ifamericansknew.org

Hudson, Michael C., "The Palestinian Challenge to US Policy," in *The Palestinians: New Directions*, ed. Michael C. Hudson (Washington: Centre for Contemporary Arab Studies, 1990).

Hunter, Robert F., *The Palestinian Uprising: A War by Other Means* (Berkeley: UC Berkeley, 1991).

Merrill, Noah, "Celebrating Nonviolent Resistance," *Peacework* (February 2006). American Friends Service Committee, http://www.afsc.org/pwork/0602/060210.htm

Pal, Amitabh, "A Pacifist Uncovered," *The Progressive* (February 2002), http://progressive.org/?q=node/1654

Paxton, Bill, "Eyes Without a Country: Searching for a Palestinian Strategy of Liberation." Weatherhead Centre for International Affairs, 1994, http://www.wcfia.harvard.edu/ponsacs/seminars/Synopses/s94dajan.htm

Peretz, Don, *Intifada* (Boulder: Westview Press, 1990).

Qur'an, ʿAbdullah Yūsuf ʿAlī translation.

Shivers, Lynne, "Inside the Iranian Revolution," in *Tell the American People*, ed. David H. Albert (Philadelphia: Movement for a New Society, 1980).

Sinha, Shall, "Books Which Influenced Gandhi's Life and Thought," (1/2/05), www.ssinha.com/bksmgrd.htm

Thoreau, Henry David, "Civil Disobedience," (1849), http://thoreau.eserver. org/civil.html

RAANA BOKHARI

Places and Perspectives: Gujarati Muslim Women in Leicester

Introduction

> *The elephant was in a dark house: some Hindus had brought it for exhibition. In order to see it, many people were going ... into that darkness. As seeing it with the eye was impossible, (each one) was feeling it in the dark with the palm of his hand. The hand of one fell on its trunk: he said, "This creature is like a water-pipe." The hand of another touched its ear: to him it appeared to be like a fan .... Another laid his hand on its back: he said, "Truly this elephant was like a throne".... On account of the place of view, their statements differed .... The eye of sense-perception is only like the palm of the hand: the palm hath not power to reach the whole of him (the elephant).*[1]

MAULANA RUMI TOUCHED UPON THE KEY epistemological problem of academia, that is, whose knowledge is acceptable? Whose discourse will be given prevalence? This is not only a debate that Western feminists have struggled with, but also one which Muslim scholars have grappled with in the West, particularly in the portrayal of Islam and Muslims. On the specific subject of women, there is a plethora of literature which pertains to, *inter alia*, their bodies, minds, cultures, economies, and social participation. But the elephant comes to haunt us continuously, for in portraying Muslim women, indeed, Muslims in general, the picture is inevitably partial: that is, in true Rumistic style, it is partial, situated knowledge. Not only that, but Rumi also captured the essential problem in presenting research in an atomistic way, as we are so in the habit of doing in the West: if the participants in question are not viewed holistically, then we distort the real picture. Thus, for a truer vision, we ought to consider the people we observe as embodied, whole individuals, rather than atomistically.

155

Hence, this paper then begins with an admission that it is partial, situated knowledge but also aims to overcome the barriers of labelling and categorising (the elephant) under the pretence of academic objectivity, by allowing those observed to fully participate and speak. That is, this research is a phenomenological study of women's lived experiences, using their voice – the voice of a minority religious group – to define themselves, employing a feminist framework to shift epistemic power away from academics as researchers and theorisers, to the researched as a participant in the process, not a 'subject.'

Drawing on postcolonial theories which stress 'difference,' this paper begins with an Islam-centred worldview synergised with Western womanist and postcolonial thought, as these women are inheritors of both traditions. They are located as whole bodies, voicing their opinions on how they perceive themselves as part of the British society, how they feel they are perceived, and their definitions of 'sacred,' 'public' and 'private' spaces, theologically, and societally. It is an exploration of their worldview, thoughts and aspirations, both epistemologically and ontologically, on the questions of defining and occupying public and sacred space in new settled environments in the West.

On a simplistic level, identity, as we know it today, not only comprises of religion, gender, ethnicity, class, and language, but also of political, economic, and social forces re/configured on a local, national, and global level.[2] Identity, however, is not simply about definitions: it is more importantly in today's political climate about state loyalty and cultural belonging.[3] Indisputably, identities are both multiple and shifting. What is interesting is the growing trend of multiple identities being particularised into homogenous religion-based identities, seemingly a result of the interaction between the state, and individuals and communities – that is, identities with reference to politicised religion. It is often claimed that for women, this homogenisation of identities is experienced on two counts: religion, and gender, often at the expense of equal citizenship.[4] This paper is not so much concerned with the gender disparity of citizenship but more the reconfiguration of Gujarati Muslim women's multiple identities in new spaces. Our definition of place is affected not just by our culture but by the very fact that we cannot conceive of place as exclusivist settled geographies any more in a world where all spaces seem to be opened up by economic, cultural and ecological forces.[5]

Places and Perspectives: Gujarati Muslim Women

If place then is a geographical site, then space suggests its social con-struction and power relations.[6] Migration then forms and re-forms this social space. If as Massey and Jess assert, space is stretched-out social relations,[7] then the key question for me is, how the space in Leciester has been 'stretched' by the Gujarati settlement. Further, how has a seemingly secular space been sacralised by a minority religious presence? Roald claims that Islamic perceptions of women undergo a change in the Western context, as a result of the influence of Western culture and thought – new negotiated cultural identities as far as settled Muslim communities are concerned.[8] This chapter examines how far this is true of the Gujarati women in Leicester.

Leicester is a model multicultural city in England. The Muslims repre-sent 11 percent of the city's population, majority being of Gujarati descent having migrated and settled from India and East Africa. Space is a particularly important and interesting notion in Islam, geography having been sacralised in Islamic history at various moments, the conse-cration of cities giving them religious meaning and authenticity. This research focuses on the theological and sociological manifestations of Gujarati Muslim women in Leicester and space. The questions that will be addressed in this paper are, how Leicester as a city has been sacralised by Gujarati Muslim women, and how, if at all, the city, in turn, has empowered and reshaped the women. In conclusion, I examine whether it is possible to distil generic ideas about Muslim women's reconfigured identity and movement in the West in a way that reflects their epistemo-logical and ontological makeup. This will be done by exploring the importance of sacred space in Islam, followed by presenting and analysing interview data.

The research has been shaped by data collated via local history archives, observation of the community in question, and in-depth semi-structured interviews of 30 Gujarati Muslim Sunni women in Leicester. It reflects a cross-section of age groups, ranging from 18 to 70 years of age, and mirroring a cross-section of women's lives, from students to housewives, lawyers, teachers, qualified scholars, charity workers and mothers. Interviews were conducted in English and / or Urdu from 2005 to 2006, and fieldwork generally was carried out over a period of almost three years. The responses given to questions concerning sacred spaces are included below.

RAANA BOKHARI

The Multicultural City of Leicester, Britain

Muslims number over 2 million in Britain. The largest minority racial group is of Indian descent: according to the 2001 Census figures, Britain's Indian / British Indian population makes up 2 percent of the total population, those of Pakistani descent making up 1.4 percent; however, the former figure includes different religions; hence, it is estimated that Pakistanis are the largest ethnic Muslim group. Indian Muslims are very influential, particularly Gujarati Indians as they herald from the theological school of learning in Deoband, north of Delhi in India which is the impetus behind the national *Dar ul-Uloom* centres in England. Leicester City has a total population of just under 280,000 (2001 Census), the Indian population being 72,000, that is 25.7 percent made up largely of Hindus, Sikhs and Muslims. In terms of religion, the Census shows that Hindus account for 14 percent of Leicester's population (41,000), and Muslims 11 percent (31,000). This influential community is attracting a lot of interest.

The riots of Oldham and Bradford are a far cry from the reality of the co-existence in Leicester: Leicester is considered to be an ideal multicultural city of co-operation and good community relations.[9] The city prides itself in its diversity: it appears to be 'ahead of the rest of the UK and Europe in developing a policy to make diversity, as manifested in the place of religious buildings for all faiths, central to all relevant planning deliberations.'[10] Leicester was the first in setting records: it was the first planning authority in Europe to produce a policy on places of worship in 1977. It was the first place where in 1954 it was debated during a court case which version of the Qur'an witnesses ought to swear on – English, or Arabic.[11] Bonney mapped out the diversity in Christian worship Leicester in the 1851 census, with Baptist, Anglican, Methodist, Catholic, Quaker and Mormon presence having been recorded. By 1874, there was a Jewish community present. In the 1960s, there was a well-established Hindu community, 1969 seeing the inauguration of the first Hindu temple.[12] Indeed the only Jain Temple in Europe started building work in Leicester in 1979 and was opened in 1988.[13] Ravat records 14 faiths being present in the city,[14] with 76 percent of its population having named religious adherence in the 2001 Census,[15] practically all faith groups being involved in social projects.[16] Furthermore, it is the first city in the UK that will probably have an ethnic *majority*, as

158

currently 50 percent of its primary school intake is from ethnic minority communities.[17] For all intents and purposes, Leicester appears to have been sacralised on many fronts.

Gujarati Muslims of Leicester

Leicester's Gujaratis came from India and East Africa.[18] Ahmed Andrews notes from census data that overall South Asian migration into Leicester increased dramatically between 1951 and 1991. In 1951, there were 636 South Asians in Leicester: 569 Indian, 49 Pakistani, and 18 East African. These figures include various faiths.[19] By 1971, these had increased to 11,510 Indians, 1305 Pakistanis, now also 685 Bangladeshis, and 66,835 East Africans. By 1991, there were 20,841 Indians, 1155 Pakistanis, and 17168 East Africans. During this period, however, not only had Enoch Powell made his 'River of Blood' speech, but the National Front had organised marches and stood in the local elections of the city. In these times of great confusion and change, Bonney notes that, on the one hand, planning permission was being granted for the establishment of mosques, Hindu temples and Sikh gurdwaras from 1969 to 1971.[20] Yet, at the same time, with the imposition of Idi Amin's Ugandan Africanisation policy, the resettlement of Asians into Britain in 1972 was unwelcomed by Leicester with the City Corporation placing its infamous advertisement in the *Ugandan Argus*, warning Ugandan Asians that thousands of families were on council house waiting lists, children were on school waiting lists, hence 'do not come to Leicester.'[21] The MP for South West Leicester, Tom Boardman, aired fears about the strain on race relations. Ironically, then, the Leicester City Council, in its haste to put off Asians resettling in the city, drew attention to Leicester and put it on the world map. In 1971, there were 6835 East Africans in the city. By 1981, there were 18,622. That is, almost 10 percent of UK's South Asian immigrants were from East Africa.

The 1991 census shows that 23.7 percent of Leicester's population was Asian, and in terms of religion, 4.2 percent of the people in Leicester were Sikh, 14.7 percent Hindu, and 11 percent were Muslim. The 2001 census indicates that out of the total population of just under 280,000 44.7 percent are Christian, 14.7 percent Hindu, 11.3 percent Muslim, 4.2 percent are Sikh, 0.4 percent Other, and 17.4 percent of No Religion (with a further 7 percent not stating any religion).[22] The 2001 Census also shows that 87.5 percent of the overall British population is white British with 2 percent being British/Asian Indian.[23] At 30,885, Leicester's Muslim community is the tenth largest in England and Wales.[24] Ahmed Andrews, however, argues that the population has always been underestimated as Gujarati Muslims often share surnames with Gujarati Hindus.[25]

There are now 20 mosques. Indeed the Council was proactive in its advice to communities seeking places of religious worship, as early as 1977.[26] Most places of religious worship are converted buildings, but there are two purpose built mosques: the Central Mosque on Conduit Street, behind the railway station, and Masjid Umar in Evington which opened in 1993 and 2001 respectively.[27] However, 'none has gained primacy over the diverse Muslim population of Leicester.'[28] Perhaps the concept of diversity, the heterogeneity of Islam, and the cultural nuances of its practise, defy homogenising the faithful and indeed their places of worship.

For all intents and purposes, the Muslim Gujaratis are self-sufficient, and have community structures which could allow many to operate without having to interact much with others outside that community. But politics and political participation shape the development and infrastructure of communities. Andrews states that there were Hindu councilors at City and County level before Muslims: Hindus were present from 1983 onwards, Muslims from 1991.[29] In 2002, 14 out of the 56 councilors were from ethnic minority communities, and by 2003, 4 out of the total 54 were Muslim, all representing the Liberal Democrats, and all from Highfields.[30] The presence of Muslim councilors has helped to bring funding and resources into the community.

Space

In Western discourse, space, place and gender are hotly debated areas, but tend to be viewed polemically: a binary dichotomy of male/female is constructed which hails the first category as the normative (male) becoming embodied in the notion of public (male) and private (female), knowledge (male) and experience (female). Second wave feminism claimed that 'the personal is political' and the categories of public and private had to be examined and re-examined. Undoubtedly, for majoritarian feminists this division of spheres is linked to sexual subordination: if space is gendered, then the door to inequality is and, indeed, has been opened. However, one woman's freedom is another woman's oppression, that is, privacy can represent freedom or oppression; publicity can represent intrusion or, indeed, liberty. Feminisms then might have upset these clear divisions – for while they campaign for public space, they also advocate personal identity, privacy, safeguarding the body – but space is not necessarily a simple case of male and female domains: in reality the categories are often blurred.

Iris Young fears that categorising space as public and private homogenises space and excludes significant groups such as women.[31] I would argue that Western feminism in turn homogenises Muslim women and excludes culture, race and ethnicities as signifiers of multiple identities, Islam being one facet of that identity and, in turn, its manifestation being indigenised, that is, shaped by culture. Nor does it adequately offer an examination of 'sacred spaces.' By 'sacred space' is meant, spaces which are sacralised and hence made holy (see below), or space used for religious purposes. Minority women in the West are invisible from feminist discourse on space. Space in fact is not necessarily geographic: its definitions, however, ought to be left to the occupiers of that space.

Gujarati women's language of religious instruction, whether at home or in a madrasah is Urdu although their language generally at home is Gujarati (and hence to some degree their interpretations of and discussions on Islam would be in Gujarati). There are several theological primary sources in Urdu that shape the women's understanding of their religion and their own identity: *Bihishti Zewar* ('Heavenly Ornaments') being the main one.[32] A fundamental theme which runs through the text is that of a binary division between the sacred and the profane, be that in the form of place or time. This mirrors Mircea Eliade's symbolic phenomenology, where religious symbols are mediators between human beings and the sacred.[33] The mosques and madrasahs are focal points in symbolising the sacred for Gujarati Muslims. The question then arises as to what is considered to be sacred space by Gujarati Sunni women and whether public and private, sacred and profane spaces reflect gender and cultural roles and expectations. Whether 'religious texts' in question dictate these categories or 'culture,' is significant.

Doreen Massey asserts that space may generally connote simultane-ous and multiple realms or structures, and place may indicate mobility, positionality, and even social belonging.[34] Ultimately, for her, what is more meaningful is relating space and place to social relations, not only from a traditional class perspective but also gender and the consequen-tial construction of gender relations.[35] Thus, space is not an absolute dimension, a void, independent and uninfluenced by its setting, but dynamic, bound, and indeed reconfigured by time and society. Whilst we acknowledge that geographies are important in these connections of space, place, and gender, equally valuable are their 'culturally specific' constructions.[36] And because,

> social relations are inevitably and everywhere imbued with power and mean-ing and symbolism ... such a way of conceptualising the spatial, moreover, inherently implies the existence in the lived world of a simultaneous multi-plicity of spaces: cross-cutting, intersecting, aligning with one another.... [T]his is so because the social relations of space are experienced differently, and variously interpreted, by those holding different positions as part of it.[37]

Not only then are space and place culturally nuanced, but are also influenced by gender roles and the cultural / religious / social dictates of how and where men and women should move. This is very significant in a traditional eastern community like Gujarati Muslims living in the heart of the West – Leicester. If the world is a place where exclusivist claims to places are made, then it is inherently political: by binding places, we try to guarantee their authenticity and meaning, fixing their identities in time and culture nostalgically, at the same time as claiming them as 'ours.' But, who is the 'we' in this equation: a religious group, as in the occupied West Bank, or a gendered group, as in the men in mosques? Whatever the answer, claims to space are inevitably excluding of others.

Let us turn to Islamic notions of space: since all the world and universe is a creation of the Divine, the Holy, then indeed all space is sacred and holy. Since Muslims can pray almost anywhere in the world, be it a mosque, or street, or shop, then all space is sacred. Hence, if God is ever present in the natural, social, psychic and spiritual sphere, then all spaces at all times carry a sacralised element. This is interesting because in reality, in true Orwellian style, some spaces are more sacred than others. For example, the three sanctified *ḥarams*, certain sites where prophets and saints performed miracles, or lived and, indeed, areas where general worship is carried out, are far holier than others. So, we are constantly oscillating between the social and spiritual realms. Does that denote a tension between the sacred and the profane? In a secular world, perhaps, but in an Islamic framework, I think not: the profanity and mundanity of space is related to deeds and intentions: the office is work space when working; it is praying space when praying. But at all times, it could be sacred space as the Divine dwells in it. That is, if one stands in awareness of the presence of God at all times, then one is always standing on hallowed ground.

Western feminist discourse has challenged the notion of space as stasis and, yet, when it views traditional Muslim women, it still tends to bind them and their society in a fixed time-space. This research offers an alternative formulation to definitions of space, as voiced and experienced by the participants. For example, the absence of the Gujarati women from the mosques appears to be an indictment of the community's misogyny. Yet, for the majority of the women interviewed, the mosque is not central to their identity and ontology. Cemeteries often feature as important in women's lives in the Indian subcontinent: that is not so much for the Gujarati women in Leicester. There is a configuration of cemeteries and shrines as sacred spaces, altered by the migration and settlement process: community centres offering weekend Islamic learning circles, mills converted into Islamic schools are just as important as mosques. Prayer – concretised in the mosque – is just one form of ritual worship then: supplication, dreams, fasting, *dhikr* sessions, give different expressions to piety and spirituality, especially when conducted in the privacy of the home.

If there is an essential social difference between men and women, then perhaps their experiences and manifestations of the five ritual pillars are different; hence, sameness of experience does not denote equality in experience. But if there is not an essential difference between men and women spiritually, then still, experiences of the divine will be different. The aim here is not to atomise the categories of man and woman so that they become meaningless, rather to suggest that gender can stereotype, and that we are individuals, whether man or woman. Multiple forms of the sacred, acculturated to the Western scene, satisfy the Gujarati women's spirituality, especially the setting up of girl's Madrasahs and women's morning Qur'an circles, prayer spaces in shopping centres, and charity fundraising events.

Some of the spatial themes that were raised in interviews examined whether articulations of holiness change in new spatial contexts. The question was also raised whether the new social reality which theology did not envisage meant that women engaged with their texts and environments differently now.

Let us turn to the theology which most Gujarati women follow and, indeed, their history in India, where their sacred spaces and public movements were different from those in Leicester.

The Anti-Colonial Past of India

An important fact, which underpins the Gujarati Muslim community's presence in Leicester, is the colonial past: the British Raj faced great opposition in the 1857 mutiny, and at the forefront of the anti-colonial movement was the Deobandi school north of Delhi which, indeed, was subsequently set up to resist the British Raj. Opposition to the British rule was gathering momentum for quite some time but the 1857 rebellion showed the might of the British Empire to suppress such disorder. The following decades were the height of the empire but Muslim scholars in the north of India began to resist: Sayyid Ahmad Khan founded the Aligarh University, where Islam was combined with a social identity that was to harness the European sciences and arts.[38] Muhammad Qasim Nanautwi (1833–1877) and Rashid Ahmad Gangohi (1829–1905) were instrumental in founding the Deoband school of learning.[39] It is not clear how far a role they played in the 1857 Mutiny[40] although Deobandis believe that they were engaged in active resistance.

Metcalf points out that Deobandi literature pre-1920 insisted that the scholars had been apolitical but post-1920 they presented the founders as freedom fighters and took a firm political stance after the First World War, supporting Gandhi in opposition to British rule.[41] I would argue that the Deobandi school was political from its inception: resistance to the Raj was the impetus for its establishment. Despite the differences in scholarly opinions, what is agreed upon is that in the aftermath of the failed 1857 Mutiny, the founding scholars moved to their home villages, away from the heavy presence of the British in Delhi, and concentrated on educational institutions so that Muslims could be empowered through their own tradition.[42]

Their initial quietist work found fruition in Deoband, a small town where all the founders had links and found spiritual inspiration, that is, Deoband had been divinely decreed in 1866. The teaching involved traditional learning of Qur'an, hadith, Shariʿah and the fiqh of Abū Ḥanīfah, the emphasis being on a reformist empowering Islam, in opposition to the imperial rule, "showing that their standard of correct belief and practise defined them as a group not only separate from but morally superior to the British."[43] This mother school's teachings were spread to other schools set up to follow the same curriculum and teachings.[44] In time, Deobandi teaching came to be known as 'Indian Islam' with students from Peshawar, Bengal and Madras.[45]

The Deobandis were not only scholars of the Ḥanafī fiqh, but also Sufis: Ashraf Ali Thanawi being one of the most influential Indian sufis, was not only a Deobandi but also the author of *Bihishti Zewar*, published in the early 1900s, the primary text at the heart of this paper's theological enquiry.[46] Today, the *dar ul-uloom* at Deoband has over 3000 students enrolled, and many from overseas, indeed England, travel there for their religious training.[47]

Ashraf Ali Thanawi

Thanawi was a second generation student and scholar of Deoband, born in 1864. In his thirties, he retired to his small home town of Thana Bhawan, in U.P, northern India. There, he wrote prolifically, was visited by many who sought his guidance and, indeed, was famous for the spiritual guidance that he offered. As a reformer, Maulana Thanawi was facing the challenges of Muslim political dominance having been replaced by British rule which encouraged a new religious identity. The new ensuing social dislocation, together with other cultural values emerging, led to the Deobandis, and Thanawi, in particular, responding with a call to renew one's Islamic identity. And for the first time in Indian Muslim history, it aimed its mainstream Islamic teaching at women.[48]

Bihishti Zewar, The Text

The book is considered to be one of the most influential scripturalist reform texts: anti-colonial freedom movements in India aimed at raising self-esteem and pride in one's religion – hence, *Bihishti Zewar* was a guide for the 'respectable woman.' It was written initially for well to do women from privileged families supporting the reformist agenda. Over time, however, the book was accessed by ordinary working class women and, indeed, the text was edited by Maulana Thanawi to include new categories of people. The 'Heavenly Ornaments' are not women but metaphorically the virtues and traits that will "earn them (men and women) the pearls and bracelets of heaven."[49] The treasures that await in Heaven would be immeasurable – hence this book is often a gift given to brides at their wedding. Indeed today, it is taught as the seminal textbook in Deobandi madrasahs for girls throughout England, particularly those run by the Gujarati community.

Up to the writing of this text, Muslim women in India had not been seen as the guardians of tradition and knowledge: that was left to the men in the public domain. The text is an example of the cultural transformations that were taking place on the Indian landscape in the modern world, for Thanawi advocates at the beginning of the text, that men and women, being the same in intellectual ability, need education in order to become good moral citizens. Society was seen as degenerate, in need of reform, and this could only be done by reforming the individual. For some critics, the text is interesting, not only because it instructs women to take individual responsibility for learning, but also in that it does not point to any physiological, spiritual, emotional or intellectual differences between men and women.[50]

However, this new responsibility to learn was in the context of a separation of roles, that is, men were still the authority in the home set up. "Women were meant to be socially subordinate to men and adhere to the Shariʿah standards of seclusion, when possible, inside the home."[51] Thanawi's aim then, was to rescue the Shariʿah, the law, embodied in the Qur'an and Sunnah and local scholarly opinions, from cultural superstitions, and to allow women direct access to these sources, so that social order would prevail. This could only be done by reforming the private lives of women and restricting their public movements, even in sacred spaces.

Unlike many other patriarchal texts, the *Bihishti Zewar* challenged cultural traditions within the home and defined the role of the ʿulamāʾ distinct from the state. Thanawi did not envisage reform as state led but as individual policing, self-reform. In aiming the text at women and equipping them in their usually private roles with a depth of Islamic knowledge which up to then had largely been the privilege of men in the public domain, the text aimed to enlighten women and allow them equal rights as men to education. But at the same time, it cleverly extended the authority of men into the private sphere in areas where men did not dictate to women previously.[52]

The work is encyclopaedic. Its language is quite emotive. At the same time, Thanawi brings Urdu prose into its own, using colloquial Urdu, rather than the Begamati Urdu of his family, to make his work accessible.[53] Thanawi avoids ecstatic poetry, relying heavily on legal ritualised principles. He uses irony upon irony for literary affect, for example when referring to local customs which he often condemns, he uses the term 'Shari'ah' (divine law), indicating his disapproval that the Indian Muslims have replaced the authentic Shari'ah with their own Shari'ah.[54] Although claiming that men and women are equal in seeking knowledge, he also claims in Book Ten that women are associated with the lower soul, the *nafs*.[55] In women, men see their own lack of control – hence an obsession with trying to control women.[56]

The text is divided into Ten Parts, ranging from beliefs, ablutions, daily prayers, to marriage, divorce, loans, contracts, hobbies, manners, and life after death. Let us take a few examples of women and the public domain: the text does not have specific sections on defining the public sphere, nor does it dictate how and when women can move in the 'public arena.'[57] The lack of definition of what is public and what is private may be because there was no call for it: Indian Muslim society at that time was clearly demarcated: the market place and work place was male dominated and the home was the place for women folk – where women were free to move and, indeed, men were excluded.

For our purposes then, to elicit Thanawi's comments and construction of the public sphere, we have to probe those sections of his text where he refers to women's covering and veils, outdoor pursuits and celebrations. He urges women, in Part 6, to be careful in dropping everything in order to go out visiting friends: the sins accumulated could be immeasurable, for example, pride in women wanting to show off their garments, putting financial pressure on the husband to cover their expenses, envy and greed in seeing what their friends have and they don't.[58] In going to mosques, women might tempt men and distract them from their prayers or, indeed, neglect their domestic duties; therefore, it would be better for them to offer their prayers at home. Indeed, Thanawi claims that even going to weddings is not a good practice, and visits to the parents' home are sanctioned, but once or twice. So, what are 'legitimate' reasons for women entering the public domain? Earlier in Part 4, women are urged, amongst other things, to cover themselves completely in the company of men who are not from the immediate family, including the hands, feet and face.[59]

The impact of this text cannot be under-estimated: the Deobandi Seminary has over 3000 students enrolled and many outpost colleges. Today, the text is still taught in madrasahs to Muslims of Indian descent world over: the Gujaratis in Leicester are no exception to this. Its impact is now far-reaching due to several English translations available, allowing migrant Muslims and their settled/Western-born children to access the source. Whatever assumptions Thanawi makes about women ought to be understood in their Indian context at the turn of the last century. However, the tension that is interesting, from my perspective, is how the Gujarati community in Leicester uses the text – a hundred years after it was written, ironically in the heartland of the former colonial master, Britain – and whether the women apply Thanawi's manual, opting for privacy and withdrawing from public life.

New Spaces, New Women?

That this Gujarati Deobandi community then settles in England is interesting: the sanctification of Deoband was in opposition to the profanity of the Raj and its people. This research examined how the community sanctified its very move to Leicester and whether there were any rites to consecrate new spaces involving the women. Hermansen claims that biographical literature is very important for this purpose in Muslim South Asia, for new spaces are configured in the sense that the established tradition is integrated with new terrain by linking South Asian Muslim individuals with the territories of Makkah and Madinah.[60]

Hence, permanence, security, and cultural meanings are given to new spaces. The blessings of saints are remembered to invoke the sanctity of the new place.[61] This is very much the case with the 'Islamicising' of Deoband: the founding fathers had inspirational dreams about the Prophet urging them to set up a school, thus, 'creating a "new" home, configuring "new" spiritual and intellectual centres, and laying out "new" circuits of pilgrimage.'[62] Hermansen quotes Eaton's examination of Bengal, and how from *Dār al-Ḥarb* it became *Dār al-Islām* 'institutionally, economically and ideologically.'[63] Thus, moods of nostalgia and sacred history are recorded in hagiographical works – very much like those of the Deobandi 'freedom fighting' founders. Memorialisation of cities then, creates new spaces, as with Delhi, Gujarat, Lahore[64] and allows for the sanctification of those new soils.[65] How this had been done, with Leicester, then, was discussed during interviews with the participants.

To the question of what makes Leicester a special space for the Muslims, all 30 women interviewed commented that the number of Muslims settled here was the largest factor in Leicester being a kind of 'sacred' space. That is, where in Gujarat and Deoband it was the setting up of centres for learning that sacralised the cities and towns, here it was the large presence of Muslims. But for one respondent, it was because of the visit and prayers of revered scholars from Deoband that actually made Leicester into a 'blessed' land.

'I have a sense of security here, absolutely' as one participant, a 32 year old housewife said:

> The fact that it has so many mosques…. And the women have added to this process I think. I think women in Leicester do a lot compared with other places. You forget how lucky you are and don't realize that, like the hijab … is a struggle for others …. And then the provision of Muslim schools. My daughter would have gone to a western school but I have the choice to send her to a Muslim school.

An 18 year old student respondent answered:

> You just feel safe here, and have the freedom to speak up, do what you want, to limits obviously. You feel pleased of who you are, and confident … I think it's because of the high number of Muslims here. We have so many mosques, my friends who come from Wigan, a smaller town in the north of England, said that they have no Muslim community there, so Leicester is a big thing for them.

This participant also commented that the women's activism involved organising charity fetes where local business and groups would sell their goods to raise money for charity. One such event that I attended as part of this research saw the women raise £20,000 in one day. With the majority of women interviewed practising veiling in the form of black outer garments that also cover the hands, feet and face, on face value, it appears that the women from this traditional austere community are silent and removed from the public. But on closer examination, that could not be farther from the truth.

Whilst another participant commented that the number of mosques, shops and Gujarati community centres helped collective identity, she felt that she belonged more so because of the multicultural mix in the city. Indeed, having lived most of her life in a non-Muslim part of Leicester, she was always known by an English name and felt more British than Gujarati: the mixed identity did not suitably define her. In the same way, a 35 year old teacher stated that her sense of dress – a headscarf and face veil – were a part of her wherever she went, but having said that, 'I do find it very comfortable here. As a Londoner, I never thought I'd settle here. Now, I'd never want to go and live in London. And the women have added their mark. We play a great part, women always do!'

For my 70 year old respondent, concentrating on educating the younger generation was what led to the community's success in maintaining a religious and cultural identity: 'The women have done a lot by setting up their own learning circles. If you stay indoors, you'll never learn.'

To the question of what Leicester as a city offered the women, again the responses were very similar. 'Leicester City Council does a lot. Even little things like Eid celebration street lights recognises that Muslims in Leicester are an important sector of the community.' A student replied that the Muslim leaders are active in working closely with the city council: 'You know they asked for prayer rooms in the shopping centre, and hospitals.' The 70 year old respondent commented that Leicester had given her a lot: 'Thank God, Leicester has given me the chance to learn. People come from other cities to learn here! I like this atmosphere, especially living with other faith communities. We women have more rights here in the West than in India.'

But for a 32 year old teacher, 'Space is not tangible for me … it's about the personal relations that you have, and about attitude. I don't think the categories are clear.'

Places and Perspectives: Gujarati Muslim Women

The important question of women's movements in the public, and Thanawi's views that women should stay home elicited the following responses: a 28 year old housewife and mother of four stated:

> You see, I would challenge those bits – on the bits about your religion, I think he's very good, but on women, he's derogatory. He says you can only visit your parents once or twice a year, but Maulana Mohammed (a local Indian scholar in Leicester) says you can go to your parents every week, without permission, it's your right. I find that some parts of the *Bihishti Zewar* are not following the Sunnah. Things have to be applicable in your environment. E.g., it's normal to hold hands with your husband in England when you're out and about, but not in India ... So I leave bits out ... You can't live according to the Indian subculture 100 years ago .... Even at weddings, we aren't totally segregated. I have my veil on, but we're not in separate rooms always – it's not possible here .... But I can't imagine that when the Prophets' companions travelled, he didn't encourage them to adapt the existing culture...

On the question of whether new spaces change Muslim theology and its application, a locally educated Imam stated:

> I don't favour the use of such texts, because they aren't relevant here. I run a private madrasah, and this book is not taught there. Only the young women study it, and this is for the sections on women's personal hygiene and purification laws etc. I don't consider myself a Deobandi. I have no connection there, I've never been. We have graduates from the western hemisphere like myself who might have been taught by Deobandi scholars, our seminaries might have an affiliation with Deoband, but we have moved on. We are not Deobandi, we are not in India. The Deobandi school is the most influential in India, but we live in a different environment.

When asked about women's movements in the public, he responded: 'You can't say women can't go out. They go to work, they study – if they are upholding their Islamic values, why should they not ....We need youngsters out and about in this society.'

There was only one participant who felt that the women had not done anything to contribute to the presence of Islam in Leicester. As a community worker, she felt her constant battle was community apathy.

All the participants said that they did not attend mosques or cemeteries, even when their own children had passed away, as they were told it was not a good practise for women. Some felt extremely excluded from the mosques as they symbolised real sacred Islamic space. A small number felt that it was better for women not to go to mosques and distract the men. But, the majority of respondents had no particular desire to go to the mosques as it was considered male space. To this degree, living in the West had not reconfigured their use of mosque space. But in as much as being active visible public women, the new Western home had significantly changed the spaces that were women's areas.

Epistemology and Ontology

What conclusions can we then draw about women's ontology and, indeed, their ways of knowing, their gender specific epistemology if there is one, from this research? I would argue none: the political academic struggle to claim epistemic power and formulations regarding women's ontology is not the purpose of my research, simply because, whilst this research gives us an insight into Gujarati women's ways of knowing and moving in new space in a new context, it does not transport neatly onto another community's experiences. Gujarati women's wholeness and holiness are a facet of their life in Leicester: but that does not allow generic conclusions to be drawn about all Muslim women in the new Western context and all reconfigurations of space in the West. That is, in criticising Western academia for homogenising Muslim women, it would, indeed, be ironic to simply offer an 'Islamicised' homgenisation!

In Western academia, for black feminists, not only is there a problem of male-controlled knowledge, but also white-based knowledge, hence, the need for a race- and culture-specific feminist epistemology.[66] This standpoint theory is promoted by both Patricia Collins[67] and also Sandra Harding. Rather than the essentialist position outlined above, it gives us a more historically, socially and culturally based understanding of women from other cultures and groups having gained other forms of knowledge through lived experience, such as Collins' research on black women.

Sandra Harding is in favour of objectivity, but with a difference: she draws on the works of Third World and postcolonial feminists who articulate understandings of the world that do not conform to Western assumptions. Standpoint is not just about viewpoints, but about knowledge of lived realities, correcting the 'distorted world' picture. Hence, there is a strong objectivity in Harding's work as it produces a better account of the world. If the task of epistemology then is to update objectivism so that it is useful to the current world, then better objectivity is reflexive knowledge.[68]

Donna Haraway offers an alternative: she claims that feminism, in thinking about knowledge production, is trapped by viewing all knowledge as socially constructed. She argues that we need to hold onto some form of objectivity but without it being a strong objective claim. Her solution is 'situated knowledge' – all knowledge is embodied, therefore, particular, located in bodies, and always partial.[69] The knowledge is not invalid; therefore, we can make claims to objectivity and validity, but on the understanding that it is partial. Partial knowledge will inevitably mean that there is accountability and interaction with the real world as a result of which knowledge can be changed. Central to Haraway's theory is learning to see faithfully from another's point of view. Haraway's theory is very useful when researching Muslim women in the West, as her idea of situated knowledge is central to this research – that is, that the view of Muslim women in defining themselves is fundamental, even in the face of any existing paradigms of knowledge, for those paradigms cannot be fixed in time as absolutes. That is, as with Rumi's elephant, paradigms shift constantly, depending on time, location and people. So perhaps objectivity is not so much about epistemology as about politics: who has the power to make knowledge?

Yet still, religion is an important factor that Western feminists omit from their discourse. And whilst some of the Gujarati Muslim women in Leicester have experienced colonialism and have attempted to reshape themselves post-colonially, others are fully the products of Islamic Western life and thought. Their societal and community infrastructure is interesting to examine as they oscillate between a very strong 'Gujarati' identity linguistically and culturally, yet located in a Western acculturated Islam. However, what these women consider to be public and private, how they apply their primary religious texts, in the Western context, and what constitutes sacred space is an evolving theme.

Conclusion

I began this research by examining what is sacred space in the West, and how Gujarati Muslim women's use and occupation of it has been reconfigured by virtue of their Western citizenship. In the Indian context,

Gujarati women led very private, domesticated, yet vibrant busy lives. In moving to Leicester, their use of space has been transformed enormously by politics, social practises, and necessity. Gujarati women's presence in shops, learning centres and schools cannot go unnoticed. Their overtly religious presence gives a sense of the sacred to these spaces. Yet, other sacred spaces, such as mosques, are not accessed by the women as a whole. Sacred spaces then vary, as do experiences of them. As Roald states:

> Change is an inevitable feature within all systems of life which promote adaptation, survival and growth. Thus religion nurtured in one cultural context and transplanted into another is bound to be subject to different forms of expression in the new environment.[70]

Hence, by virtue of being British citizens in Leicester, the women have a new sense of empowerment, security and movement. Yet at the same time, as space is not detached from people, but affected by them, Leicester in turn has been made 'sacred' by the presence of Muslim motifs and symbols. That is, we have a double reconfiguration: of Leicester as a sacralised city and of Gujarati Muslim women as British citizens.

This research aimed at shifting epistemic power to those researched, to allow for real self-definition. It is, therefore, only fitting to end with a quote from one of the participants:

> My Tunisian Arabic teacher has really shaped my identity. You see, I don't feel Indian, because we have no one there. My great grandfather moved to South Africa, and so my parents were born there. And I feel African. Yet ethnically I'm Gujarati. I feel the whole world is my space, whether public or private.... At the end of the day, no matter what *Bihishti Zewar* or anything else says, I am an Abdullah (servant of Allah). Everything else – any other rule, or description – is just an adjective.

REFERENCES

Andrews, A., "Muslim Women in a Western European Society: Gujarati Muslim Women in Leicester," in *Religion in Contemporary Europe*, ed. J. Fulton and P. Gee (Lampeter: Edwin Mellen Press, 1994).

Places and Perspectives: Gujarati Muslim Women

Bonney, R., *Understanding and Celebrating Religious Diversity in Leicester's Places of Worship Since 1970* (Leicester: University of Leicester, 2003).

Chhachhi, A., "Identity Politics: South Asia," in *Encyclopedia of Women and Islamic Cultures*, ed. Suad Joseph (Leiden: Brill, 2005), vol. 2.

Collins, P.H., *Black Feminist Thought: Knowledge, Consciousness and the Politics of Empowerment* (London: Routledge, 1991).

Eliade, M., *The Sacred and the Profane: the Nature of Religion*, trans. W. Trask (London, Harcourt: Brace Johanovich, 1959).

Gilani, I.S., *Citizens Slaves and Guest-Workers: The Dynamics of Labour Migration from South Asia* (Islamabad: Institute of Policy Studies, 1985).

Haraway, D., *Simians, Cyborgs and Women: The Reinvention of Nature* (London: Free Association Books, 1991).

Harding, S., *The Science Question in Feminism* (Ithaca: Cornell University Press, 1986).

_____ "Rethinking Standpoint Epistemology: 'What is Strong Objectivity?'" in *Feminist Epistemologies,* eds. L. Alcoff and E. Potter E. (London: Routledge, 1993).

Hermansen, M., "Imagining Space and Siting Collective Memory in South Asian Muslim Biographical Literature *(Tazkirahs),*" *Studies in Contemporary Islam* (2002), vol. 4, no.2.

Mahomedy, M., trans. *Heavenly Ornaments, Bahishti Zewar, A Classic Manual of Islamic Sacred Law by Maulana Ashraf Ali Thanvi* (Karachi: Zam Zam Publishers, 1999).

Martin, J. and G. Singh, *Asian Leicester* (Gloucestershire: Sutton Publishing, 2002).

Massey, D., *Space, Place and Gender* (Cambridge: Polity Press, 1994).

_____ and P. Jess., *A Place in the World* (Oxford: Open Univeristy Press and Oxford Press, 1995).

Metcalf, B., *Islamic Revival in British India Deoband, 1860–1900* (Oxford: Oxford University Press, 1982).

_____ *Perfecting Women: Maulana Asraf 'Ali Thanawi's Bihishti Zewar* (Oxford: University of California, 1990).

_____ *Traditionalist Islamic Activism: Deoband, Tablighis, and Talibs* (Leiden: ISIM, 2002).

Modood, T. and P. Werbner, eds. *The Politics of Multiculturalism in the New Europe* (London: Zed Books, 1997).

Nicholson, R.A., trans. and ed. *The Mathnawi of Jalalu'ddin Rumi* (Karachi: Dārul Ishaat, 2003).

Ravat, R., *Embracing the Present, Planning the Future: Social Action by the Faith Communities of Leicester* (Bury St Edmunds: Leicester Faiths Regeneration Project, 2004).

Roald, A.S., *Women in Islam: The Western Experience* (London: Routledge, 2001).

_____ "Who Are The Muslims? Identity, Gender and Culture," in *Gender, Religion and Diversity: Cross-Cultural Perspectives*, ed. U. King and T. Beattie T. (London: Continuum, 2005).

Robinson, F., *Varieties of South Asian Islam*, Research Paper no. 8 (Coventry, CRER: University of Warwick, 1988).

Saroha, M.M.K., *Heavenly Ornaments*, English Translation of Maulana Ashraf Ali Thanvi's *Bahishti Zewar* (Karachi: Darul Ishaat, 1991).

Young, I., "Impartiality and the Civic Public: Some Implications of the Feminist Critiques of Moral and Political Theory," in *Feminism, the Public and the Private*, ed. Joan Landes (Oxford: Oxford University Press, 1998).

Online Census 2001, accessed in August 2005.

www.about-leicester/demographic

www.leicester.gov.uk/councillors

www.leicester.gov.uk/about-leicester/city-statistics/keyfacts/demographic-and-cultural

LUCY MICHAEL

Securing Civic Relations in the Multicultural City

Introduction

COMMUNITY COHESION AND SOCIAL inclusion programmes have demanded new alliances across old divides established by historical processes of exclusion and marginalisation which have visibly ordered the 'multicultural' city along ethnic and religious lines. This work draws on analyses of interviews and observations conducted across Muslim communities in Manchester and Stoke-on-Trent (UK). The paper[1] looks at the evolving community-level systems of formal and informal representation and collective action that operate within and alongside institutions of local governance, and reflects on their capacity to manage conflict, cohesion and civility within those communities, and improve their capacity to access public institutions and mobilise effectively for a 'fair' share of social resources. It also reflects on how those issues of security and participation are presented by community representatives to institutions of local governance, and within the new alliances that they have formed, and the consequences of these portrayals in ameliorating the position of their communities.

> The prisms through which British Muslims are viewed, and the solutions that are being sought, see Muslims first and foremost as a potential threat.[2]

Muslim communities in Britain today find themselves at the sharp end of a number of broad trends that have coalesced in the political context. These trends include a development of governance upon communitarian lines, with reliance on the existence of social capital[3] and the increased 'responsibilisation' of citizens,[4] the introduction of ambient police strategies which are appearing in high crime societies such as Britain and

177

the USA to deal primarily with insecurity rather than crime,[5] and a risk management approach to governance.[6] The relationship between risk control and race relations is not new but critical analysis of this relationship in the past has focused singularly on 'law and order' issues or socio-economic contexts. Risk control has been aimed at reducing the segregation of disadvantaged groups, and the associated social phenomena such as crime, disorder and self-segregation.

Discourses focusing upon the risks inherent in multicultural and multi-faith societies have become commonplace across Europe, particularly since 2001. In Britain, multicultural policies have been blamed for causing cultural and physical segregation, language barriers, and a decreased commitment to national citizenship amongst minorities through integrative and isolationist practises in governance and the provision of welfare services. Since 2001, the Government has pushed 'community cohesion' as a way of promoting integration at a local level in order to reduce the negative effects of segregation for both minority and majority ethnic populations within cities, and as a crosscutting format for national engagement. What can be seen in these developments is a race relations agenda that is moving rapidly from a basis in anti-discrimination and equality to one which is based on social control and influenced heavily by these trends. Under a new social control agenda, risk management has impacted upon minority communities in two ways: firstly, in the provision of state resources, and secondly, in relation to the role and capacity of representatives. It is on the second of these that this paper will focus. This paper explores the role of leadership in this changing context, as civic relations at both national and local levels are altered and leadership itself is established in broadly new terms.

The simultaneous promotion of the equality agenda, community cohesion, and social control requires a huge depth of leadership within minority communities. The equality agenda requires both activists and technocrats to continuously challenge inequalities on a consistent basis on behalf of minority communities at local and national levels. Community cohesion requires leadership of local communities into engagements with other local communities on a continuous basis. The simultaneous operation of these different agendas within and across a wide range of political and social arenas has impacted upon the development of leadership within British Muslim communities in significant ways. The social control agenda, now, requires leadership that can engage with and influence extreme positions within minority communities, whilst maintaining the normative status quo. This paper argues that the impact of this new agenda must be considered in any discussion of leadership and representation of minority communities. We start with an account of civic relations under the equality agenda, before proceeding to an examination of the changes introduced by the new agenda of social control.

Civic Relations: The Equality Agenda

The equality agenda has its roots in the anti-discrimination movements of the British Left in the 1970s which pushed for an end to racism and the integration of immigrant communities as well as increased provision for particular sectors of minority communities that suffered further inequalities, such as women. Since that period, equality campaigns have been established within the state, embodied within the Commission for Racial Equality and other institutions. This agenda assumes, however, that citizens of minority groups are willing to engage with a process of challenging discrimination and fulfilling the full array of rights and duties associated with citizenship in all aspects. One of the groups considered least likely to have benefited from these developments, because of self-segregation,[7] are South Asian Muslims. Like Anwar, Ansari has argued that the immigrant generation's initial adoption of 'accommodation' rather than 'integration' or 'assimilation' as their main strategy was a response to the social rejection of them by much of the host community, and the result was cultural encapsulation and minimum involvement in British life and institutions.[8]

However, equality movements have provided an important space within which minority groups have been able to establish civic relations with the state. Della Porta and Diani suggest that collective action of this type can be interpreted as the formation and consolidation of new value systems, as well as having symbolic importance in allowing participants to identify themselves collectively.[9] The 'Black' political identity of the 1980s, for example, to which many Muslim South Asians subscribed during that period, had its origin in the equality movements of that period. The move away from the 'Black' identity has been a gradual one, but it is nonetheless valuable to note that it was a basis upon which many

Muslims initially engaged with the state, before it was largely replaced by a 'faith' identity (reflecting their needs and values) rather than a specifically 'political' identity. Purdam has argued that after the 'Rushdie affair,' Islam became a powerful strategic political constituency in Britain, and therefore use of the term 'Muslim' is a political strategy, 'both as a target for demonisation and a source of unity for Muslims.'[10]

Within early equality movements, there was a deep distrust of electoral politics,[11] but the integration of equality movements and electoral politics developed sufficiently in the intervening years that by 1996 there were over 160 Muslim Councillors across England and Wales.[12] Political participation is often used as a measure of the integration of minority groups in equality terms, because it suggests a commitment to citizenship and the development of civic relations between the minority citizen and the state. High political participation with established political parties has therefore been interpreted as a sign of increasing integration. Over the 1980s and 1990s, the political structure began to allow access to minority political representatives. As strong supporters in many cities of the Labour party, South Asian communities were at the forefront of this development. Recent trends in voting amongst minority ethnic groups, including Muslims, have however provided cause for debate. Low political participation amongst younger minority ethnic adults has been suggested both to be a result of feelings of inefficacy arising from the socio-economic positions of Muslim communities and simultaneously a signifier of integration into an inner city culture which does not value political participation.[13] With the increased physical and ontological insecurity that accompanies exclusion, there is a deep impact upon the individual's sense of efficacy. It is already evident that political participation amongst minority ethnic citizens is diminished severely by this, as well as by factors of access and discrimination.

A more holistic view of the relationship between state and citizen, in terms of minority groups, is seen through the lens of leadership, and it is to this that we now turn. 'Leaders' in various forms and contexts act as mediators in civic relations, and an analysis of the development of leadership within minority communities reveals much about the development of civic relations in Britain.

Leaders

The mediation role of 'leaders' begins early in the story of immigrant Muslim communities in Britain. Ethnic 'community leaders' constituted a key section of race relations actors from the 1960s onwards when Caribbean, Pakistani and Indian workers were coming to Britain for industrial employment. The influence of these 'leaders' was enormously strong, particularly in South Asian communities, because of chain migration and the establishment of residential communities along kinship lines, and to some extent it can be inferred from a variety of accounts that this role included elements both of representation and social control. Religious advisors were largely employed in the new mosques at the behest of particular community members who paid their salaries, and thus in many cases supported this system of informal leadership.[14] Independent religious figures were scarce at this point, but held much influence where they did reside.[15] Today, many of Britain's Muslim communities outside London are constituted largely of traditionally mono-ethnic South Asian communities and continue to utilise the established religious and educational institutions of those communities. Because of that, it is important to understand the ways in which leadership has been conceptualised and envisioned in those contexts.

Wider recognition in governance of the unrepresentativeness of many of these early leaders came about in the 1980s.[16] The provision of welfare and social support for fellow immigrants is the first point at which minority communities accept responsibility for one another's well being. In Britain, ethnic and religious organisations were recruited and legitimised by the local state to help to reverse the exclusionary processes which minorities experienced, by direct provision and by consultation with the local state and they continue to play an important role in this regard. At this stage there was movement from engagement with ad hoc community leaders of patronage to what Cain and Yuval-Davis have called 'salaried professional spokespeople.'[17] It soon became clear however that the new representatives often lacked the ability to mobilise community membership. In recent years, policy-makers have increasingly recognised the importance of the 'social' in the stimulation of economic and cultural growth and know that 'communicative action' is more politically legitimate and 'adds value.'[18] Community capacity-building programmes have thus become important in developing this type of leadership to combine professional leadership with cohesive representation.

With a proliferation of representation opportunities over the last decade, 'leadership' today can be observed in an array of different political and social arenas, provided both by those who are religious leaders, and those who represent and mobilise Muslims in relation to non-faith issues. Representations are made at a national level by umbrella organisations established around faith identity, such as the Muslim Council of Britain, and around the faith itself, as well as by political representatives through the electoral process. Nationwide membership organisations, such as the Muslim Association of Britain, provide representation alongside a number of other Muslim and Islamic-based campaign and welfare groups. Representations also come from formal arenas, such as Racial Equality Councils and City Council consultative forums, local political representatives and informal groups that coalesce around the provision of welfare services.

Spaces of Engagement

With a growing and increasingly segmented population, it was inevitable that there would be an increase in the number and type of 'community' organisations, places of worship and education, and social spaces that they used. The legitimisation process operated by the local state also had an impact in this regard as it created a proliferation of informal associations each competing to be the legitimate 'voice' of their community. This trend, however, has also increased the spaces in which Muslim communities could collectively negotiate the norms and values to which they hold, and establish a basis for their development. Alongside the work to reverse social exclusion, ethnic and religious organisations provided a space for discussion and often a formal basis upon which to debate such issues. It would be misleading however to suggest that these, as primary spaces of engagement for the 'Muslim community,' were spaces in which disparate sections of the 'community' were able to engage freely with each other.

In British society, there are few spaces that bring together a whole identity population from different social, economic and political positions. Likewise, in the Muslim 'community,' these spaces are often divided by residence, class, religious and ethnic identities, age and gender, as well as by political outlook. Mosques, for example, have been observed to be the site of much conflict over positions on the management committees, whilst ethnic organisations have split and reformed, as various factions struggle for control of valuable resources across the community, sometimes competing with each other across ethnic, religious and political arenas.[19] There are particular social constraints upon these spaces too. Gender segregation as a faith practise requires that there are men and women who can engage with each other across this divide and facilitate wider debate within both gender groups, particularly amongst younger adults[20] who are the most affected by this practise. A longstanding emphasis on age (not unlike that in all other communities) also means that younger adults do not have the same access to discussions on the community's developments. These issues are significant not because of the ethnicity or religion of the communities, but because of the limited arenas in which these kinds of discussions can be held. We might therefore ask how effective these spaces of engagement were.

Conflict and dissent appears to have created a separation of these spaces as well as change within these spaces. The establishment of new organisations was easily facilitated by resources from the state which supported groups with visible needs not met by existing organisations. The separation of these arenas can allow for a more radical change to the development of the community than might occur under a deliberative engagement between all members of the community. This schism can create both positive and negative outcomes. An example of this can be found in Stoke-on-Trent, where it is broadly possible to talk about a community of youth in each of the residential clusters in a way that it is not possible to talk about the older generation, either as a functional imaginary or as a real normative grouping. Even across the city, such a community of youth is much more visible. Young people in this city have used cross-community cohesion as a basis for new alliances across the boundaries created by those earlier generations, not just between Muslim and non-Muslim, but between the smaller Pakistani communities built upon biraderi obligations, and kinship and economic transnational links. The most visible alliances are between the young people of these residential communities, formed through common use of institutions like the city's College, and increasingly drawing in more of their contemporaries. These have grown at least partly in response to exclusion from the decision-making processes within the community organisations and an absence of in-community spaces in which they had the freedom to express their distinct viewpoints.

Changing Agendas

In Britain after 2001, there came a new agenda in race relations, with an emphasis upon social control rather than equalities. The social control agenda visibly comes into play after the events of September 11th and the increased security assessments that followed, but arguably it comes from a long history of race relations that were based around 'community leaders' and their ability to influence the political participation of their fellow citizens. The substantive change is that while the equality agenda has as its aim the protection of citizens belonging to recognisable minority groups from the negative effects of the majority's 'way of life,' the aim of the social control agenda is the protection of the majority's 'way of life' from citizens belonging to recognisable minority groups. Tony Blair was the first to indicate the new agenda in his speech, just one week after the London bombings of July 7th, when he said:

> What I'm trying to do here is, and this will be followed up with the action in the next few weeks as I think you will see, is to send a clear signal out that the rules of the game have changed.[21]

The new agenda, as expressed by the Prime Minister, emphasised the interdependence of rights and responsibilities in citizenship, and paved the way for a 'partnership' between government and the 'Muslim community' to promote that duality. The normative statements that he made during 2005 left little room for negotiation of the norms and values to which Muslims should subscribe in the aftermath of the bombings. The 'rules of the game' were expressly related to the deportation of foreign national 'extremists,' to refugees and immigration, and finally in relation to faith schools, and were positioned as the basis for the protection of a British 'way of life.'[22] By juxtaposing the multiculturality of Britain with the 'new rules,' Blair linked a non-commitment to an unspoken 'British way of life' to the Muslim communities which were already under pressure to explain and moderate the extremist positions on the edges of their communities. In the latter half of this paper, I will examine the impact which this changed agenda has had, firstly, on civic relations and, secondly, on Muslim leadership.

Changing Civic Relations

The changed agenda has two main effects on civic relations between Muslims and the British state, which I will discuss in more depth below. Firstly, the prioritisation of social control, most recently couched in the language of Blair's 'new rules,' has defined multiculturality as a risk to be controlled in order to avoid the danger of extremism. Secondly, Muslim communities have undergone a process of 'dangerisation'[23] which labelled them as groups to be avoided rather than engaged with.

Why does multiculturality pose a risk? Under multiculturalist policies[24] of the British state, immigrant populations are imagined to have developed ways of life that pose risk (self-segregation, non-participation in civic life and apparent non-commitment to British values), and they therefore constitute the risk to be managed. Risk, Beck has argued, has to do with its consequences for individual and societal 'forms of life' which might be endangered in the future.[25] Management of risk has therefore become the central social practise for risk societies. So it is that the multiculturality has been connected with a number of prioritised risks in relation to terrorism and violent public disorder.[26]

As multiculturality is increasingly framed as a risk, the process of 'dangerisation' of minority groups creates a number of anxieties for the communities or groups that are the subject of those processes. This process is described by Lianos and Douglas as the way in which 'sensibility to threat is built by cultural means.' Through future projections of danger, ethical evaluation is made irrelevant in governance, or at best deflected on to safety concerns. The populations who are 'dangerised' are not, however, described as deviant. Like the Muslim populations of Britain discussed at length in the public debates on terrorism, they are known to be disadvantaged. Thus,

> they are not to be morally condemned, but they are to be contained. They are not to be patronizingly treated, but they are to be avoided, They are not detestable but they are disposable. They are simply 'dangerous,' 'suspicious,' 'aggressive,' 'threatening,' 'dodgy.' They do not need to break rules to be excluded .... What is important is their perceived probability of being dangerous and this can even be associated with completely legal behaviour ...[27]

Dangerisation of Muslim communities in Britain has arisen from the amplification of the terrorism threat by government and the media. Increasingly, Muslim communities are described as culture-bound to immigrant traditions, insular, and self-segregating through language and lifestyle. Containment of this population is however dependent, in contrast to the populations described by Lianos and Douglas, on the exposure of the 'ways of life' of these communities in order that they can be more easily visible to the state. Along with this surveillance, formal social control of these citizens imposes the restrictions of rights, and imposes the risk of over policing and criminalisation processes on these citizens.

During the latter part of 2005, it was clear that the Government's strategy was to co-opt Muslim citizens into public support of the Government's 'war on terror.' This strategy was vocalised by the Prime Minister shortly after the London bombings. He explicitly described the new partnership between the Government and the Muslim 'community' in the following terms:

> Time and again over the past few weeks I've been asked to deal firmly with those prepared to engage in such extremism, and most particularly with those who incite it or proselytise for it. The Muslim community, I should emphasise, have been and are our partners in this endeavour. Much of the insistence on strong action to weed out extremism is coming most vigorously from Muslims themselves, deeply concerned lest the activities of the fanatical fringe contaminate the good reputation of the mainstream Muslim community in this country.[28]

Blair was, of course, right. Some of the most vociferous rejection of terrorism did come from Muslim citizens in the aftermath of the attack. It is doubtful, however, that the Muslims who called for 'strong action' to weed out extremism intended that they become subject to the kinds of controls which were later introduced. Rather it might be suggested that their calls were underpinned by a concern that *in*action on the Government's part would contribute to the processes of dangerisation which they were experiencing.

Changing the Role of Leadership
The rewriting of the 'rules of the game' by the Government clearly

involved too a rewriting of the role of Muslim leadership in relation to the state. By inviting 'leaders' from Muslim communities, the Government showed a clear strategy for engagement on the issue. Humera Khan observed,

> Having in the past set up numerous ineffectual working groups and finding that it's investment into producing a viable representative voice for the Muslim community was not delivering the goods, it had to think quickly and think new. Enter the 'Preventing Extremism Together Working Groups' (PET), the so-called 'Muslim task force.' While the title might be a little kitsch the format was definitely new. What was new about this group was that it provided that when the government wanted to get a more representative cross section of the Muslim community together it could.[29]

The real change to the format of engagement was that rather than inviting those perceived to be leaders of the Muslim community, the Home Office looked for leaders from the Muslim community. Politicians, religious and welfare experts, academics and individuals who were pioneers in economic and social arenas were all invited and contributed their expertise. The 109 prominent Muslims who constituted the 2005 working groups on tackling extremism themselves provide a useful example of the way in which the concept of 'leadership' has been engaged with loosely in government-community relations. Invited as individuals, not as representatives of organisations or communities, their contribution was wide-ranging and full of expertise, but not tied to any visible group or section of Muslim communities. Within the reports, these prominent individuals set out a sizeable number of recommendations relating to the use, development or creation of leaders. Overall, the role assigned to 'leadership' within these discussions was problematic.

Emphasis, in earlier reports on the 2001 disorders,[30] was specifically placed upon the re-establishment of informal social control mechanisms within ethno-religious communities, and upon the establishment of formal structures (like youth forums) within which risks could be identified early on. Recommendations from these reports made the position of leadership central to formal and informal control and cohesion strategies, and to the identification of risky groups. In the reports that followed the 2005 bombings,[31] produced by government appointed working groups, alienation and exclusion of young Muslims were a key focus.

Leaders were designated as having a central role in socio-economic development, religious reconciliation, and capacity building in civic participation. Central to both sets of reports was a holistic concept of 'leadership' which brought together competent representation, dialogue with government, capacity-building in the community, the development of faith dialogues, community cohesion activities, recognition of exclusionary practises and the ability to connect with the excluded.

The central role of 'leaders' in the 2001 reports was hardly surprising, given the prominence of 'community leadership' in previous inquiries into race-related disorders throughout the 1980s and New Labour's citizen responsibilisation[32] agenda, but its appearance in the 2005 reports established a new precedent because of its proponents. Welfare and political leaders have traditionally been critics of 'community leadership' that is informal, unelected and accorded access to government on an ad hoc basis. The leadership proposed by the reports, however, did not move away from a holistic representation of a 'leader' but rather awkwardly bound 'community leadership' into the language of the new partnership. The 'leadership' which is to take forward almost two-thirds of the recommendations is largely imaginary, made up of a variety of representatives and activists already engaged in this kind of work at government behest and dealing with fragmented systems of representation and resources. The roles they play, as representatives and activists, are themselves largely fragmented roles, operating across and between institutional structures of the local state.

Evidence from political representatives and Muslims working within voluntary organisations at a local level,[33] presented later in this paper, will provide some insight into these divisions, and into the consequences of making 'leadership' a cornerstone, once again, of race relations policy and practise. But it is important to note that even before the 2005 consultation process was over, there were concerns from those prominent Muslims within it. The most cautious report produced by the working group on Security and Policing, clearly expressed its authors concerns about the present engagement with Government. The working group

> ... retained significant reservations about the Government's intentions for and commitment to the process. This is partly based on the rushed and poorly organised nature of the current consultation process; and the impression

conveyed by the dialogue to date that these consultation meetings were designed more for effect than for any meaningful input.[34]

Careful reading of the later report, 'Preventing Extremism Together: Progress,'[35] reveals that these concerns may well be borne out. The report makes it clear that the onus for tackling extremism has ultimately fallen to Muslim communities. Of the 64 recommendations from the working groups, only 27 were deemed appropriate to be adopted by government, with the remainder 'for the communities themselves to take forward.'[36] The consequence for Muslim communities of this 'opportunity to respond in a constructive way which was inclusive, positive and forward looking'[37] was ultimately an extension of the government's responsibilisation strategy which endorses the role of an imaginary Muslim 'leadership' in which informal social control features heavily.

The British Government has not singled out Muslim communities for this type of responsibilisation; rather it is symptomatic of a wider trend in advanced liberal societies. Nikolas Rose has observed that this trend combines what he calls 'ethopolitics,'[38] that is the regeneration of ethical values and shared moral norms and values, and an emphasis on self-governing community. The role of community leadership can be seen as crucial to the success of this governance project. Rose describes how community self-governance holds an interest for government by utilising inside knowledge about crime, and thereby removing risks for wider society:

> Community is not simply the territory within which crime is to be controlled, it is itself a means of government: its detailed knowledge about itself and the activities of its inhabitants are to be utilized, its ties, bonds, forces and affiliations are to be celebrated, its centres of authority and methods of dispute resolution are to be encouraged, nurtured, shaped and instrumentalised to enhance the security of each and of all.[39]

The responsibilisation of Muslim communities with regards to extremism can be viewed in the same light. It is the community's detailed knowledge about itself that is intended to be harnessed and its own mechanisms of informal social control used to draw in and moderate the extremist positions on its edges. Greater Manchester Police, for example, wrote to each mosque in Manchester in July 2005 describing the London attacks as creating 'a difficult time' for all communities in the area, and urging people to be alert and vigilant in relation to terror threats. This open letter illustrates the language of responsibilisation that was prevalent during this period:

> We must ensure we don't let these awful events divide the strong communities that we have in Greater Manchester. We all have an important part to play in protecting and reassuring our communities. Extremists will not survive in our communities if we unite together and we work to drive terrorism out. We must divert those who are vulnerable and impressionable away from being drawn into terrorist activity.[40]

It is within this new context that Muslim 'leadership' now operates, and must develop in order to challenge the new agendas introduced by the state in pursuit of greater social control. One pertinent criticism of Muslim 'leaders,' such as those prominent individuals involved in the Home Office working groups, representatives of the Muslim Council of Britain and Muslim politicians, is that to date they have not sought (or have not had the capacity) to challenge sufficiently those new agendas.

Critical Distance

I want now to turn to an examination of criticisms that have been aimed at 'leaders' under this new agenda by other Muslim citizens. The criticisms have to some extent been argued and responded to in the media and constitute a large body of material which is revealing about their proponents in many ways. However, my particular interest here is the understanding of these criticisms as expressions of insecurity at a local level.[41] Four main concerns emerge from the criticisms levelled at the 'leaders' working on a national level with government. These criticisms largely were based upon media coverage of the Home Office working groups reports and Muslim Council of Britain engagements over the issue of the regulation of Imams, and upon communications which had come through the organisations and networks of which these local 'leaders' were members. These concerns focused on leadership: on the acceptance of dangerisation; on the acceptance of responsibility for extremism; on a lack of challenge to the social control agenda which undermined work on equality and on a retreat from providing a critical voice in relation to government policy in other areas.

Securing Civic Relations in the Multicultural City

Firstly, there was a concern that the engagements between Muslim 'leaders,' and government implied an acceptance of 'risky' label by allowing government to phrase equality in risk terms. Public representation by the Muslim Council of Britain and by the working groups were seen to demonstrate a preference for government dialogue over publicly challenging the insecurities experienced by their communities. By engaging with government in the way it did after the London bombings, the Muslim Council of Britain was thought to allow government to set the race relations agenda along the lines of risk management, and to define the role to be played by national and grassroots Muslim leaders and activists. The following quotation, from an interview with an ex-City Councillor, reflects this concern:

> There isn't one Muslim who considers them [the terrorists] to be a Muslim. Muslims themselves ostracise – but because we cannot control them – why is that onus on us? Instead of saying that the Muslim community is the most law-abiding citizens in the country and the people perpetrating these acts are on the fringe, why are they saying they're within our community? I was horrified when Muslim leaders were asked *'how will you stop them?'* And they said *'we'll try harder.'* How if you don't know who?

It also highlights the second concern, that Muslim communities who actively excluded those who held extremist positions in the past would be put into a position where organisations responsible for these exclusionary activities now had to actively try to engage with them. Post September 11th, some Muslims had felt pushed into an identity that they had not previously owned. That identity was a stereotyped cultural-religious identity, linked with ideas about disloyalty to Britain, disrespect for human rights of other cultural-religious groups, the promotion of violent conflict via terrorism, an all-encompassing commitment to an invisible unknowable Ummah.

> Then came September 11th – they all became Pakistani. All of a sudden you were a terrorist, or a latent terrorist. And that's where we're at now .... At each step it further alienates the British Muslims because they feel very very unfairly treated by the British government and the people themselves. (Male, late 40s)

Pushed into such a deviant identity, many people strove to adopt a visible and oppositional non-deviant Muslim identity, one that cherished British citizenship, respect for law and for human rights, and promoted peace, denouncing a 'Western' predilection for war along the way. The exclusion of those who held extremist views from community organisations and from the use of community facilities was a practise that was apparent before 2005, particularly since Muslim communities were fearful of police raids in counter-terrorist activities after the 2001 World Trade Centre attacks. Groups holding unpopular views were excluded from community centres and mosques in Stoke-on-Trent and Manchester during the research, and it was clear that this was as much because their views did not fit with the moral norms and values of the community as because of a fear of increased police surveillance.

From an academic perspective, conflict is both unavoidable and essential to community life. Conflict occurs in the spaces in which the community grows and develops, and it allows the community's membership to reiterate and to challenge the established norms of the community. But conflict also introduces insecurity to the group, about who is included and excluded, and who has access to the group's resources. Conflict between groups within a community of origin or faith, or between communities, may create insecurity by posing questions about the validity not only of the group's claims on societal resources, but about the established norms of that community around which the boundaries are drawn.[42] In a group already excluded from the resources of the political community, such conflicts can be enormously damaging, particularly when spaces for open engagement are disappearing. The second concern, that Muslim communities would suffer further criticism and suspicion for not being able to control those excluded groups, and would experience new problems of internal cohesion, in this light appears to be well founded.

The third concern, which emerged from the criticisms voiced in the research, was orientated towards the provision of welfare and social support within these still disadvantaged communities. Several local 'leaders,' including youth workers and elected city councillors, reported that their time and energy was increasingly consumed with being constantly on call to police and to the City Councils to deal with issues of concern around disadvantaged teenage males in the inner city. Such issues were mainly based in crime and disorder but also specifically in relation to their modes of expression of their religious identities in their schools and their neighbourhoods. Such included graffiti, gang formation and challenges to authority within those environments. Reports of a variety of organisations in both cities make specific mention of the efforts put into reducing the alienation of teenage males from the institutions of their community and providing a space for them within those institutions. The concern is that intense focus on disadvantaged teenage males will divert attention away from the equalities agenda and the distinct needs of females and older age groups. This may occur through a prioritisation of applications for funding which emphasise work with young disadvantaged males, or prioritisation of engagement with organisations who carry out this work, or in any case, a perceived prioritisation which encourages community organisations to divert their valuable resources away from other groups.

The fourth theme emerging from these critical narratives concerns the willingness of national figures to provide leadership that challenges the state in other ways. Two specific issues captured these concerns: the British role in Iraq and the extradition of Babar Ahmad, a British Muslim suspected of terrorist activities, to the USA. Currently, both of these issues attract support from a wide range of Muslim citizens and 'leaders,' but the perceived reticence of 'leaders' in national arenas to challenge government foreign and extradition policies during 2005 formed a central theme in local discussions. Voicing their criticism in this way appeared to allow participants to vocalise other feelings of insecurity which they experienced and therefore form an interesting record of those, although they are sometimes based on errors in fact. Criticisms were levelled both in relation to the direct representational roles of national leader figures (as can be seen from the first quotation), and in relation to their role in expressing the position of Muslim citizens to other British citizens (as is suggested in the second quotation below).

Muslim leaders are not democratically elected. If you look at the war on Iraq, all the leaders were supporting it when they should have been supporting anti-terrorism. They should focus on external issues, not our own [state] terrorism. There's terrorism in India, Pakistan, Russia, Italy – but no one wants to address these. With Iraq, a lot of information filters down to Muslim communities and it has an impact on religion – like the killing in the mosque, or in

Palestine of a 13 year old. These atrocities are not visible. MCB – are they proactive? They didn't have a hard stance on that originally – NOW they're against the war. (Male professional, voluntary youth leader, 30s, Stoke-on-Trent)

The MCB never stood up. Margaret Hassan – when she was beheaded, Sacranie – it was all so disgusting – they said it was inhuman, barbaric that she'd been killed. It sounds fantastic to the white community. But if you're Iraqi, Muslim, there was not a word about the thousands of Iraqis killed every day. Not one word about them. It's barbaric but given how many are killed, there comes a time when frustration comes out. That kind of statement would have won them the support of the Muslim community. (Male, 40s, Manchester)

This perception of reticence was reflected in observations that other national organisations seemed also to be holding back on direct action. They perceived that fears around the closure of mosques were similarly affecting people involved in these organisations and the threat of governmental backlash.

I said [to the senior members] 'you haven't done anything for Babar Ahmed' – they said 'we're doing it behind the scenes.' But it's not visible. Therefore, it's not worth it. They think they're going to be the next target. (Female activist, 30s, Manchester)

The actions of national organisations, however, also carried another implicit meaning. A stark depiction of apparent compromise at a national level sent a message to the communities indirectly represented by the Muslim Council of Britain that would have had a huge impact on the ontological security of those communities. Even national organisations which had been critical voices prior to the London attacks appeared to be in retreat; that message was that the atmosphere in Britain for Muslims was so full of danger that it was no longer possible to speak plainly about the insecurities suffered by Muslim communities.

Conclusion: Secure Civic Relations?

Throughout this paper, we have seen that there are a number of roles to be played by 'leaders' across a range of social and political spaces of engagement. In principle, the challenge for leadership remains the same under the social control agenda as it does under an equalities agenda. For minorities, it is still a fight to gain equality and at the same time to protect the right to be different and to express that difference. For leaders, it is still a challenge to recognise threats to those rights, and react to them in ways that do not undermine the future of those rights. In practise, however, within the social control agenda, there are additional challenges: to ensure that the full diversity of opinion in the Muslim community is represented; to protect the 'reputation' of the minority population; to protect faith-associated resources that are considered by government to add risk, such as faith schools; and to maintain access to resources and representation opportunities related to equalities rather than risk management.

Leadership itself then is a focus for future debate. What is it that may be required of leaders, and by whom? Clearly, there is a conflict within the roles set out in this paper. Evidence from Manchester and Stoke-on-Trent of community practise depicts strong exclusionary tendencies that strengthen the cohesion within these communities. Exclusionary processes aimed at protecting the reputation of the community and decreasing internal conflict have long been aimed at 'extremist' groups and individuals who are in conflict with the norms and values of the majority number. Government-led initiatives however have at their heart a notion of containment and moderation of extremist positions within Muslim communities by Muslim leaders. They are reliant upon the social influence of Muslim 'leaders' who, as we have seen earlier, already face difficulties in mobilising and influencing the diverse sections of the communities they work for or represent.

Of particular importance in this discussion is the suggestion that the adoption of a social control agenda of this type by Muslim 'leaders' appears to significantly increase the levels of insecurity experienced by their communities. Processes of dangerisation, which are under way in relation to Muslim communities, cannot easily be reversed. They are also now amplified by dangerisation processes within Muslim communities aimed at those with 'extreme' perspectives. The capacity of leaders to manage conflict and cohesion within these communities is thus fundamentally challenged. Particular difficulties are posed for the development of civic relations as distrust in the state's institutions of governance and of social control is increased by the social control agenda promoted by the state, and the increased promotion of separatism in response to that agenda. The conclusion to be drawn from this, therefore, is that this new agenda significantly decreases the capacity of leaders to carry out the functions which the state requires of them at precisely the time when capacity-building is recognised as key to good civic relations.

REFERENCES

Ansari, Humayun, *The Infidel Within: Muslims in Britain since 1800* (London: Hurst, 2004).

Anthias, F. and Nira Yuval Davis, *Racialised Boundarie*s (New York: Routledge, 1992).

Anwar, Muhammad, "Muslims in Britain: Issues, Policy and Practise," in *Muslim Britain: Communities under Pressure*, ed. T. Abbas (London: Zed Books, 1991).

Beck, Ulrich, *Risk Society: Towards a New Modernity* (London: Sage, 1992).

Burlet, Stacey and Helen Reid, "Riots, Representation and Responsibilities: The Role of Young Men in Pakistani-Heritage Muslim Communities," in *Political Participation and Identities of Muslims in Non-Muslim States*, ed. W.A.R. Shadid and P.S. van Koningsveld (Kampen, The Netherlands: Kok Pharos, 1996).

Cain, Harriet, and Nira Yuval Davis, "The Equal Opportunities Community and the Anti-Racist Struggle," *Critical Social Policy* (Autumn, 1990), vol. 29.

Cantle, Ted, *Community Cohesion: A Report of the Independent Review Team* (London: Home Office, 2001).

Cohen, Anthony P., *The Symbolic Construction of Community* (London: Tavistock, 1985).

Della Porta, Donatella and Mario Diani, *Social Movements: An Introduction* (Oxford: Blackwell Publishing, 2006).

Department for Communities and Local Government. 'Preventing Extremism Together' Progress Report (London: Home Office, 2006), http://www. raceand-faith.communities.gov.uk

Electoral Commission, Voter Engagement among Black and Minority Ethnic Communities: Research Report (July) (London: The Electoral Commission, 2002).

Faulkner, David, "Civil Renewal, Diversity and Social Capital in a Multi-Ethnic Britain," Runnymede Perspectives series paper (January) (London: Runnymede, 2004), http://www.runnymedetrust.org

Home Office, "'Preventing Extremism Together' Working Group Reports, August–October" (London: Home Office, 2005), http://www.raceandfaith.communities. gov.uk

Home Office, "Building Cohesive Communities: A Report of the Ministerial Group on Public Order and Community Cohesion" (London: Home Office, 2002).

Hussain, Akhtar, *The Four Tribes of Nottingham: The Story of Pakistanis and Kashmiris in Nottingham, England* (Karachi: Awami Publishers, 1999).

Hussain, Yasmin and Paul Bagguley, "Citizenship, Ethnicity and Identity: British Pakistanis After the 2001 'Riots,'" *Sociology* (2005), vol. 39, no. 3.

Innes, M., "Reinventing Tradition: Reassurance, Neighbourhood Security and Policing," *Criminal Justice* (2004), vol. 2, no. 4.

Lianos, Michalis, with Mary Douglas, "Dangerisation and the End of Deviance: The Institutional Environment," *British Journal of Criminology* (2000), vol. 40, no. 2.

Macey, Marie, "Class, gender and religious influences on changing patterns of Pakistani Muslim male violence in Bradford," *Ethnic and Racial Studies* (September, 1999), vol. 22, no. 5.

Ouseley, Herman, *Community Pride not Prejudice* (Bradford Vision: Bradford, 2001).

Purdam, Kingsley, "The Impacts of Democracy on Identity: Muslim Councillors and their Experiences of Local Politics in Britain." PhD dissertation (Manchester: Manchester University, 2003).

Ritchie, D., *Oldham Independent Review*. Oldham Panel, One Oldham One Future: Oldham (2001), http://www.oldhamir.org.uk/

Rose, Nikolas, "Government and Control," *British Journal of Criminology* (2000), vol. 40, no. 3.

Shirlow, Peter and Brendan Murtagh, "Capacity-building, Representation and Intra-community Conflict," *Urban Studies* (2004), vol. 41, no. 1.

Solomos, John and Les Black, *Race, Politics and Social Change* (London: Routledge, 1995).

Webster, Colin, "Race, Space and Fear: Imagined Geographies of Racism, Crime, Violence and Disorder in Northern England," *Capital & Class* (December, 2002).

Werbner, Pnina, *Imagined Diasporas among Manchester Muslims: The Public Performance of Pakistani Transnational Identity Politics*. World Anthropology Series (Oxford: James Currey Publishers, 2002).

Political Islam

ABDELWAHAB EL-AFFENDI

Islamic Revivalism and the Elusive Ethical State: Revisiting the "Damascus Model"

Introduction

IN LATE 1987, AT A TIME when the Iranian parliament and the Council of Guardians reached a deadlock over legislation relating to the role of the state in the economy, the Speaker of Parliament at the time, Hashemi Rafsanjani, appealed to the Supreme Leader of the Revolution, Ayatollah Ruhollah Khomeini, to intervene to resolve the dispute. The Council of Guardians, empowered by the constitution to rule on the conformity of legislation to Islamic norms, had objected to proposed laws in view of their negative impact on private property rights. The government, by contrast, wanted more powers to intervene in the economy to implement some of its social programmes. It was backed in this by the parliament. A deadlock ensued, prompting the appeal to Khomeini.

The Ayatollah did intervene, this time supporting the government. While acknowledging that the legislation in question did indeed contradict Sharicah provisions, he argued that it was permissible for the ruler to override Islamic law provisions if the public interest dictated it. According to the principle of *Wilāyah al-Faqīh* (the mandate of the jurist), Khomeini argued, the Supreme Leader (*al-Wāly al-Faqīh*) can override Islamic law to safeguard the public interest, especially when the survival of the Islamic state was at stake.

Commenting on the Leader's ruling, the then President Ali Khamenei tried to expound on the principle involved during his Friday sermon in Tehran, arguing that it was indeed permissible for the Leader to override some specific Islamic rules, provided, of course, that he continues to observe the overall dictates of Sharicah and not contradict any categorical imperatives of Islamic law. A few days later, on January 6, 1988,

Khomeini fired a letter of rebuke to the President, who was told that he had apparently completely misunderstood the ruling. The Islamic Government, Khomeini wrote, was the most important of all divine ordinances, and safeguarding it took precedence over all other religious obligations. In the interest of safeguarding the Islamic state, all other Islamic obligations, including such fundamental obligations as performing prayers, fasting or going on pilgrimage (considered to be the "pillars of Islam") could be rightfully suspended or prohibited by the Imam (Leader). Even mosques could be destroyed if necessary. Khomeini termed this the principle of the "Absolute Mandate of the Jurist" (*Wilāyah al-Faqīh al-Muṭlaqah*).[1]

For many observers, including some of Khomeini's astonished followers, this sounded suspiciously like the theses of Niccolo Machiavelli and Thomas Hobbes about the amorality of politics and the supremacy of the "reason of state." What the judgement effectively said was that the state could accept subjection to no norms outside itself. The principle was soon enshrined in the 1989 amended constitution, and the Expediency Council was set up and tasked with determining the "interests of the regime" (*Maṣlaḥah al-Niẓām*), which was to become from then on the supreme value to which all other considerations, including Islamic norms and laws, were to be subjected.

End of the Virtuous State Dream?

For a number of commentators, this clear announcement of the supremacy of decidedly secular criteria, and specifically of regime interest, as the final arbiter of the conduct of the affairs of a presumed Islamic state signalled the "bankruptcy of the Iranian regime," and was a telling indication of the dead end in which political Islam finds itself.[2] The resulting "failure of political Islam" underlines the barrenness of the "the Islamic political imagination," in which the vision of the Islamic state was grounded. That vision was "dominated by a single paradigm: that of the first community of believers at the time of the Prophet and of the first four caliphs" and offered the militants an ideal of an "egalitarian, undifferentiated society, placed under the auspices of a man who didn't legislate, but who stated the revelation."[3] However, since this paradigm which denied the existence of autonomous politics, has admittedly been irretrievably lost, the prevailing attitudes tended to reject the legitimacy of any existing political order, making this vision an element of constant destabilisation.[4]

In any case, the Islamist quest for the recreation of an Islamic order suffered from an inescapable circularity: in order to recreate a virtuous Islamic community, a virtuous state must exist; however, this state can only be put in place by virtuous leaders supported by a virtuous community. Moreover, if and when such a state is created, it would immediately wither away. For

> once the Islamic state is in place, justice results not so much from state actions as from the convergence of men who are virtuous at last, who spontaneously conform to the *sharia* without any external pressure .... The state has a purely pedagogical role: to make men virtuous, then harmony automatically exists among men. The state is not a mediator between citizens; it does not construct civil society. The more virtuous the society, the more the state withers.[5]

But before this could happen, a circle had to be squared. "Islamic society exists only through politics, but political institutions function only as a result of the virtue of those who run them, a virtue that can become widespread only if the society is Islamic beforehand. It is a vicious circle."[6] It is, in addition, a dead end which also describes "the limits of the politicisation of religion, any religion."[7]

Roy's depiction of the Islamic revivalist dilemma is not entirely accurate, as the normative appeal of the early Islamic model is much more complex than that, a point to which we shall return. On the other hand, this dilemma is not exclusive to religious models of the state, but faces any ethical political project. Indeed the modern political debate has been characterised by a polarisation around two alternative solutions to the problem. The first vision, espoused by authors like Ibn Khaldūn, Machiavelli and Hobbes, among others, regarded society as essentially an amoral, or at least pre-moral, arena of a fierce struggle for survival between self-interested individuals or groups, where all is fair and brute force is the ultimate arbiter. It is thus the responsibility of the state to instil a modicum of order into this lawless arena of unmitigated egoism. For this end, the state may have to match the viciousness of its recalcitrant subjects, and absolve itself from observing moral constraints as this could hamper its efforts to bring order to society and enable civilised life to exist and continue. The second view, outlined by liberals harking back to Locke, Bentham, Mill, etc., holds the reverse: that the state is the repository of amorality and will to domination, while society (nowadays "civil society") is the fountain of good. The state, and power holders within it, must therefore be treated as suspect and subjected to constant supervision and monitoring by representatives of various social groups.

The Islamic vision (and this includes "Islamist" as well the more general inclination which Roy describes as the "Islamic political imagination") tends in fact, contrary to Roy's suggestion, more towards the Hobbesian paradigm than the rival one. Far from advocating the withering away of the state and the reliance on virtuous society, Islamic theorists have been preoccupied with thinking up "guardianship" schemes to constrain the inherently virtue-challenged masses. Whether this could take the shape of caliph, *faqīh*, or council of *ʿulamā'*, it has to somehow stand outside society and above it. The idea is that society, left to itself, without a suitable "guardian" in the shape of a virtuous ruler, is likely to drift away into sin and chaos. Ideally, of course, a virtuous society combined with a virtuous ruler could create a virtuous cycle, where the ruler continues to guide society onto the path of virtue, while society gallops along willingly. That, of course, is how the Righteous Caliphate model was viewed. There was never a question of the state "withering away," for vigilance is always necessary.

The core of the revivalist dilemma could not thus be summed up by Roy's vicious circle, for Islamist leaders were clear about the priority of a virtuous society, and constantly recalled the Prophet's model of carving out such a society out of the world of "*jāhiliyyah*" without any need for a state. The state was supposed to grow "organically" out of the community once it reached a "critical mass." The idea was summed up in Hassan al-Banna's famous slogan: "The Muslim individual, then the Muslim family, then the Muslim Society" (the state is not even mentioned here). Abu'l A'la al-Maududi's thesis (which was later taken up and reinforced by Sayyid Qutb) similarly argues for a vanguard community that must exist and convert the bulk of society to its vision in advance of any Islamic political order. Where some Islamists faced a problem was in entertaining recurrent delusions that such a conversion had already taken place and all they needed to do was to take charge of the emerging Muslim society, and persuade it to surrender its will completely to their "guardianship" which could henceforth assume the task of keeping it virtuous.

In this regard, it was the much maligned Maududi-Qutb hardline position which appears at once more consistent and inherently pacifist. For if one believed, as they did, that no genuine Muslim society exists, then what was needed was to create one, and that can only be done peacefully, by preaching the message until one can gather a large enough following to make a viable community. But if one did believe, like al-Banna, Khomeini and others that the virtuous community is already here, but either did not know it yet or was awaiting the right leadership, then that is when one would enter the contest with rivals to wrest out this leadership. It is this belief in the "miraculous" and transformative role of virtuous and charismatic leadership which is the inspiration for present day (conflictual) activism.

The Caliphate Model

The origin of this belief is not simply a harking back to the Golden Age model of the Righteous Caliphate, but the inspiration of an earlier revivalist moment where a simple change of leadership appeared to work a miracle on its own. The crucial figure who inspired this outlook was the Umayyad caliph ʿUmar ibn ʿAbd al-ʿAzīz, also known as ʿUmar II (99–101/717–720), renowned for his obsessive scrupulousness and reforming zeal, a trait romanticised by historians since it contrasted sharply with the conduct of the dynasty from which he had emerged. If he could not be considered the "first Islamist," ʿUmar II is nevertheless widely regarded as the one who has achieved most success in the attempt to restore the early model in admittedly adverse circumstances.

The characteristics of that model on which ʿUmar II focused came to define it in the minds of later generations. His starting point was the insistence on strict adherence to the Qur'an "without modification, reservation or respect for persons" as a guide for the formulation and implementation of state policy, and the affirmation that the "first duty of a Muslim government is to propagate the Faith."[8] Other features included, scrupulousness in the dispersal of public funds, exemplary moral leadership, establishing a just order perceived as such, avoiding resort to violence in inter-Muslim relations, and trying to promote a consensus based on Islamic norms. Another related issue he had considered, but did not manage to resolve, was that of the selection of political leaders. He was about to conclude a peace deal on the issue with the implacable *khawārij* rebels who insisted on the right of the community to choose its own leaders when he died suddenly.[9]

As part of his approach, ʿUmar II also tried to minimise conflict with non-Muslims by recalling armies sent to attack Constantinople and by putting restrictions on warfare with foreign enemies, stipulating that peaceful alternatives had to be offered to them first.[10] He outlawed torture to extract confessions from suspects and any form of illegal or excessive punishment, and specifically prohibited violence against political opponents and critics of the regime. He even made the emphatic point that he would not try to push his reforms if that involved bloodshed, and rebuked governors who asked his permission to use harsh policies against dissidents or suspects.[11]

The restraint in using violence as an instrument of politics was regarded as a defining feature of the original caliphate model as it emerged during the reigns of Abū Bakr (11/632–13/634) and ʿUmar I (13/634–23/644). There was an irony in this, for although a rare and probably unique instance of an "ethical state," the establishment of the caliphate was not free from violence. In fact, it was only set in place after a series of very intense wars known as the "Apostasy Wars." Abū Bakr, who was acclaimed as the first *khalīfah* (successor) of the Prophet, took a belligerent stance against tribes which refused to acknowledge his authority, and waged a relentless war against the rebels until he vanquished them and succeeded in reuniting Arabia under his rule.[12]

Apart from this initial deployment of violence to establish the authority of the state as a state (since it was not just the rule of Abū Bakr which the rebels rejected, but the very notion of being ruled by a central authority from Madinah), Abū Bakr and ʿUmar I did not use violence to enforce their personal authority, and did not need to. The rulers did not even have bodyguards. This principle was carried to an extreme when the third caliph ʿUthmān (23/644–35/656) faced a direct challenge to his authority from armed rebels, but rejected all offers from supporters to defend him even after the rebels occupied Madinah and besieged the ageing caliph's house.

What was remarkable about ʿUthmān's principled pacifism was that it had stood the question of the state on its head. In this conflict, it was not the state which monopolised violence, but the rebels. While ʿUthmān continued to plead his case vociferously, in sermons at the mosque, in meetings, in letters he sent to the provinces and to the pilgrims in Makkah, he gave strict instructions forbidding the spilling of blood in his defence. This inverted relation of state violence and the freelance violence of self-styled advocates of reform was to have a lasting impact on the subsequent course of Muslim politics, for it became the starting point for a prolonged cycle of violence and counter-violence in which the restraining effect of "legitimate" state violence had no place.

Following the murder of ʿUthmān and the accession of ʿAlī (35/656–40/661), this equation began to change. ʿAlī spent all his reign fighting those who challenged his right to rule. Interestingly, the level of state violence decreased considerably in the early part of Umayyad rule. In spite of his reputation as a ruthless politician, the reign of the founder of the Umayyad dynasty, Muʿāwiyah I (41/661–60/680) was not characterised by excessive violence, apart from the case of rebellious Iraq, where his governor, Ziyād (44/664–53/673), was not so scrupulous about resort to violence. Muʿāwiyah relied more on his shrewd political manoeuvrings and the liberal use of public funds to attract or neutralise powerful opponents. The reign of his son Yazīd (60/680–64/684), however, was very bloody, culminating in the murder of the Prophet's grandson al-Ḥusayn (in 61/680) and the sacking of Madinah by his vengeful troops (in 63/683). The reliance on cruelty and violence reached a peak under ʿAbd al-Malik ibn Marwān (64/684–86/705) and his sons, especially under his governor for Iraq, al-Ḥajjāj ibn Yūsuf (75/694–95/715), whose name became a by-word for cruelty and wanton violence. ʿUmar II came into direct conflict with al-Ḥajjāj during his term as governor of Madinah under his cousin, al-Walīd, as al-Ḥajjāj accused him of providing a safe haven for Iraqi dissidents fleeing persecution. These accusations led to ʿUmar's dismissal from his post as governor of Madinah, and has influenced his later thinking.[13]

During ʿUmar I's reign, some very strict criteria of public authority were introduced, including the barring of close relatives from top jobs in the state or from receiving special benefits from the public treasury. The personal privileges of the ruler were reduced to the lowest common denominator, with further cuts in times of hardship, as happened in the famine year of year 18AH. The ruler also employed no bodyguards or personal retinue, and the dispersal of public funds was completely transparent.

One other vital reform introduced by ʿUmar I, with momentous consequences for his successors, was to occasion a more decisive shift away from the demands of power politics accepted even during the time of the Prophet. It was customary during the earlier period to show special consideration for powerful individuals, such as tribal chiefs and other dignitaries. The Qur'an even acknowledged this necessity by establishing a category of *al-mu'allafah qulūbuhum* ("courted persons," or, more literally, "individuals whose hearts are to be won"), who could legitimately benefit from state funds. The Prophet also used to accord influential tribal chiefs material and symbolic privileges in recognition of their status. ʿUmar I, in his uncompromising drive to create an "ethical state," abolished this category during his reign, arguing that the Islamic state had by then become powerful enough to dispense with the need to court the favour of any individual, no matter how powerful.[14]

The system began to unravel during the latter part of ʿUthmān's reign, partly through no fault of his own. The fast expansion of the Madinah city state into an empire created many new difficulties, as the administration of the expanded state became too complicated for the city state model of management as it evolved up to that time. It was in the end rebellions fomented by residents of two key provinces, Iraq and Egypt which brought about the collapse of the caliphate/city-state model.

But the rebellion also took place against the background of a wider crisis of legitimacy, occasioned by a widely shared perception that ʿUthmān had deviated considerably from the original *khilāfah* model as developed by the "two venerable men" (*al-Shaykhayn*) Abū Bakr and ʿUmar I. The rebels had made specific demands all pertaining to the reversion to earlier policies guaranteeing a fair and equitable treatment for all. They wanted ʿUthmān to abandon favouritism of his relatives and to appoint governors more acceptable to the provincial elite.

The crisis revealed a central flaw in the original model which had no provision for resolving disputes of this nature. Abū Bakr's earlier resort to force to bring to heel recalcitrant tribesmen who refused to acknowledge state authority had been justified in terms of religious doctrine, as many of the tribes in question joined forces with non-Muslim groups or abandoned Islam altogether, making that a fight to restore the authority of the Islamic community, and not that of the caliph. However ʿUthmān's critics, far from abandoning the faith, had posed as its defenders, accusing the ageing caliph of having betrayed basic Islamic principles. They could thus be regarded as the earliest "Islamic revivalists."

Far from restoring the model, however, the rebellion signalled the collapse of the system. While ʿAlī's reign which followed is regarded by Muslims as a continuation of the system of the Righteous Caliphate (and by the Shia as its beginning), in fact ʿAlī's brief and stormy reign was a doomed and unsuccessful attempt at restoration which highlighted even more dramatically the limitations of the model as it was then understood. ʿAlī never managed to assert his authority over the whole Islamic territory, as he was challenged from the beginning by the pro-ʿUthmān faction, led by Muʿāwiyah, and by factions consisting of alienated supporters from his own camp. The latter known as the *khawārij* (rebels), were a group of disillusioned but fanatical former supporters who charged he had given too many concessions to opponents. ʿAlī was forced to abandon the caliphate seat in Madinah, and base himself in Iraq, where he was soon to face a series of challenges that did not end until his murder in 40/661. His eldest son al-Ḥasan then made a deal with Muʿāwiyah which further splintered his volatile supporters.

The Problem of "Republican" Instability

Some analysts viewed the conflict that led to the collapse of the caliphate system in terms of attempts by entrenched provincial elites to defend "positions and interests which they had either lost or were in the process of losing."[15] The "religious aristocracy" empowered by ʿUmar and the other "early comers" to the provinces were facing a threat both from the rise of old tribal elites who had been sidelined by the advent of Islam, and from the centralising policies of ʿUthmān.[16] There is some truth in this, although it may be inaccurate to describe ʿUthmān's policies as favouring increased centralisation in contrast to ʿUmar's, for the complaints of the rebels do not seem to have focused on this issue. If anything, their complaint was that ʿUthmān had given his governors too much leeway. Given the poor lines of communications in the extended empire, and given ʿUthmān's more relaxed attitude compared to ʿUmar's strict hands-on policy, the problem appeared to have been the considerable autonomy which ʿUthmān's governors enjoyed, rather than the reverse.

In any case, the Madinah model experienced powerful destabilising forces due mainly to inner tensions between the vision and reality. The model has emerged from the struggles which followed the death of the Prophet, and was shaped by the hard-line centralising stance adopted by Abū Bakr, who was of the idea that the unity of the community depended on its submission to one central authority. But his success in suppressing the rebellions against this authority launched the dynamics that led to break-neck expansion in Muslim-controlled territories and the dispersal of the "citizenship" body made up mainly of Arab Muslims throughout the new territories. A flood of new adherents to the faith, who theoretically had equal rights with the Arab Muslims, also began to swell the ranks of the community. As a result, tensions arose due to the increasing autonomy of the provinces and provincial governors, and the difficulty of communications with the centre. Some provinces, like Egypt and Iraq were the main source of revenue for the state. Others, like Syria, had a significant weight in political and military terms due to its position as the frontier province facing the Byzantine Empire. The centralising tendency of the system which privileged the khalīfah and gave him supreme authority contrasted with the de facto autonomy of the provinces while the distance from the centre made it difficult to address grievances against governors or the centre.

The resulting tensions put unbearable pressure on the original model which depended on the active consent of a cohesive citizenship body with opportunities to communicate effectively, usually face to face and on a daily basis. It also depended on deference to the legitimate central authority. In the twelve years following the murder of ʿUmar by a disgruntled Persian ex-slave, the authority of the khalīfah and the cohesiveness of the citizenship body suffered serious erosion, while the line of communications faced virtual breakdown.

The instability which characterised the Madinah model cannot thus simply be attributed to its alleged utopian character, for this instability has been a characteristic of all pre-modern republican and democratic experiments from Rome and Athens to Italy's Renaissance republics. It has also been the fate of most modern democracies in the world until the final quarter of the last century.

It is intriguing to note here the astonishing parallel between the Roman republican experience and the Muslim caliphate at the moment of their collapse. The murder of Caesar by an alliance of convenience grouped around the ideal of protecting the republic from the threat of alleged monarchic ambitions mirrors ʿUthmān's murder by a similar alliance which raised the banner of restoring the pure caliphate and safeguarding it against the encroachment of semi-monarchical privilege of the pre-Islamic Quraysh elite. The role played by Octavius as Caesar's aggrieved nephew is mirrored by Muʿāwiyah's role as the caliph's avenger, and the propaganda used to mobilise support was also similar in its attempt to appropriate the very republican/ caliphate legitimacy it was proceeding to subvert and replace by a new imperial order. It was no surprise therefore that Muʿāwiyah's critics immediately labelled his system of rule "Caesarian."

There was also a sense in which the crisis in both instances, in fact, represented a clash between two "restoration" models, even as it also harkened back to an even earlier model, unnameable because it was the antithesis of the whole ethos of the republican system. While Brutus and his associates called for the restoration of the original republican model, and ʿUthmān's opponents had called for the restoration of the system established by Abū Bakr and ʿUmar, their opponents also held the banner for a pre-existing normative order against alleged usurpers. The Octavius/Marcus Antonius camp relied on the charisma of Caesar, a popular hero now depicted as wronged victim, while the Umayyad camp led by Muʿāwiyah defended ʿUthmān as the "wronged caliph" murdered by criminal usurpers. In both cases, the forces of the Caesarian/Umayyad camp had also been working from a position of relative advantage, since they had occupied entrenched positions within the republic, especially in the case of the Umayyads and their allies, who had occupied key positions of power during ʿUthmān's reign, and were fighting either to safeguard or regain those positions. In both cases, charisma or legitimacy claims also masked aristocratic interests that could only be served by a monarchical restoration or the conversion of aristocratic privilege into a monarchy.

The "Damascus Model"
An additional significant factor in the collapse of the caliphate model was the emergence of an alternative model of governance which offered the promise of stability. This model emerged from Damascus, the capital of the province of Syria. Damascus had been under the governorship of Muʿāwiyah, the son of Abū Sufyān, the acknowledged leader of Quraysh

and Muhammad's archenemy until the surrender of Makkah in 8/630. Later Abū Sufyān and his sons worked hard to atone for their long enmity to the Prophet and participated in military campaigns. Muʿāwiyah himself worked as a scribe for the Prophet, and his elder brother, Yazīd, became one of the commanders of the armies in Palestine and Syria during ʿUmar's reign. Muʿāwiyah's sister, Umm Ḥabībah, was an early convert to Islam and became one of the Prophet's wives.

Muʿāwiyah was appointed as governor of Damascus in the early days of ʿUmar's Caliphate, and proved such a competent governor that ʿUmar left him at this post throughout his reign. His domain was expanded by ʿUmar and later by ʿUthmān so that it comprised most of Greater Syria.[17] Like other governors, he successfully protected his borders against outside enemies, in his case the formidable Byzantine Empire which, unlike its Persian counterpart, was still alive and well. He also expanded those borders, and undertook some remarkable military exploits, being the first governor to build a fleet and conduct successful maritime expeditions, starting with the conquest of Cyprus which he undertook jointly with the governor of Egypt. Unlike most other governors, Muʿāwiyah succeeded in keeping his province stable and free of internal dissent. His soldiers were fanatically loyal to him and there was scarcely a complaint against his rule. This was a testament to his political and administrative skills, given the difficulties faced by other governors, notably those of Egypt, Yemen and Iraq. Interestingly, Muʿāwiyah's style of realpolitk and disregard for Puritanism (ʿUmar reprimanded him for his lavish lifestyle) hardly evoked the kind of criticism the lesser transgressions of his boss, the caliph ʿUthmān, had to endure.

Unlike the austere ʿUmar, Muʿāwiyah did not hesitate to use public finances judiciously to reward loyalty. His style thus contrasted fundamentally with the "ethical" model promoted by Abū Bakr and ʿUmar. He was not too strict in applying the laws and principles of the caliphate, whether in matters of enforcement and punishment, or in dispensing public funds, being careful not to antagonise important actors or sectors of the population, and keen to cultivate loyalty. Muʿāwiyah was also reputed for his consummate political and diplomatic skills and for his legendary forbearance.

The "Damascus model" was not a repressive or despotic one, and could not afford to be. For the governor, not being supreme ruler, could not afford to antagonise his subjects and run the risk of being removed from his post if complaints against him were to persist. Rather, Muʿāwiyah relied on applying the values of the tribal aristocratic system in which he was brought up. The tribal chief was no king, and could not impose his authority by force, but has to earn it through acts of generosity, compassion, wisdom, heroism and delicate negotiations. Muʿāwiyah had the required qualities and his control of the purse of a rich province meant that he could afford to be generous. His troops were also surprisingly disciplined and fiercely loyal. His model had thus based itself on astute leadership, administrative competence and a realistic (not to say Machiavellian) approach to politics. The main selling point of his model was its success, first and foremost, in achieving a stability and prosperity based on modest ethical demands.

The original caliphate model which the anti-ʿUthmān rebels sought to revive, had its own attractions, and a wider appeal as it was perceived to be a much fairer one which did not reward mainly those with power. It was also popular within a community which defined itself in ethical-religious terms, and it was seen to work, having generated for many prosperity, fairness and ethical fulfilment. However, attempts to revive the earlier model were not motivated exclusively by ethical considerations, but involved grievances by interested parties. The battle lines inevitably became drawn across tribal, clan and regional lines. New identities began to emerge: Iraqis and Egyptian versus Syrians, Yemenis (southern Arabs) versus Mudaris (northern Arabs), Kufah against Basra, and Arabs vs. non-Arabs, etc.

Of equal significance has been the tendency of the "ethical party" (or the "religious party" as it is often called) to undermine itself by endemic indiscipline. Those claiming to stand up for the "pure" model deferred only to their own conscience and accepted no earthly authority. This made for poor discipline and endless fragmentation. Leading figures would endorse one policy one day and condemn it the following day, and there appeared to be as many factions as there were strongly held political opinions. This has proved fatal in the final analysis, given the relative discipline of the other side. The "ethical" side, in anticipation of later "Islamist" trends, has shown a readiness to resort to violence at the slightest pretext, given its self-righteous pretensions and the moral assurance which made proponents of this vision ready to sacrifice life and limb for the cause.

The fact that many were in the "ethical party" for less than ethical reasons also made it easier for Muʿāwiyah to woo many leaders by making them offers they could not refuse. The ethical model also found it difficult to rally its ostensible supporters to defend it due to the paradoxical requirement that to join this party one has to deliberately sacrifice one's own interests. To join the ʿAlī camp meant to impose on oneself an austere lifestyle and to accept a system that did not reward loyalty. ʿAlī made a point of offering no favours to relatives or loyal supporters, and of trying to be fair even to those who declared war against him. This did not endear him to his loyal followers and did not win the loyalty of his sworn enemies who accepted his largesse and used it against him.

The "Damascus Model" by contrast, made fewer demands, offered more rewards and was thus inherently more stable precisely because of this. It recommended itself for its practicality, and because it had fewer self-imposed restrictions on engaging in "normal" politics which meant recognising existing balances of power, and giving the influential elites what was "due to them."

The Struggle for Restoration

Nevertheless, few people accepted the new order based on the "Damascus Model" as fully legitimate, even after ʿAlī's elder son and leader of his camp, al-Ḥasan, formally accepted Muʿāwiyah's rule in a deal which would have allowed al-Ḥasan to succeed as ruler. Al-Ḥasan, however, died shortly after this deal was concluded, and this led to further fragmentation in the ʿAlid camp and the "religious party" as a whole. "Islamist" groups and entrepreneurs then proliferated with rival projects to revive and restore the cherished caliphate model. The first of these was the ultra-radical and extremely violent *khawārij*, who continued to wage their violent campaigns with singular and fanatical determination for centuries, but remained a largely fringe movement. A more mainstream movement began to coalesce around the figure of al-Ḥusayn, al-Ḥasan's younger brother.

But when al-Ḥusayn was killed among many of his close followers and members of his immediate family as he was making his way to Iraq to join prospective supporters, his martyrdom (in 61/680) became the founding event of Shiite Islam. And it did not take long for a related "Islamist" movement to emerge in Iraq. Led by Mukhtār al-Thaqafī, the so-called *al-tawwābūn* (the Penitents) movement made it its goal to avenge the death of al-Ḥusayn and atone for having let him down after promising support. The result was the establishment of the first Shiite State in Iraq in 66/685. It lasted for only two years and turned out to have more affinities with its rival Umayyad power state than the presumed model it sought to emulate. The mantle of revivalism was then taken over by ʿAbd Allāh ibn al-Zubayr, who had barricaded himself in Makkah towards the end of Yazīd's reign, and survived a campaign to dislodge him from there in 63/683. He later extended his rule to Iraq and Egypt and followed more faithfully the caliphate model, advertising its limitations in even starker light. His rule collapsed a decade later when he was killed after a long siege of Makkah in 73/692, allowing the Marwanid offshoot of the Umayyad dynasty to consolidate its rule.

Ironically, even supporters of the Umayyad dynasty continued to acknowledge the dream of restoration. However, their interpretations of the model and their explanations for its demise differed. Debates over why the model seemed to face problems date back to the time of ʿUthmān, who explained the rebelliousness he faced as having been due to his more lenient methods, in contrast to what he said was ʿUmar's harsh approach. Later interpretations focused on the decline of the standards of the community as a whole, a view given a stark exposition by the Umayyad caliph ʿAbd al-Mālik, who told a congregation in Madinah in 75/695: "You demand from us the standards of the early *muhājirūn* (migrants), but you do not stick to them yourselves; you order us to fear God but forget to do so yourselves. I swear by God that if I ever hear someone say to me 'Fear God!' after today, I will have him beheaded!" (Ibn al-Athīr, *al-Kāmil*, classic Islamic history book written circa 1231).

Ziyād, Muʿāwiyah's governor in Iraq, combined rebukes to the people, who he accused of falling short of the ideal Muslim standards, with brutal repression, claiming that his policy of "firmness without excessive violence, and leniency without weakness," was the essence of the caliphate approach. His many victims did not concur, though.

Countless other revivalist movements continued to emerge, with varying degrees of succuss. However, those which succeeded in taking power found themselves inevitably reproducing the Umayyad model rather than the much vaunted "righteous caliphate" model. This was the case with the Abbasid revolution (132/750) and the Fatimid movement which established its own state in North Africa (297/909), and many subsequent uprisings and movements, including those which had established the present day Moroccan and Saudi states.

The Model Re-Evaluated

ʿUmar II's experiment appears unique in having succeeded effortlessly in restoring the original model, albeit briefly and in a transient manner, with no bloodshed, and without the expected transformation of the community into a "more virtuous" entity. He rebuked one governor who tried to sell him the old idea that the people's standards had deteriorated and could only "respond to the sword and the whip." "You lie!" ʿUmar II wrote back. "They respond to justice. So institute justice among them."

ʿUmar II did indeed adopt harsh methods, but it was harshness on himself, his family and the remnants of his Umayyad clan. His moral stature and his resulting popularity ensured from then on that his authority remained beyond serious challenge. However, his success, like the failures of his predecessors and many who came after, could not conceal the serious problems facing the model he had aspired to restore. The model was based on a number of assumptions and demands, such as extreme austerity at the top, and the abstinence from using public funds to bolster one's authority, demands that were unrealistic and unsustainable over the long term. A ruler who is sustained on a starvation diet and had to juggle his personal finances daily while watching his family suffer in silence may not be able to dedicate sufficient energy to the affairs of the state which were becoming more and more complex and demanding. More important, a ruler who refuses to use public funds to reward loyalty or violence to punish opponents, surrenders most of what state power is all about. Even though ʿUmar II did not stick to the interdiction against having bodyguards which, together with the ethos of unrestricted access, had resulted in three out of the four first caliphs being murdered, he still maintained a marked aversion to political violence and to playing the game of power politics. In the process, he had created many powerful enemies and limited his repertoire of political tools.

ʿUmar II was not totally unaware of the exigencies of power politics, however. When the Umayyad princes refused to heed his demand to voluntarily restore to the public treasury or rightful owners properties they had illegally acquired, he held back from enforcing his order, fearing, as he said, that they would "mobilise against me the very people to whom I seek to restore these rights."[18] He also rejected his son's insistence on taking drastic measures to dispossess the princes, arguing that he wanted to avoid bloodshed. "By God I would prefer to see the end of the world before seeing a single bottle of blood shed on my account."[19] Like all successful idealists, ʿUmar II was acutely aware of the demands of reality, but only just.

The serious restrictions on the use of public funds to accommodate the dictates of power politics put severe constraints on the system and on state power. The assumption here was of a "purely ethical" authority which one had to obey regardless of the impact on self-interest. While there were many who were prepared to comply with such severe demands (provided those at the top set the example, of course), these demands were unsustainable in the long term. It is ironic that while ʿUmar II's policies were beneficial to the majority, leading to unprecedented widespread prosperity, this did not translate into effective popular support, since the policies were not specifically targeted to create an effective constituency or attract powerful supporters. One illustration of the problem was the way poets were treated under the regimes of ʿUmar I and ʿUmar II, who both argued that Islamic rules on public expenditure made no allowance for rewarding poets. Those poets who frequented the court hoping for remuneration were turned away empty handed, or given small payments as "wayfarers." By contrast, the Umayyad court before and after ʿUmar II (and the Abbassids who replaced it) rewarded poets generously. This did not only contribute to the flourishing of culture, but became also an important instrument of state power, since poets at that time played the role of today's media, advertising the ruler's (mostly imaginary) virtues, publicising his policies and shoring up the system's legitimacy.[20] Similarly, and following his namesake, ʿUmar II neglected the imperative of cultivating and rewarding influential leaders, such as tribal chiefs and ambitious military commanders. This caused these to drift to the other camp and contributed to the collapse of the system when it was challenged, as had been the case with ʿAlī.

The Crisis of Revivalism
While ʿUmar II's experiment fired the imagination of "revivalists" ever

since, the challenges of the time also pointed to the limitations of revivalism (or "Islamism") and the problems faced by movements which based themselves purely on the alleged moral requirements of the lost system. This was evident from the case of the *khawārij*, the hardliners within ʿAlī's camp, who were arguably among the earliest bearers of this banner. The fervent followers of this trend, who also happened to come mainly from marginal Bedouin tribes with no large stake in the power politics dominated by Quraysh and other leading tribes, saw the conflict between the two opposing camps as one between good and evil, with no room for compromise. While ʿAlī agreed in principle with this, he was realistic enough (a paradox of all "idealistic" tendencies) to accept a proposal for arbitration in the conflict. When negotiated settlement agreed fell apart, the incensed hardliners accused ʿAlī of betrayal, and argued that violence was the only way to deal with their opponents, whom they accused of apostasy.

The extremism of these groups proved self-destructive, especially since they adopted the same violent approach with regards to intragroup schisms. As a result, the groups (there were many to start with) splintered into myriad warring factions which nevertheless remained a serious threat to authorities for many centuries. However, what their career demonstrated was that the ideological alternative they presented was incapable of resolving intra-group conflict, let alone forming the basis of a political system capable of society-wide conflict resolution.

The other major "Islamist" groups which emerged in the early Islamic period with a revivalist agenda was the Shia. Originally a political faction (the shia, or party, of ʿAlī), it began to coalesce into a coherent group following the martyrdom of Ḥusayn, achieving an early minor success with the institution of a mini state in Iraq as mentioned above. Later, it became the centre of a broader "Hashimite" (in reference to the Prophet's clan of Hāshim) coalition which succeed in 132/750 in toppling the Umayyad dynasty. However, the Abbasid branch of the coalition decided to monopolise power, sending the ʿAlid branch into opposition again. Through the trials and travails which followed, a distinct Shiite tendency emerged, which in turn splintered into three major branches, the Ismailis, the Twelvers and the Zaidis. The Ismailis were the most successful in the short term, capturing the state in North Africa and Egypt (where they were known as the Fatimids) from 297/909, while other Shiite states rose in Persia, Iraq and Syria during the fourth century. However, the trend of Shiite ascendancy declined sharply afterwards, and Ismailism survives today only in small enclaves in Pakistan, Southern Arabia and East Africa. The Zaidis achieved more long-term, if regionally limited, political success, capturing the state in North Yemen and achieving dominance there for the best part of the last millennium, until modernity caught up with them in the shape of a secular military coup in 1962. The Twelvers are the most ideologically successful, to the extent that today when the term Shia is used it generally refers to this sect.

The Twelvers follow a line of imams that was interrupted in the 4th/9th century with the disappearance of the twelfth imam of that line, and had since evolved the rather novel belief that the going into hiding of that imam, regarded in the beginning as a prudent political precaution, was in fact a cosmic act of mystical "occultation." The imam survives in metaphysical space, waiting to appear as the *Mahdī*, the Guided One, when the time is right to restore justice and righteousness.

By transforming the task of the restoration into a *metaphysical* one of which Heaven alone could take charge, the Twelvers appeared to have resolved the *political* problem conceptually, and became a quietist movement engaged mainly in the ideological elaboration of the doctrine and the management of the private and communal affairs of its members. This universe of detachment which was momentarily disturbed by the rise of fourth century Shiite states, was again challenged by the rise of the Safavid Shiite State in Iran in the 16th century. The sect reached a modus vivendi with that state without radically transforming its ideology. However, it was convulsed again by the restatement of the doctrine of *wilāyah al-faqīh*, originally a device to regulate the internal affairs of the community in a "hostile" environment, and its transformation into a political ideology by Ayatollah Khomeini in the 1970's. This transformed the sect again into a revivalist movement committed to activism in the here and now. But that is another story.

Many other revivalist movements emerged, most were localised in space and short lived in time, with most being crushed in their early stages. In addition, sufi revivalist movements, concerned mainly with personal spiritual edification of followers, proliferated all over the Muslim world and are today followed by hundreds of millions. Some of these experienced a metamorphosis into active political revivalist movements, but the majority remained largely apolitical or only partially politicised.

What is remarkable about all these movements was that, when successful, the states which they established were not different in style or ethos from the traditional states they tried to replace. They adopted the same power politics tactics and repressive measures, espoused the hereditary principle, and showed no resemblance to the early model they purported to revive. Their modern heirs, whether the Saudi or Moroccan monarchies, the Khomeinist republic or the Sudanese one, could also hardly be distinguished from their secular rivals. This fact, coupled with the disastrous consequences of many failed "idealist" revolutions, had led Muslim jurists and other thinkers to draw early conclusions against regarding the matters in stark contrasts of black and white, and accept that one has to make many compromises in order to keep the peace.

The Khaldūnian Prognosis

It was left to the fourteenth century historian, politician and thinker, Ibn Khaldūn (1332–1406), to point out the obvious: there is a fundamental problem with the vision itself, rather than its attempted implementations. Ibn Khaldūn's argument outlined the now familiar premise of modern social science: values are one thing, reality another, or as Hume would say, "ought to be" does not necessarily mean "is." Zealous Islamic reformers, Ibn Khaldūn argued, have been fixated on the "ought" part and thoroughly oblivious to the "is" question. There is an internal logic to human societies in general, and political power in particular, that was independent of religious beliefs and moral aspirations.

Ibn Khaldūn reiterated the traditional view on the deterioration of the caliphate into monarchy which took place in three stages. In the first stage, the two institutions were combined, with the new monarchs striving to also fulfil some of the spiritual functions of the caliphate. Later, the caliphate acquired a purely symbolic role, standing beside the monarchy and providing it with some legitimacy. Finally, the system relapsed into pure despotism without any vestiges of spiritual or moral authority.[21]

The error of those attempting to reverse this process, he argued, was that they remained oblivious to the laws of governing power. Those guilty include "those rebels both from jurists and from the masses who rise up to redress wrongs." Their repeated failure is no accident.

> These leaders soon gather a large following among the rabble and the mob;
> and yet they expose themselves to destruction, till most of them are in fact
> destroyed and get no thanks but only blame, for God ... demanded only that
> men should seek to redress those evils which lie in their power .... For the
> power of kings and dynasties is great and deep-rooted and can be shaken and
> overthrown only by a vigorous attack, supported by the solidarity of a tribe
> or clan, as we said before.[22]

And this takes us to the heart of Ibn Khaldūn's theory of power which
anticipates the Hobbesian derivation of power from social relations and
individual inclinations. The premises are as follows: a) individuals are
dependent on each other for survival, since none can subsist on his own;
b) individuals are naturally aggressive and self-seeking, so this interdependence can lead to conflict unless a restraining authority keeps the
peace among people and enables continued civilised interaction; c) this
authority needs a social force to underpin it, and such a force is found
naturally in the cohesion provided kin solidarity "ʿaṣabiyyah;" d)
authority is initially established within the kin group by a senior figure
who is acknowledged as leader, but commands no coercive powers over
his followers. However, he soon moves to assert his authority through
the mustering of independent resources, and thus becomes a king whose
authority is underpinned by coercive power.

Thus kingship, or statehood, emerges naturally from within the evolving kin relationship. Kin solidarity could be, and inevitably is, also used
to establish authority over other groups, usually through building a
broad coalition of tribes and clans around a dominant one, and using
the combined force to subjugate other groups and control territory.
However, no sooner has the state been thus established, then the
supreme ruler begins to dispense with clan solidarity, using the resources
of the state to rule through the recruitment of mercenaries, slaves and
bureaucrats. The state, so to speak, asserts its autonomy. However, the
resulting weakening of clan solidarity, combined with the rising costs of
maintaining despotic power, ushers in inevitable decline and collapse,
making the ageing state ripe for a takeover by a fresh coalition of clans
not yet corrupted by power, or even from a marginal branch from the
same ruling clan.

Reformers and other aspiring politicians have to be mindful of these
laws of social action, and need to seek sources of power where they

naturally lie. It is no use championing a noble cause if one cannot deliver the striking capability needed to carry it to victory. A reformer has thus to enlist the support of a powerful solidarity group for this purpose. God selects prophets only from the leading clans within strong tribes.

There are a number of flaws in Ibn Khaldūn's pioneering theory, in particular in the apparent contradiction between his theses about how clan solidarity is indispensable for state formation and maintenance, and his contention that the first thing the state did when established was to detach itself from the clan. This indicates that the state does indeed have resources to fall back on independent of the clan. However, the main point he was trying to make was that politics does have its own logic which was internal to it, and that the dynamics of power are related to actual social processes which are independent from the moral sources of legitimacy that are needed to underpin them. And this principle remains central to modern political and social theory, and part of its problem.

Revisiting the Khaldūnian Paradox

The tensions inherent in what I have elsewhere[23] called "the Khaldūnian paradox" (seeking to legitimise politics according to its own logic, or locating "rationality" in "reality" *à la* Hegel), are at the heart of most deliberations in modern political theory. The line of thought inaugurated by Ibn Khaldūn was later formulated and elaborated upon (independently, it would seem) by a long line of thinkers who laid the foundations of modern political thought in the West. The first of these was the much maligned Niccolo Machiavelli (1469–1527) who argued that politics has a logic (and an ethics) of its own. In order to maintain order in the state, rulers need not observe values such as honour, truthfulness, mercy etc., although it pays to appear to do so.[24] The successful ruler thus should strike terror in his enemies, put up a façade of virtue, attempt to do good, but not shrink from doing evil if need be. He should also think nothing of breaking his word if that proves to his advantage. "If all men were good, this precept would not be good; but because men are wretched creatures who would not keep their word to you, you need not keep your word to them."[25]

Machiavelli's reasoning is thus very straightforward, expressing the general belief that politics is a dirty business, and those who wish to immerse themselves in it must wear the appropriate moral dirty suit, and act as half beast and half man. But if Machiavelli argued that men tended to behave in immoral ways, Thomas Hobbes (1588–1679) believed that morality itself has no meaning in a pre-state society. Starting from premises similar to Ibn Khaldūn's about the equality of men in physical endowments and their natural aggressiveness, he concludes that in pre-state existence men lived in a state of war "of every man, against every man."[26] Under those conditions, every individual is perfectly entitled to use any means at his disposal to defend himself and his interests. However, this unrestrained conflict would disadvantage all, preclude civilised existence, and cause men live in "continual fear, and danger of violent death; and the life of man, solitary, poor, nasty, brutish, and short."[27]

Trying to take refuge in collective security by joining a Khaldūnian-type clan for protection is not going to resolve this problem, for the same dangers faced by individuals would be faced by larger groups, and may even be greatly magnified. The only way to exit from this unhappy situation was for men to confer "all their power and strength upon one Man, or upon an Assembly of men, that may reduce all their Wills, by plurality of voices, unto one Will." This would mean the creation of the state as the "*Mortal God* to which we owe under the *Immortal God*, our peace and deference."[28] And with any god, this creature cannot be subjected again to the questioning of its actions, whether on moral or other grounds, since any such questioning would defeat the purpose of erecting an entity that should remain above the very disputes it is charged with resolving.

The state, therefore, is the natural growth of man's worst qualities, and is necessitated by them. And since men are by nature self-seeking brutes prone to evil, the state must be permitted to sink to their level when necessary in order to protect them from themselves. In order to do good and fulfil its functions of safeguarding civilised life, the state must remain above, and act outside, those values. Effective governance is largely an exercise of absolute power which cannot be questioned, divided or ceded, and the sovereign determines rules as well as values.[29] Idealist perceptions, such as the erroneous beliefs that men can have independent moral judgement values, are a dangerous "disease" which threatens the state, and must thus be combated. A similar stern stance must be taken against unhelpful religious notions, such as the Christian admonition to turn the other cheek which are useless, even counterproductive, in the business of state building and maintenance. So is the misguided search for inspiration from ancient models of republicanism and democracy, or even from different neighbouring constitutional orders.[30]

The Machiavelli/Hobbes (one should add Ibn-Khaldūn) "discovery" of *realpolitik* or *Machtpolitik* as the guiding principle of social life is seen as the defining moment of modern political thought, and it also marks the genesis of the modern secular state.[31] What these thinkers seemed to say is, in effect, that the rather unethical manipulations needed to gain and maintain supreme political power were not an aberration, but inherent in the very nature of politics. Politics is about safeguarding order in society, a task that could only be fulfilled by an agency which monopolised supreme authority, was subject to no other, and in particular had the sole power to deploy and use capabilities of violence superior to that of any actual or potential rival under its jurisdiction (or even outside it). How and by what means this is achieved may be interesting in itself, but the first task is to achieve it, for failure to do so would be catastrophic for society. Success in monopolising the capabilities of violence in a society is what matters, not its *legitimacy*. The latter was seen as incidental. For Ibn Khaldūn, what could be termed the "iron law" of power politics (that the basis of all power is *ʿaṣabiyyah*, or clan solidarity) appeared to be a regrettable fact of life inherent in human nature and its weakness. Machiavelli appeared to accept the logic of power without regret or enthusiasm, while Hobbes embraced it with vigour, arguing that regarding power as its own justification was the only rational and legitimate way to view things. Introducing extraneous ethical or religious considerations into the matter could only undermine the efficacy of power which would destroy it, given that the efficacy of political power was its *raison d'être*.

A number of modern theorists have provided variations on this theme. Charles Tilly argued that politics in general, and state making in particular, was not just amoral, but outright immoral. Tilly disputes the prevalent conception of the state as "the ultimate source of ethical authority,"[32] and thus society's first and last line of defence against crime, arguing instead that the modern state's function is more akin to racketeering in that most of the dangers it purports to protect against are of its own creation.[33] To attempt to distinguish the violence deployed by the state from that of more mundane racketeers by labelling state violence as "legitimate" may beg the question. For governments gain legitimacy less by securing the consent of the ruled than by obtaining the acquiescence of other governments. The international actors, concerned as they are with maintaining stability within the international system, tend to support those who command de facto superior capability of violence against those who command less.[34]

Marx and other theorists have restated the idea in radically novel terms, arguing that grand claims of states to uphold collective values and interests are no more than a camouflage for the naked self-interest of the privileged dominant class.[35] The only ethical state, Marx argued, was one which ceases to exist, since the state is a reflection of class divisions and class domination. This had caused Marx's Leninist heirs to deduce the conclusion that, since all states are instruments of class domination, the best among them was that which sought, through the dictatorship of the proletariat, to prepare for the ultimate abolition of all class divisions and consequently the withering away of the state as such.

Tilly's pessimistic characterisation of state building as essentially criminal is tempered by the realisation that this endeavour had developed its own internal and international dynamics, which "constrained the rulers themselves, making them vulnerable to courts, to assemblies, to withdrawal of credit, services and expertise."[36]

The stark realism inaugurated by Ibn Khaldūn, Machiavelli and Hobbes has been influential, even among those who condemned this realism, including such leading liberal theorists as Locke.[37] The Machiavellian/Hobbesian paradigm still survives at its starkest in the realist schools of International Relations theory, from Morganthau onwards, and in the realist inclinations of US policy makers, who nevertheless vehemently deny any charges of Machiavellianism.[38]

As mentioned above, it has been argued that the problem is inherent in the state itself, and in "the problematic character of any attempt to conduct politics honestly and rationally."[39] Politics is by nature the realm of the expedient, an arena of compromises. The insistence on "moral purity as the exclusive guide for political action" inevitably collapses into fanaticism, as was demonstrated by the French revolutionaries' "quest for a virtuous republic [which became] inseparable from the use of terror against its enemies."[40] This attitude could also "encourage the virtuous to abandon public life [and cede] the field to the vicious." But even more seriously, it could promote the notion that "the judgment that this disengagement is necessary because a life of integrity is impossible in this corrupted world."

> When integrity is viewed as purity, anything less may be condemned as unpardonable. And if this standard is in fact too high, we may be led to condemn behavior that is not only tolerable but necessary. The result is not only ceding the field to the vicious but weakening the good ones who remain in the fray. Crucial moral distinctions are obliterated when all who are engaged in the world are condemned as equally corrupt.[41]

This point which is a subtle variation on the Khaldūnian-Hobbesian thesis of the irreducible autonomy of politics has been given a recent postmodern spin by Brian Latour, who similarly argues that the current disillusionment with politics has its roots in a fundamental misconception of politics. Thinkers since Socrates have taken it on themselves to disparage politics and judge "political talk" by standards external to it, ones that originate in, and are more suitable for, other discourses. It is consequently found to lack truth, transparency, honesty and immediacy.[42] This, however, is a fundamental error, since political discourse has to be judged on its own terms as the art on which the very existence of political groups depends.

> Political truth appears to be untruthful only in contrast with other forms of truth. In and for itself it discriminates truth from falsehood with stupefying precision. It is not indifferent to truth, as it is unjustly accused of being; it simply differs from all other regimes in its judgement of truth. What then is its touchstone, its litmus test? It aims to *allow to exist* that which would not exist without it: the public as a temporarily defined totality. Either some means have been provided to trace a group into existence, and the talk has been truthful; or no group has been traced, and it is vain that people have talked.[43]

The Democratic Solution

Liberal democracy emerged as one possible solution to the perceived problem of the amorality of politics, a device whereby the acknowledged autonomy of politics would not make it necessary an "ethics-free zone." Post-Hobbesian theory and practise had started from the same premises of pre-state lawlessness and suspicion of all human beings, but did not spare the state from its condemnation. The ideas of Hobbes, which represented "a point of transition between a commitment to the absolutist state and the struggle of liberalism against tyranny," offered "at once a profoundly liberal and illiberal view."[44] They provoked a debate which departed from the same Hobbesian premises of pessimism about human nature, and argued for extending the suspicion of man to state power holders, who they suspected were equally human, and thus equally bent on the use of violence and crooked means to further their own private ends. An individual would not be wise, as Locke countered, to seek protection from foxes in the embrace of a lion. The state must thus be constrained by subjecting it to constitutional limits on its power and making it accountable to the people through their representatives.[45]

In time, this debate led to what appeared to be a complete reversal of the Hobbesian theses about the state being the fountain of virtue and pre-state society being the source of many dangers. Through progressive contributions from Montesquieu, de Tocqueville, Mill, Rousseau, Paine, etc., the argument was developed that self-organising society is in fact a repository of many virtues. The state's function is thus to protect and safeguard these self-organising capabilities. Its role is to maximise individual freedoms, and thus its powers should be restricted and limited to the achievement of this goal. After a detour inspired by Marx's restatement of the Hobbesian argument in a new guise, and by practical exigencies of stabilising capitalist democracies through welfarist policies and Keynesian interventionist measures, the pendulum of modern democratic thought have now shifted back to arguing for the capacities of civil society for self-management and for playing a pivotal role in the political and moral regeneration of the political community.

Thinkers such as Locke, Montesquieu, Tocqueville, Mill, Marx and others based their writings on observing modern political developments signalling the transition from the absolutist state to the bourgeois, and were responding to them. The dialectic involved culminated in some fine tuning of theory in order to reduce the Hobbesian gap between autonomous politics and social values. This was done by minimising demands on, and scope of, state power. The state should not dictate religious values (it has become increasingly secular and somewhat culturally neutral), it should intervene minimally in personal affairs or the economy, it should be subject to the rule of law and remain accountable to the people through their representatives and through such surveillance devices as the media.

According to some schools of liberal thought, assuming the worst about human beings may be just the way to get the best out of them. If we submit that man is a self-obsessed, greedy, pleasure-seeking and aggressive creature, why not harness these very qualities to the good of society through the right form of government and social organisation? Utilitarianism and laissez faire economics inspired by Adam Smith tried to do just that: harness greed and self-seeking inclinations of man to the good of the whole through regulated and state-policed competition. This ingenious formula worked out wonders for the lucky few in the short term, and for many more subsequently, even if the price has often been rather high for the losers in this high stake game.

The features which came to define democracy as a system of government and a body of thought emerged from all these considerations. On the face of it, defining democracy should be a pretty straightforward affair. As one early leading democrat, the famous Athenian fifth century BC leader, Pericles, succinctly put it: "Our constitution is called a democracy because power is in the hands not of a minority but of the whole people."[46] Put simply thus a democracy is a system of government in which all members of the community are permitted to participate in public decision making in some manner found acceptable to all or to the majority. It is the rule of the people (or the many), in contrast to rival forms, such as monarchy (rule by one person), oligarchy (rule by the few), plutocracy (rule by the rich) or anarchy (rule by no one). The core idea behind it (that of "a political system in which the members regard one another as political equals, are collectively sovereign, and possessing all the capacities, resources and institutions to govern themselves"[47] also appears to be simple enough.

This, of course, says little about the content or direction of such system, a matter of concern for the system's early and many critics, who included such prominent figures as Plato and Aristotle. For these early critics, democracy had a connotation of "mob rule." The "people" referred to the commoners, even the "rabble," and there was no telling where the whims of the masses could lead the polity. However, from very early on, democracy was associated with a constellation of substantive values, chief among which were liberty, equality, tolerance, public-spiritedness, respect for laws, direct participation and popular sovereignty. Liberty or autonomy is seen by Aristotle as central to the democratic idea, where the ideal is "'not being ruled,' not by anyone at all if possible, or at least only in alternation."[48] This ideal of self-government is closely related to tolerance. Again as Aristotle puts it, a central idea of democracy is "to live as you like" which is the essence of being free, "since its opposite, living not as you like, is the function of one being enslaved." Pericles also emphasises tolerance as a central quality (and virtue) of the Athenian democracy, where people do not "get into a state" with one's next door neighbour "if he enjoys himself in his own way," and do not even "give him the kind of black looks which ... hurt people's feelings."[49]

The concept did undergo significant changes in the intervening centuries, but the general idea remains the same. According to one contemporary author, democracy is

> a mode of decision-making about collectively binding rules and policies over which the people exercise control, and the most democratic arrangement [is] that where all members of the collectivity enjoy effective equal rights to take part in such decision-making directly – one, that is to say which realises to the greatest conceivable degree the principles of popular control and equality in its exercise.[50]

Democracy as a concept is, therefore, "uncontestable," as it is to be contrasted to systems where people are totally or partially excluded from political participation. In this sense, disputes about the meaning of democracy "which purport to be conceptual disagreements are really disputes about how much democracy is either desirable or practicable."[51]

It can be a matter of argument whether values such as civic virtue, obedience to the law and to those put in authority, tolerance and liberty are intrinsic to the concept of democracy. Equality certainly appears to be, since it is of the essence of democratic rule to limit privileges that are not based on merit. Liberty is also essential, but as Pericles points out, so is obedience to public authority and the law. While the ideal of democracy is maximum freedom and autonomy, the very concept of rule involves limits on freedoms. On the other hand, the principle of tolerance involves self-imposed limits and restraints on even such spontaneous reactions as showing distaste to other people's private life-styles.

ABDELWAHAB EL-AFFENDI

In its modern manifestation, democracy has come to be closely associated with two distinct principles, constitutionalism and liberalism. The dominant model of "liberal representative democracy" is centred around "a cluster of rules and institutions permitting the broadest participation of the majority of citizens in the selection of representatives who alone can make political decisions, that is, decisions affecting the whole community."[52] This cluster includes elected government; free and fair elections in which every citizen's vote has an equal weight; a suffrage which embraces all citizens irrespective of distinctions of race, religion, class, sex and so on; freedom of conscience, information and expression on all public matters broadly defined; the right of all adults to oppose their government and stand for office; and associational autonomy – the right to form independent associations including social movements, interest groups and political parties.

Conceived as "a way of containing the powers of the state and of mediating among competing political projects," democracy manages these tasks by holding out "the possibility of the entrenchment of a principle of legitimacy based on the one hand, on the political involvement of each and all and, on the other, on a process of decision-making which can mediate differences and distill (by virtue of its adherence to this process) acceptable outcomes."[53] In this regard, democracy can be viewed both as incorporating constitutionalism and the self-imposed limits on the will of the majority, and also as a mechanism for peaceful conflict-resolution between competing interests and visions.

However, both constitutionalism and liberalism are distinct principles from, and at times contradictory to, democracy. Liberalism could and did exist without democracy, while constitutionalism could be, and has been, used to curb democracy. American constitution makers in particular had used complex constitutional curbs on democratic rights (indirect elections of the president and senate, special role for the Supreme Court, etc.) in order to guard against the "tyranny of the majority" as much as to guard against the tyranny of the few.[54]

In contrast to constitutionalism, which is pessimistic about human nature and seeks to limit government and access to power, democracy is based on an optimistic view of the rationality and the benevolence of the masses.[55] Not only this, but democrats are also optimistic about the essentially beneficial outcome of the blind processes of popular choice in the same way as liberal economists believe in the ultimate benevolence and consummate efficiency of the market. One reason for the popularity of the concept is the connotation that democratic systems conform to the magical formula of safeguarding the interests and wishes of the majority while satisfying the basic rights of all. It is this claim that democracy has something for everyone which underlines its normative power. Any definition of democracy must be able to capture this fundamental aspect of the concept: it is a system endowed with a mysterious self-corrective capability which also translates into stability.

Democratic politics claims to resolve the central ethical question of reconciling pubic authority with individual autonomy. The corresponding Muslim political ideal of autonomy expresses itself in the concept of a "nomocracy," a polity where only the law is supreme. For 'Umar I, the state tended to disappear as the ruler dissolves himself into the law, turning into a walking conscience for the community. The ruler opts to fall silent, leaving only the law and conscience to speak. Here, we have what Latour describes as complete autonomy, (the very ideal that Hoffman says is unattainable):

> 'What you are telling me to do is what I would have liked to do' ... the expression of obedience; 'What you are saying is what I would have said if I had spoken' ... the expression of representation; and 'So I do only what I wish and I am free' ... autonomy.[56]

It has been argued by some that the ideal of complete autonomy cannot be reconciled with the function of the state which "cannot escape being an instrument of domination."[57] Failure to recognise these limitations on political action, and the fanatical pursuit of ideals in politics, could be counterproductive and do more damage than good, it has been argued. The best one can do is to engage in exercises of damage limitation and compromises, the best example of which is the practise of modern democratic politics.

In any case, the more prevalent Islamic conception of the state as "guardian" tends to do away completely with autonomy. In Khomeini, this formula is turned on its head: the ruler/religious leader towers so imposingly over the community that he ends up eclipsing the community, the law and conscience. The state becomes a substitute for the (absent) conscience, like *Pinocchio's* Gemini Cricket.

Achieving the Democratic Compromise

But if the state's defining characteristic is violence and coercion, and its very rationale, the *rasion d'etat*, it is to be recalled, rests ultimately on a mistrust of the totally free society, the state of nature in which men are free to do what they liked, and if politics is the realm of the amoral, then how can democracy's apparent trust in civil society be justified? How can this circle be squared? As the ultimate arbiter in civil conflicts, the state has to be able to say: here discussion and dialogue end, and coercion begins. And if no such authority is acknowledged to have the right to resolve disputes in this ultimate case, then we have civil wars, as America did in 1861, and many other countries before or since.

On the other hand, democratic systems are deemed to be unique for being "open systems," where parties are allowed to compete freely and the outcome of such competition has to remain uncertain. As Przeworski argues, democratisation "is a process of subjecting all interests to competition, of institutionalizing uncertainty." In contrast to authoritarianism, which is marked by the existence of "some power apparatus capable of overturning the outcomes of the institutionalised political process," the "essential feature of democracy ... is referential uncertainty: in democracy outcomes of the political process are to some extent indeterminate with regard to positions which participants occupy in all social relations."[58] However, this uncertainty has its limits. For unless key actors are guaranteed respect for their vital interests, each party concerned will be "better off seeking a full realisation of its interests," i.e., seek to impose its will. As a result, "the outcome will not be democracy but either a continuation of the old dictatorship or the establishment of a new one." Consequently, democracy only becomes possible "when the relevant political forces can find institutions that could provide reasonable guarantees that their interests would not be affected in a highly adverse manner in the course of democratic competition."[59]

This is a paradoxical aspect of democracy which "seeks to institutionalize uncertainty in one subset of political roles and policy arenas, while institutionalizing certainty in others,"[60] and it is one reason why the concept of democracy is such a contested one.

However, proponents of democracy are also acutely aware that democratic systems had been notoriously unstable and short-lived, both in pre-modern times as well as in the modern era. Hence the preoccupation with safeguarding or "consolidating" democracies. Past democratic systems exhibited a tendency to collapse very quickly into despotism or chaos, a feature which critics since Plato regarded as an inherent one. The reasons for this related first to the absence of international guarantees, and second to the inability to contain violence as a factor in politics. Democracies were most of the time vulnerable to predatory neighbouring states and empires. Democratic city-states tended to lose their democratic systems when they expanded into empires or when incorporated into ones. In addition, since all members of the political community in the ancient democracies used to bear arms, disputes often degenerated into violent conflict which brought the system down by favouring generals as opposed to politicians.

Democracy has thus to be seen as a system which has a twin foundation: an ideal-typical image of a system of perfect harmony in society which recognises and guarantees rights and values, and a realistic component which seeks to construct a sustainable system of governance which makes concessions to human weaknesses and accommodates the realities of power. Unlike rival systems which also accommodated the realities of power politics, democracy aspired to a normatively defensible compromise, one which did not completely neglect the values of equality and individual liberty, even if it did not completely conform to them. The democratic compromise seeks to accommodate the values as well as the interests of the relevant (usually powerful) parties, so that no one feels unduly aggrieved or completely excluded. The principle of "bounded uncertainty" also provides the indispensable predictability, as all democratic systems are based on written or unwritten constitutions limiting the range of possible outcomes within acceptable limits.

Democratic thought and practise achieved success in stabilising and sustaining the new systems by alternating between pessimism about human nature (especially when the human beings in question were in power) and optimism and trust in man (especially when out of power). This led to a variety of complex systems of safeguards and precautions against abuse of power, as well as safeguards against chaos and or system collapse. In polities where democracy was won in a gradual struggle against monarchies, the continued existence of the monarchy acted as a stabilising factor. Where monarchies were done away with, such as in France and America, the monarchy had to be restored at some point, or complex safeguards incorporated in constitutions, making it very difficult for even a majority to change the rules of the game at will.[61]

It can thus be concluded that it is not uncharacteristic for democratic systems, especially in their early stages, to require "extra-democratic" stabilizers. However, like organ transplants for ailing bodies, these components cannot be completely external, and have ultimately to be incorporated seamlessly into the body politics. A "foreign" component can only be temporary and transient in this regard. Constitutionalism, as mentioned above, makes it possible to come up with devices to provide such stabilizers.

Conclusion

One can argue that the dilemma of Islamic revivalism is, on one side, related to its long history of chasing the ideal of an elusive ethical model, coupled with the belief in the miraculous powers of "righteous" leadership. The crisis does not relate merely to the taxing attempt to emulate a highly ethical model, but to the inherent instability of that model which itself suffered from numerous inner contradictions.

The instability of the "ethical model" of the Madinah State was caused in part by the unrealistic demands it put on leaders and followers. But it also needs to be seen in the wider context of the challenges facing pre-modern "republican" models of government, in particular city states during a period of fast expansion. The Muslim experience was complicated by the fact that, unlike Athens or Rome, the central authority had no control over citizenship rights. While in those earlier city states, citizenship devolved only on the original inhabitants of the city-state and those granted it by the authorities, in the Muslim state any person who embraced Islam became, theoretically at least, instantly a citizen with full rights. Thus the geographical expansion of the state territory was accompanied here by an explosion in the number of citizens (from myriad cultural and ethnic backgrounds) with claims on the state. The administration that had to deal with all these problems simultaneously simply did not have the institutions to do it.

The problems faced by such systems invite the rise of political entrepreneurs who find it opportune to step into the resulting vacuum which demands the combined skills of competent administrators, shrewd politicians and skilled military commanders, capable of addressing the complex problems of fast expanding empires. The problem was that theory and ideology had failed to catch up with reality in these instances. While Muslim thinkers, like their Roman counterparts, had effectively acquiesced into imperial rule, they continued to deny it legitimacy. The resulting divergence between ideal and reality spelt a dangerous moral vacuum, which continued to infect Muslim politics down the years, and accounts for much of its pathology, as we attempt to show.

At another level, the elusiveness of the "ethical state" model could be viewed in another wider context. In this sense, the problem is captured by the realism of modern political theory and its Khaldūnian antecedent, where the problem is seen as the problem of excessive political idealism in general. In this regard, politics is not seen as the translation of social ideals into reality, but of reconciling conflicting demands of power and balancing the requirements of justice and privilege.

Based on this, the democratic compromise is seen as a solution to this dilemma, since it assumes the amoral (or pre-moral) character of politics. Modern democratic theory can thus be seen as the attempt to elaborate a method of doing politics without the burden of the counterproductive and age-old assumption which demands that politics be the realm of virtue, but ends up giving us a realm of crime, or as Latour puts it, to evolve a language that is unique to politics.

The lesson for Islamic revivalism (and Islamic political discourse in general) is to also move from the traditional language, which tasks political leaders with undeserved and unattainable qualities of virtue, and also see both politics and Islamic history in a more realistic light. This would mean to look at the broader picture, both historically and now. The challenge of reconciling Islamic ethics and democracy must thus be met by going beyond the habitual exercise of constructing tables with one column for democracy and another for Islam and try to tick what is common and what is divergent. Rather, one should first reassess the historical Islamic models in realistic terms, and then try to capture the essence of the achievement of modern democratic practise which is the success in evolving the most realistically ethical and the most ethical practical political system possible without lapsing either into utopian idealism or crass Machiavellianism.

This paper, hopefully, shows how we could start going about this exercise.

REFERENCES

Al-Aqqad, Abbas, Mahmud, ʿAbqariyyah ʿUmar (Cairo: al-Maktabah al-Tijāriyyah al-Kubrā, 1943).

Arjomand, Said Amir, *The Turban for the Crown: The Islamic Revolution in Iran* (Oxford: Oxford University Press, 1998).

Ayubi, Nazih, *Overstating the Arab State: Politics and Society in the Middle East* (London: IB Tauris, 1995).

Bayart, Jean-Francois, "Republican Trajectories in Iran and Turkey: A Tocquevillian Reading," in *Democracy without Democrats? The Renewal of Politics in the Muslim World*, ed. Ghassan Salamé (London: IB Tauris, 1994).

Beetham, David, "Liberal Democracy and the Limits in Democratisation," in *Prospects for Democracy*, ed. David Held (Polity and Stanford University Press, 1993).

Binder, Leanard, *Islamic Liberalism: A Critique of Development Ideologies* (Chicago: University of Chicago Press, 1988).

Dahl, Robert A., *Democracy and its Critics* (New Haven: Yale University Press, 1989).

Dunleavy, Patrick and Brenda O'Leary, *Theories of the State. The Politics of Liberal Democracy* (Basingstoke: Macmillan, 1987).

El-Affendi, Abdelwahab, "Al-Shuʿarā' kānū Ajhizah Iʿlām al-ʿArab" [Poets were Arab Media Organs], *Al-ʿArabī* (December, 1976).

Elster, Jon and Rune Slagstad, eds., *Constitutionalism and Democracy* (Cambridge: Cambridge University Press, 1988).

Enayat, Hamid, *Modern Islamic Political Thought* (London: Macmillan, 1982).

Entelis, John P., ed., *Islam, Democracy, and the State in North Africa* (Bloomington: Indiana University Press, 1997).

Evans, Peter B., Deitrich Rueschemeyer, and Theda Skocpol, eds. *Bringing the State Back In* (Cambridge: Cambridge University Press, 1985).

Gellner, Ernest, *Conditions of Liberty, Civil Society and its Rivals* (London: Hamish Hamilton, 1994).

Gibb, H.A.R., "The Fiscal Rescript of Umar II," *Arabica* (January, 1955), vol. 2, no. 1.

Grant, Michael, *A Short History of Classical Civilisation* (London: Weidenfeld and Nicholson, 1991).

Grant, Ruth W., *Hypocrisy and Integrity: Machiavelli, Rousseau, and the Ethics of Politics* (Chicago: University of Chicago Press, 1997).

Habermas, J., "Hannah Arendt's Communications Concept of Power," in *Power: Readings in Social and Political Theory*, ed. Steven Lukes (New York: New York University Press, 1986).

Hall, Stuart, "The State in Question," in *The Idea of the Modern State*, eds. Gregor McLennan, David Held, and Stuart Hall (Milton Keynes: Open University Press, 1984).

Hawting, G.R., *The First Dynasty of Islam* (London: Croom Helm, 1987).

Held, David, "Central Perspectives on the Modern State," in *The Idea of the Modern State*, eds. Gregor McLennan, David Held, and Stuart Hall (Milton Keynes: Open University Press, 1984).

_____Ed., *Prospects for Democracy* (Cambridge: Polity Press, 1995).

_____*Models of Democracy*, 2nd edn. (Cambridge: Polity Press, 1996).

Hinds, Martin, *Studies in Early Islamic History* (Princeton: Princeton University Press, 1996).

Hobbes, Thomas, *Leviathan*, ed. C.B. Macpherson (London: Clarendon Press, 1968).

Hoffman, J., *Beyond the State* (Cambridge: Polity Press, 1995).

Hussein, Taha, *Al-Fitnah al-Kubrā* (Cairo: Dār al-Maʿārif, 1947), vols. I-II.

Ibn al-Jawzī, Abd al-Raḥmān, *Al-Muntaẓim fī al-Tārīkh* (Beirut: Dār al-Kutub, 1992).

Ibn-Khaldūn, ʿAbd al-Raḥmān ibn Muḥammad, *Al-Muqaddimah* (Beirut: Dār al-Mashriq, 1967).

Issawi, Charlies, *An Arab Philosophy of History: Selections from the Prolegomena of Ibn Khaldun of Tunis* (Murray, 1950).

Jessop, Bob, *State Theory: Putting the Capitalist States in their Place* (Cambridge: Cambridge University Press, 1990).

Kennedy, Hugh, *The Prophet and the Age of the Caliphate* (London: Longman, 1986).

Keddie, Nikki, *An Islamic Response to Imperialism* (Berkeley: University of California Press, 1968).

Kepel, Gilles, *The Prophet and the Pharaoh: Muslim Extremism in Egypt* (London: al-Saqi Books, 1985).

_____*Jihad: The Trail of Political Islam*, trans. Anthony F. Roberts (London: IB Tauris, 2002).

Khalid, Khalid Muhammad, *Khulafā' al-Rasūl* (Beirut: Dār al-Shorūq, 1971).

Khomeini, Ayatollah Ruhollah, *Islam and Revolution: Writings and Declaration of Imam Khomeini*, ed. Hamid Algar (Berkeley: Mizan Press, 1981).

Latour, Bruno, "What if We Talked Politics a Little," *Contemporary Political Theory* (July, 2003), vol. 2, no. 2.

Le Glay, Marcel et al., *A History of Rome* (Oxford: Blackwell Publishers, 2001).

Lewis, Bernard, "Islam and Liberal Democracy: A Historical Overview," *Journal of Democracy* (1996), vol. 7.

Machiavelli, N., *The Prince*, trans. George Bull (Harmondsworth: Penguin, 1999).

Przeworkski, Adam, "Democracy as a Contingent Outcome of Conflicts," in *Constitutionalism and Democracy*, ed. Jon Elster and Rune Slagstad (Cambridge: Cambridge University Press, 1988).

Rahe, Paul A., *Republics Ancient and Modern: Classical Republicanism and the American Revolution* (Chapel Hill: University of North Carolina Press, 1994), vol. 2.

Rawls, John, *Theory of Justice* (Cambridge: Belknap Press of Harvard University, 1971).

_____ *Political Liberalism* (New York: Columbia University Press, 1993).

Rida, Rashid, *Al-Khalīfah aw al-Imāmah al-ʿUẓmā* (Cairo: Dār al-Manār, 1925).

Roy, Olivier, *The Failure of Political Islam*, trans. Carol Volk (Cambridge: Harvard University Press, 1994).

Rueschemeyer, Dietrich and Peter Evans, "The State and Economic Transformation: Towards an Analysis of Conditions Underlying Effective Intervention," in *Bringing the State Back In*, eds. Peter Evans, Dietrich Rueschemeyer and Theda Skocpol (Cambridge: Cambridge University Press, 1985).

Sayyid al-Ahl, Abd al-Aziz, *Al-Khalīfah al-Zāhid ʿUmar ibn ʿAbd al-ʿAzīz* (Beirut: Dār al-ʿIlm li al-Malāyīn, 1969).

Schmitter, Philippe C., "Some Basic Assumptions about the Consolidation of Democarcy," in *The Changing Nature of Democracy*, eds. Takashi Inoguchi, Edward Newman and John Keane (New York: United Nations University Press, 1998).

Skinner, Quentin, *Machiavelli: A Very Short Introduction* (Oxford: Oxford University Press, 2000).

Skocpol, Theda, "Bringing the State Back In: Strategies of Analysis in Current Research," in *Bringing the State Back In*, eds. Peter Evans, Dietrich Rueschemeyer and Theda Skocpol (Cambridge: Cambridge University Press, 1985).

Tilly, Charles, "War Making and State Making as Organized Crime," in *Bringing the State Back In*, eds. Peter Evans, Dietrich Rueschemeyer and Theda Skocpol (Cambridge: Cambridge University Press, 1985).

Waterbury, John, "Democracy without Democrats? The Potential for Political Liberalisation in the Middle East," in *Democracy without Democrats? The Renewal of Politics in the Muslim World*, ed. Ghassan Salamé (London: IB Tauris, 1994).

NOTES

Expanding Our Intellectual Vision

1   I use this phrase with Claude Addas' book in mind: Claude Addas, *Quest for the Red Sulphur – The Life of Ibn Arabi,* trans. Peter Kingsley (Cambridge: The Islamic Texts Society, 1993).

2   Muhammad 'Abduh, *The Theology of Unity* (English translation of *Risalat al-Tauhid*) (Islamic Book Trust, 2004), pp.30–31.

3   Muhammad Iqbal, *The Reconstruction of Religious Thought in Islam* (Kazi Publications, 1999), see in particular Chapter VI, "The Principle of Movement in the Structure of Islam."

4   Fazlur Rahman, *Islam and Modernity – Transformation of an Intellectual Tradition* (Chicago: The University of Chicago Press, 1982), p.132.

5   Ibid., pp.3–4.

6   Syed Muhammad Naquib al-Attas, *Islam and Secularism* (Kuala Lumpur: International Institute of Islamic Thought And Civilisation, 1993), see, inter alia, p.105.

7   Ismaʿil R. al-Faruqi, *Islamisation of Knowledge* (Herndon: International Institute of Islamic Thought, 1982).

8   Rifāʿah Rāfiʿ al Ṭahṭāwī, *Al-Murshid al-Amīn li al-Banāt wa al-Banīn* (Cairo, 1872–1873). See also Albert Hourani, *Arabic Thought in the Liberal Age, 1798–1939* (Cambridge: Cambridge University Press, 1983), Chapter II.

9   Syed Ameer Ali, *The Spirit of Islam – A History of the Evolution and Ideals of Islam* (London: Chatto & Windus, 1974).

10 Taha Husayn, *Mustaqbal al-Thaqāfah fī-Miṣr* (Cairo, 1938).

11 Sayyid Qutb, *Maʿālim fī al-Ṭarīq* [Milestones], p.32, 90.

12 Sayyid Abul A'la Maududi, *Islamic Way of Life* (Lahore: Islamic Publications, 1979), 11th edn., p.39.

13 Abdolkarim Soroush, *Reason, Freedom, and Democracy in Islam* (Oxford: Oxford University Press, 2000), see generally Chapter 12, "Let Us Learn from History."

14   Oliver Roy, *The Failure of Political Islam*, trans. Carol Volk (Cambridge: Harvard University Press, 1996), p.198.

15   Shaykh Muhammad al-Ghazālī, *A Thematic Commentary on the Qur'an*, trans. Ashur A. Shamis (Herndon: International Institute of Islamic Thought, 2000), p.576.

From Tolerance to Recognition to Beyond

1   Some material contained in this article is derived from my forthcoming book: "The European 'Other'" (Edinburgh University Press, 2009). However, this essay was delivered as a lecture to the Association of Muslim Social Scientists in Istanbul, Turkey, in 2006, as an introduction to certain themes and questions – it should not be regarded as comprehensive in scope or in depth.

2   The Runnymede Report (see Commission on the Future of Multi-Ethnic Britain, 2002). The Report of the Commission of Multi-Ethnic Britain, (London: Profile) outlined five possible models that states could emulate in order to cope with diversity:
- Procedural: the state is neutral vis-à-vis culture, and only a few basic procedures are common in society.
- Nationalist: the state promotes a single culture, and those who do not assimilate to it are second-class.
- Liberal/constitutional patriotism: there is a uniform political culture in public life, which provides for cohesiveness but diversity in private.
- Plural: in the public and private spheres, there is both unity and diversity; the public realm is 'continually revised to accommodate cultural diversity in society at large.'
- Seperatist: the state permits and expects each community to remain separate from others, confining itself to maintaining order and civility.
No state is composed of only one of these models, whether in the past or present, but shares features from all of them in different ways.

3   Commission on the Future of Multi-Ethnic Britain (CFMB). The Report of the Commission of Multi-Ethnic Britain (London: Profile 2002), pp.42–45.

4   Ibid.

5   Ibid.

6   Will Kymlicka, *Contemporary Political Philosophy: An Introduction* (Oxford: Oxford University Press, 2002), pp.365–366.

7   Most authors do neglect to mention that this is indeed a 'Western' grouping of political philosophies, and not universal; there are a number of other, non-'Western' political philosophies that have yet to be adequately analysed before we are to speak of 'contemporary political philosophy.'

8   It should be noted very clearly that this article is not entirely concerned with

abstract theoretical discussions of what normative political theory should be; rather, what is described is contemporary civil society. If it was a purely theoretical discussion, then the normative basis might be something quite different, but politics is, after all, the art of the possible.

9   Kymlicka, 2002, p.366.

10 Commission on the Future of Multi-Ethnic Britain (CFMB). The Report of the Commission of Multi-Ethnic Britain (London: Profile, 2002), pp.42–45.

11 Ibid.

12 Bhikhu Parekh, *Rethinking Multiculturalim: Cultural Diversity and Political Theory* (London: Palgrave Macmillan, 2000), pp.239–240.

13 *L'affaire du foulard* in September 1989. Other religious symbols were similarly proscribed, but it was clear from the history of the debate what was being targeted.

14 Ali Sina, "The Fall of Europe," 2005; see http://www.faithfreedom.org/oped/sina50525.htm

15 Margaret Talbot, "The Agitator," 2006; see http://www.newyorker.com/fact/content/articles/060605fa_fact

16 Melanie Phillips, *Londonistan* (London: Encounter Books, 2006).

17 Notice their annual conference in 2006 dealt almost exclusively with this theme, and gave the then Chancellor of the UK, Gordon Brown, the opportunity to deliver a keynote speech on the subject of 'Britishness,' which was then widely covered in the press.

18 See for example, Tariq Ramadan, *Western Muslims and the Future of Islam* (Oxford: Oxford University Press, 2004).

19 Amin Maalouf, *In the Name of Identity: Violence and the Need to Belong* (USA: Arcade Publishing, 2001).

20 U.F. Abd-Allah, "Islam and the Cultural Imperative," published by the Nawawi Foundation, 2004; see http://www.nawawi.org/downloads/article3.pdf

21 See Abdal Hakim Murad, "Bombing without Moonlight," published in October 2004, hosted at http://www.masud.co.uk/ISLAM/ahm/ moonlight.htm

22 This was not left unnoticed in previous years; I wrote as such in 1997 in the Muslim Peace Fellowship newsletter 'As salamu 'alaykum' and Shakir wrote in a separate volume reflections in the same vein (republished in Zaid Shakir, *Scattered Pictures: Reflections of an American Muslim*, USA: NID Publishers, 2005).

23 Amir Ben David, 'Leopold of Arabia,' 2001; see http://www.haaretz.com/hasen/pages/ShArt.jhtml?itemNo=95213

24 "A Look at the Five Pillars of Islam"; see http://www.islam-australia.com.au/revert/five_pillars.htm

25 Al-Ghazālī, Imam Abū Ḥāmid, Book VIII of his *Iḥyā' ʿUlūm-ud-Dīn* [The Revival of the Religious Sciences]: *The Condemnation of Status and Ostentation*, abridged by Shaykh Ahmad al-Shami, http://www.masud.co.uk/ISLAM/misc/MISC-Ghazali_status.htm

26 'Europe in Islam' debate hosted by Muslim Youth Helpline on 7th June 2006.

27 Islamic law forbids the consumption of some fermented substances that result in intoxicating alcohols. On the other hand, 'wine,' a fermented substance, is often used as a metaphor in spiritualist literature for love of the Divine.

Beyond the Tower of Babel

1 Genesis 11:1–9.

2 This metaphorical association began in English in the sixteenth century. The entry for *babel* in the *Bloomsbury Dictionary of Word Origins* by John Ayto (London: Bloomsbury Publishing, 1990), p.47, points out, however, that "the word has no etymological connection with 'language' or 'noise'. The original Assyrian *bab-ilu* meant 'gate of god' and this was borrowed into Hebrew as *babel*." The later Greek version of the name is *Babylon*. Popular etymology, however, links the word to a similar Hebrew root *balal*, 'confusion' or 'mixing'. Chambers *Dictionary of Etymology* observes that the English word *babble*, which folk etymology has connected with *Babel* and thus probably influenced its sense of 'meaningless or confusing chatter or prattle', does have a direct connection with language, in that "the various forms of this word in Indo-European languages are all probably formed on the repeated syllables *ba, ba,* or *bar, bar,* sounds typically made by infants and used to express childish prattle." See *Chambers Dictionary of Etymology*, ed. Robert K. Barnhart (Edinburgh: Chambers, 1988), p.70.

3 For a profound exposition of the Qur'anic basis for religious pluralism, see R. Shah-Kazemi, "The Metaphysics of Interfaith Dialogue: Sufi Perspectives on the Universality of the Qur'anic Message," in *Paths to the Heart: Sufism and the Christian East*, ed. James Cutsinger (Bloomington, IN: World Wisdom, 2002). According to Mahmoud Ayoub, "Humanity began as one and must remain one, but it is unity in diversity. This diversity, moreover, is not due to the gradual degeneration of human society from an ideal or utopian state. Nor is it the result of a lack of divine guidance or human understanding. Rather, religious diversity is a normal human situation. It is the consequence of the diversity of human cultures, languages, races and different environments." Mahmoud M. Ayoub, "The Qur'an and Religious Pluralism" in *Islam and Global Dialogue, Religious Pluralism and the Pursuit of Peace*, ed. Roger Boase (Aldershot: Ashgate, 2005), p.273.

4 Translations from the Qur'an in this paper are from *The Message of the Qur'an* by Muhammad Asad (Bath: The Book Foundation, 2003).

5   In his note to this verse from the Qur'an, Muhammad Asad explains how "unity in diversity" is frequently stressed in the Qur'an (e.g., in the first sentence of 2:148, in 21:92–93, or in 23:52 ff.).

'The expression "every one of you" denotes the various communities of which mankind is composed. The term *shir'ah* (or *shari'ah*) signifies, literally, "the way to a watering-place" (from which men and animals derive the element indispensable to their life), and is used in the Qur'an to denote a system of law necessary for a community's social and spiritual welfare. The term *minhāj*, on the other hand, denotes an "open road," usually in an abstract sense: that is, "a way of life." The terms *shir'ah* and *minhāj* are more restricted in their meaning than the term *dīn* which comprises not merely the laws relating to a particular religion but also the basic, unchanging spiritual truths which, according to the Qur'an, have been preached by every one of God's apostles, while the particular body of laws (*shir'ah* or *shari'ah*) promulgated through them, and the way of life (*minhāj*) recommended by them, varied in accordance with the exigencies of the time and of each community's cultural development.' Murad Hofmann regards this verse as a "virtual manifesto of religious pluralism" and "a *structural guarantee* for the survival of more than one religion and every Muslim should not know it by heart," and further asserts that it can be deduced from Qur'an 22:67 that "God has guaranteed the existence of more than one religion for as long as the world lasts." See Murad W. Hofmann, "Religious Pluralism and Islam," in *Islam and Global Dialogue, Religious Pluralism and the Pursuit of Peace*, 2005, op. cit., pp.238–239.

6   Muhammad Asad notes: 'Thus, the Qur'an impresses upon all who believe in God – Muslims and non-Muslims alike – that the differences in their religious practises should make them "vie with one another in doing good works" rather than lose themselves in mutual hostility.'

7   Muhammad Asad comments as follows: "know that all belong to one human family, without any inherent superiority of one over another (Zamakhsharī). This connects with the exhortation, in the preceding two verses, to respect and safeguard each other's dignity. In other words, men's evolution into 'nations and tribes' is meant to foster rather than to diminish their mutual desire to understand and appreciate the essential human oneness underlying their outward differentiations; and, correspondingly, all racial, national, or tribal prejudice (*'aṣabiyyah*) is condemned – implicitly in the Qur'an, and most explicitly by the Prophet (see Asad's second half of note 15 on 28:15).

8   These phrases are used by Diana Eck, Director of the Pluralism Project at Harvard University, in arguing that "as a style of living together, tolerance is too minimal an expectation," Diana L. Eck, *Encountering God* (Boston: Beacon Press, 1993), p.198.

9   See Omid Safi, ed. *Progressive Muslims on Justice, Gender and Pluralism* (Oxford: Oneworld Publications, 2003), p.24.

10   *Ikhtilāf ummatī raḥmah*. This hadith is quoted by Professor Fred Halliday as the penultimate sentence of his article "The 'Clash of Civilisations?': Sense and Nonsense" in *Islam and Global Dialogue, Religious Pluralism and the Pursuit of Peace*, op. cit., p.129. The final sentence is: "This sage *hadith* is a far cry from the incendiary banalities of Professor Samuel Huntington."

11   In commenting on the above Qur'anic verses, Khalid Abou El Fadl makes the important point that "the classical commentators on the Qur'an did not fully explore the implications of this sanctioning of diversity, or the role of peaceful conflict resolution in perpetuating the type of social interaction that would result in people 'knowing each other'. Nor does the Qur'an provide specific rules or instructions about how 'diverse nations and tribes' are to acquire such knowledge. In fact, the existence of diversity as a primary purpose of creation ... *remained underdeveloped in Islamic theology* [my emphasis]. Pre-modern Muslim scholars did not have a strong incentive to explore the meaning and implication of the Qur'anic endorsement of diversity and cross-cultural inter-course. This is partly because of the political dominance and superiority of the Islamic civilisation which left Muslim scholars with a sense of self-sufficient confidence. Nevertheless, it is fair to say that the Islamic civilisation was plural-istic and unusually tolerant of various social and religious denominations. Working out the implications of a commitment to human diversity and mutual knowledge under contemporary conditions requires moral reflection and attention to historical circumstance – precisely what is missing from puritan theology and doctrine." Khalid Abou El Fadl, *The Place of Tolerance in Islam* (Boston: Beacon Press, 2002), p.16.

12   Eck, op. cit., p.192.

13   I have explored the difference between *pluralism* and *plurality* in more detail in my paper, J. Henzell-Thomas, *The Challenge of Pluralism and the Middle Way of Islam* (London: AMSS UK, 2002).

14   C.S. Lewis, *Perelandra* (London: HarperCollins, 1943).

15   The three races are the Sorns, a tall race who live in the high places, are wise and have a knowledge of science; the Hrossa, who live in deep fertile crevices below the planet's surface which can no longer support life, and the Pfifltriggi, small quick people who live in the deep places of the planet and are gifted artisans and metal smiths. They all live under the guidance of beings visible to the human eye only as a patch of intense light, and who themselves act under the direction of 'The Old One'.

16   I refer to this exemplary story in a short article entitled "Diversity Provides Golden Opportunities for Learning" posted on the forum dedicated to

contemporary issues in education on the website of the Book Foundation (www. TheBook.org).

17 Nancy Kline, *Time to Think: Listening to Ignite the Human Mind* (London: Lock,1999), p.97.

18 *Islam and Global Dialogue, Religious Pluralism and the Pursuit of Peace*, op. cit., p.75.

19 Jalaluddin Rumi, *Mathnawi*, II, 3681 ff.

20 This applies particularly to the difficulty in capturing the web of associated meanings represented by the tri-literal Arabic root system. An obvious example is the Qur'anic term *taqwā*, often translated as 'fear of Allah'. Yūsuf ʿAlī, in his note to Qur'an 2:2 ("This is the Book; In it is guidance sure, without doubt, to those who fear Allah"), explains that *"Taqwā, and the verbs and nouns connected with the root, signify: (1) the fear of Allah which, according to the writer of Proverbs (i. 7) in the Old Testament, is the beginning of Wisdom; (2) restraint, or guarding one's tongue, hand, and heart from evil; (3) hence righteousness, piety, good conduct. All these ideas are implied: in the translation, only one or other of these ideas can be indicated, according to the context"* [my emphasis].

Muhammad Asad translates the same verse as "This Divine Writ – let there be no doubt about it – is meant to be a guidance for all the God-conscious" and points out that "the conventional translation of *muttaqī* as 'God-fearing' does not adequately render the *positive* content of this expression – namely, the awareness of His all-presence and the desire to mould one's existence in the light of this awareness; while the interpretation adopted by some translators, 'one who guards himself against evil' or 'one who is careful of his duty', does not give more than one particular aspect of the concept of God-consciousness."

However, it could also be said that Asad's adoption of the term 'God-consciousness', while capturing the dimension of spiritual awareness and positive mindfulness which the term 'God-fearing' may fail to evoke, nevertheless in itself may fail to evoke the moral dimension of accountability and the positive sense of 'fear' (or awe) which motivates the *mu'min* to be vigilant in exercising self-restraint and in considering the consequences of all actions (including those of the tongue and heart). For just as the term 'God-fearing' may reify the term for those familiar with a Semitic conception of God derived from the religion of the 'People of the Book', so the term 'God-consciousness' potentially restricts the meaning in other ways by its associations with Eastern religions.

Another example is the translation of the Qur'anic term *ʿaql* as 'reason' which, in the context of its restricted use in the Western intellectual tradition to refer to the purely logical, analytical, rational and *intellectualising* processes centred in the brain (Latin *ratio*, Greek *dianoia*) does not do justice to the multi-layered sense it carries in the Qur'an, where it refers not only to such rational processes but also to the higher human faculties of perceptive *intellection* or *insight* combining mind and heart (Latin *intellectus*, Greek *nous*) and the *moral* intelligence capable of distinguishing truth from falsehood.

21   "We believe in the revelation which has come down to us and in that which has come down to you; our God and your God is one and the same and it is to Him we [all] submit" (Qur'an 29:46).

22   The word *kāfir* ("one who denies the truth") from the root KFR, is commonly mistranslated as "unbeliever," and often restricted even further (without Qur'anic justification) to denote non-Muslims. See James Morris, "Ibn 'Arabi's Rhetoric of Realisation," *Journal of the Muhyiddin Ibn 'Arabi Society*, 2003, vol. XXXIV, p. 134, for further examples.

23   For example, a recent BBC radio 4 series on the Sikh community in the UK included a programme in which an artistically talented Sikh student talked about the prejudice she had experienced in secondary school from teachers and examiners who had devalued and even openly scorned her artwork because it was too "traditional" and "derivative" and did not conform to their Eurocentric modernist assumptions that all "creative" artwork must be "original" and "innovative." In this example, the diversity strand of the Citizenship programme of the National Curriculum is actively flouted through lamentable ignorance of other cultural traditions, although it may well be that this strand will more typically be simply given lip service in a curriculum overloaded with examinable content and taught by teachers deficient in inter-cultural knowledge and skills.

I refer to a further example of poorly educated teachers in an article entitled "Why Teachers need to Understand the Benefits of Multilingualism" on the Contemporary Issues in Education forum on the Book Foundation website. This described research by the University of London Institute of Education which brought together a number of studies on bilingual and trilingual children showing that children who speak at least two languages do better at school than those who speak only one. Why is it, then, that so many teachers still see multilingualism as a problem rather than an asset?

Caroline Haydon, reporting these research findings in an article in the UK newspaper *The Independent* on 9/10/03, describes how a group of six-year-olds in a school in Hackney, London, proudly told her about their language skills. "And they were quite astonishing," she says. "They speak Gujerati (and a little Urdu) to grandparents, they speak English and Gujerati to their (second generation parents), and a great deal more English to their siblings. And from age five they spend two hours a night studying religious texts in Urdu and the Koran in Arabic in the local mosque." Caroline Haydon, "The Language of Success," *The Independent* (9/10/03).

Haydon goes on to say that despite the assumption that children find it difficult to learn foreign languages, the fact is that at six they are quite capable of dealing with different scripts, and they enjoy learning to read in three languages from the age of five. "And they positively benefit from having their existing language skills recognised, and developed, by their schools. Most important of all, the consequent boost to self esteem helps them to work harder and do better in their school work."

Dr. Raymonde Sneddon of the School of Education and Community Studies at the University of East London has shown that, far from being confused by different languages, the trilingual children she studied were accomplished speakers of English and performed better on a test of reading comprehension than children who spoke only English.

Despite these findings, Sneddon's study also showed that even where schools had positive attitudes about multilingualism, some teachers often persisted in underestimating the skills of multilingual children and wrongly believed that even bilingualism (let alone trilingualism) was a problem rather than an asset.

Dr. Charmian Kenner, who researched six-year-olds growing up in London and learning to write Chinese, Arabic or Spanish as well as English, concludes: "The price of ignoring children's bilingualism is educational failure and social exclusion."

24 The word conformation is used by Muhammad Asad to translate the phrase *fī aḥsani taqwīm* in Qur'an 95:4: "Verily, We create man in the best conformation." Variant translations include "We indeed created Man in the fairest stature" (Arberry), "We created the human being in the highest station" (Sells) and "We have indeed created man in the best of moulds" (Yūsuf ʿAlī). Yūsuf ʿAlī's note gives the various connotations of *taqwīm* as "mould, symmetry, form, nature, constitution." He adds: "There is no fault in Allah's creation. To man Allah gave the purest and best nature, and man's duty is to preserve the pattern on which Allah has made him."

25 The notion of a 'standard' or 'criterion' is a key Qur'anic concept. Muhammad Asad translates the key term *furqān* as "a standard by which to discern the true from the false" (2:53). Asad's note to Qur'an 2:53 advances Muhammad Abduh's interpretation (supported by 8:41) that this term, while describing "one or another of the revealed scriptures, and particularly the Qur'an itself" … can also be applied to human reason. Asad also claims that in 8:29, "it clearly refers to the faculty of moral valuation which distinguishes every human being who is truly conscious of God." Such moral valuation according to Asad, is ultimately provided by the "*absolute* criterion of revelation – and revelation alone." In 2:53, the term refers to the "divine writ" revealed to Moses, but "since the Mosaic dispensation as such was binding on the children of Israel

alone and remained valid only within a particular historical and cultural context, the term *al-furqān* relates here not to the Mosaic Law as such, but to the fundamental ethical truths contained in the Torah and common to all divine revelations" (see note 57 to verse 21:48).

26 I am thinking here of *relationship* in the sense of *contextualisation*. To be sensitive to context is to relate to current needs and conditions and to reformulate concepts so as to make them accessible to the contemporary mind. This is not the same as the *relativism* which regards every level of reality as something "negotiated" and without any anchor in absolute truths or values.

27 Jefferson said that "Eternal vigilance is the price of liberty," and no doubt he would agree with Mark Perry's critique of the "absurdity of John Stuart Mill's assertion that 'Liberty consists in doing what one desires', an opinion which Hegel was to qualify as one of 'utter immaturity'. Intemperance is not liberty but bondage." M. Perry, *On Awakening and Remembering* (Louisville: Fons Vitae, 2000), p.285, note 109.

28 According to Thomas Jefferson, "If a nation expects to be ignorant and free, it expects what never was and never will be."

29 The underlying sense of an 'idea' in English is that which is 'seen' or 'perceived', rather than that which is 'thought'. It comes from the Indo-European root *ueid-*, meaning 'look at, see'. This root gives us Sanskrit *Veda*, knowledge, as in the sacred books of Hinduism (*vidya* is 'knowledge' – i.e. 'seeing' in Sanskrit, and *a-vidya* is 'ignorance', or at best 'imperfect knowledge', literally 'not seeing' or 'blind'). The same root *ueid-* gives us Greek *eidos* and *idea,* and Latin *videre* ('to see') from which our own English derivatives are legion.

It is worth noting also that the original sense of the Greek word *idea,* used by Plato in the specialised sense 'archetypal form' or 'ideal prototype', is the 'look' 'appearance' or 'image' of something. The early English sense before 1398 was the Platonic 'general or ideal form, type or model'. The more general and abstract sense of 'notion, mental conception' is not found in English, as far as I know, before 1645.

So, the underlying concept is that of 'seeing' not of 'thinking'. As with so many words which had kept a measure of their original meaning in the medieval period, the sense of 'idea' as something 'seen' was reduced in the post-Renaissance world to something 'thought'. A concrete experience, a 'tasting' (*dhawq*), was reduced to an abstraction.

The word 'ideology', first appearing in 1796, further extends the degraded sense of 'abstraction'. Borrowed from French 'idéologie', it has the sense of the study or science of ideas; the political or social philosophy of a nation; and, later, the connotation of impracticable theorising and even visionary speculation. The meaning of a set of ideas, doctrines or beliefs was not recorded in English until 1909.

30 For more detailed discussion of this notion of universal primordial concepts embedded in the human mind-heart (ʿaql) see my paper, "Going Beyond Thinking Skills: Reviving an Understanding of Higher Human Faculties" presented at the 10th annual conference of the International Association of Cognitive Education and Psychology, University of Durham, England, July 2004. This paper is available on the website of the Book Foundation at www. TheBook.org.

31 The most obvious expression of diversity is the underlying elemental polarity in the whole of creation, for, as the Qur'an says, "everything have We created in pairs" (51:49), and "We have created you all out of a male and a female" (49:13).

32 Qur'an (2:31).

33 A. J. Arberry, ed. and trans. *The Mawaqif and Mukhatabat of Muhammad Ibn ʾAbdi'l-Jabbar al-Niffari* (Cambridge: CUP, 1935), p.111.

34 Roland S. Barth. *Improving Schools from Within* (San Francisco: Jossey-Bass, 1990), p.169.

Public Opinion and Political Influence

1 The Association of Muslim Social Scientists (AMSS UK) and the Foundation for Political, Social and Economic Research (SETA) jointly organised a conference in Istanbul in September 2006 on "Citizenship, Security and Democracy." In this conference I gave a paper entitled "The Shadow of the Classics: Islamophobic Discourse Masquerading as Arts and Literature." Parts of the paper have been revised and updated and the new edition is being printed under the title "Islamophobic Discourse Masquerading as Art and Literature: Combating Myth Through Progressive Education" in a book on Islamophobia being jointly produced by Georgetown University and the OIC and edited by Professor John Esposito and Dr. Ibrahim Kalin. In addition, I also gave at the conference a power-point presentation on popular fiction and images on book covers stereotyping Islam and Muslims. The paper being published in this volume is based on that power-point presentation.

2 See Alex Hamilton "Top Hundred Chart of 1993 Paperback Fastsellers," in *Writers' and Artists Yearbook 1995* (London: A. & C. Black), p.256.

3 See Frank N. Magill, ed., *Critical Survey of Long Fiction: English Language Services* (Englewood, NJ: Salem Press, 1983), IV, p.1607.

4 Reeva Simon, *The Middle East in Crime Fiction: Mysteries, Spy Novels and Thrillers 1916 to the 1980's* (New York: Lilian Barber, 1989), p. v.

5 Ibid., p. vi

6 See David Lister, "The Bard Meets 'Pulp Fiction'," *The Independent*, September 9, 1995.

7   Simon, vii.

8   The same trend is also noticeable in popular French and German fiction. Among a large number of original German titles and translations are: Gerhard Herm, *Sturm am golden Horn* (Hamburg: Hoffmann und Campe Verlage, 1982); Kenize Mourad, *Im Namen der toten Prinzessin: Der Roman der letzten Sultanin* (Munich: Wilhelm Heyne Verlag, 1989), a translation from the French *De la part de la Princesse Morte* (1987); Jean Warmbold, *Der Arabische Freund* (Frankfurt: Eichborn Verlag, 1992), a translation by Susanne Aeckerle from the original American version; Waldimir Bartol, *Alamut: Ein Roman aus dem alten Orient* (Bastei Lubbe, 1993), a translation from the French *Alamut*.

9   See, for example, Oriana Fallaci, *Inshalla* (London: Chatto and Windus, 1992): and Aldo Busi, *Sodomies in Eleven Point* (London, Faber and Faber, 1992).

10 See Riad Nourallah, "Sorcerers, Straight Swords, and Scimitars: The Arab-Islamic East in Modern Fantasies of Magic and Conflict," *The International Journal of Islamic and Arabic Studies,* Indiana University, (1990), VII, no. 2, pp.1–40.

11 See Jack G. Shaheen, *The TV Arab* (Bowling Green, Ohio: State University Popular Press, 1984).

12 Published in *The Independent*, November 10, 1990. Later republished under the title "The Thriller in an Age of *Détente*" in Daniel Easterman, *New Jerusalems: Reflections on Islam, Fundamentalism and the Rushdie Affair* (London, Grafton, 1992), pp.195–7.

13 Two years after the end of the Second World War an article written by "X" (an American diplomat by the name of George Keenan who became known as 'the father of containment') appeared in the *Foreign Affairs* journal warning of expansionist ambition and power of the communist Soviet Union and recommending forceful vigilance. As a result the doctrine of containment was born. Huntington's thesis was first published also in *Foreign Affairs* in 1993 two years after the end of Desert Storm. The containment doctrine these days seem to be directed towards Muslim countries.

14 Quoted in Donald McCormick and Katy Fletcher, *Spy Fiction: A Connoisseur's Guide* (Oxford, Facts On File, 1990), p.234.

15 In *The Sunday Telegraph*, February 5, 1989.

16 R.W. Johnson, "A Suitable Enemy for Crusaders," *The Independent on Sunday*, December 30, 1990.

17 "The Thriller in an Age of *Détente*," p.197.

18 "The New Anti-Semitism," in *New Jerusalems*, p.199.

19 *The Independent*, 25th April 1992.

20 "The New Anti-Semitism," p.199.

21 Ibid.

22 Grant Hugo, "The Political Influence of the Thriller," *Contemporary Review* (December, 1972), p.289.

23 Ibid, p.285.

24 Ibid., p.284, p.285, p.289.

25 McCormick and Fletcher, p.8.

26 It may indeed be a very strange a coincidence that during the Lewinsky sex scandal and amid the numerous media speculation that the Clinton administration may try to distract attention by launching a devastating strike on Iraq even before diplomacy has run its course a film *Wag the Dog* was showing throughout the US. In the film, the President of the United States is caught having sex with a teenage girl in the Oval Office. The trouble-shooter, Robert De Niro suggests manufacturing a phone war against Albania to distract media attention to the scandal. The justification for the war was fabricated by a Hollywood director who creates in Hollywood studio scenes from burning Balkan villages. When the footage is fed to the television networks, the media and the public fall for the trap. Anyone who has seen the film or read about it will not fail to see similarity between its fiction and the reality unfolding in Washington. Simon Halls, a publicist for the film, is reported to have said: " I've got four pages of calls wanting some kind of comment of life imitating art." (See David Usborne, "Now there's and idea: let's start a war," *The Independent*, January 24, 1998).

27 Malcolm J. Turnbull, *Victims or Villains: Jewish Images in Classic English Detective Fiction* (Bowling Green, OH: State University Popular Press, 1998), p.144.

28 The Nazi anti-Semitic propaganda started with cartoons, children stories and through popular culture in general.

29 Wesley K. Wark, ed., *Spy Fiction, Spy Films and Real Intelligence* (London: Frank Cass, 1991), p.1.

30 LeRoy L. Panek, *The Special Branch: The British Spy Novel 1890–1980* (Bowling Green, Ohio: Bowling Green University Popular Press, 1981), p.15.

31 Ibid.

32 As quoted in ibid. Emphasis mine.

33 As quoted in ibid.

34 Anthony Masters, *Literary Agents: The Novelist as Spy* (Oxford: Basil Blackwell, 1987), p.4. It may be interesting to note that before the invasion of Iraq in 2003, it was rumoured that the CIA had commissioned the translation of the novels claimed to have been authored by Saddam Hussein.

35 See Terry Crowdy, *The Enemy Within: A History of Espionage* (Oxford: Osprey Publishing, 2006), p.200.

36 Ibid.

37 Ibid.

38   Wark, p.2. Emphasis mine.

39   Ibid., p.1.

40   See Marc A. Cerasini, "Tom Clancy's Fiction: The Birth of the Techno-Thriller" in Martin H. Greenburg, ed., *The Tom Clancy Companion* (London: Fontana, 1992), pp.18–19.

41   Masters, pp.9–10. However, Masters stresses that Childers had "never been recruited by any branch of the Secret Service" (p.3).

42   See Panek, p.17, 22. The same was done by Rudyard Kipling in "The White Man's burden": See my paper "Islamophobic Discourse."

43   Frances Stoner Saunders, *Who Paid the Piper?: The CIA and the Cultural Cold War* (London, Granta Books, 1999), p.5.

44   See my paper "Islamophobic Discourse." See also Elliot Colla's Response, in Letters to the Editor, *ISIM Newsletter,* (Spring, 2005), 15, p.5.

45   Elliot Colla, "A Culture of Righteousness and Martyrdom," *ISIM Newsletter*, (June, 2004), 14, p.6.

46   The work relates the story of Jesus' return to Earth where he fulfils God's will by wiping out all non-believers from the planet, a form of en masse religious cleansing.

47   (London, Hodder & Stoughton, 1975).

48   See "Fears of Terrorism Focus on Super Bowl Football Game," in *The Independent,* (January 26, 1991). In the wake of the Oklahoma bombing – and after Muslim-bashing had subsided – the CNN referred to the possible impact of fiction on reality. At 11.30 p.m. GMT on April 26, 1995 CNN's Gene Randall reported the following: "There are countless theories about the motivation for the Oklahoma City bombing. In the search for answers, some people are examining the themes of a book written seventeen years ago. At issue [are] some frightening fictitious similarities to last week's bloodshed. CNN's Bruce Morton looks at the author and the message." Bruce Morton then introduced the book *The Turner Diaries*, a work of fiction written in 1978 by Andrew Macdonald [William Pierce]. He pointed to the striking similarities between the Oklahoma bombing and the fictitious bombing in the book of the FBI building in which "the same type of explosives (ammonium nitrate fertilizer) was used for a little under five thousand pounds bomb which killed many innocent people ... [and was delivered] by a truck with a timing device." Morton said that this, and other similarities in the book, had "everyone wondering whether the Oklahoma bombers [had] read [the book]." In addition, Nick Toczek in an article entitled "Make-believe World Inspires US Terror" (*The Independent on Sunday*, August 6, 1995) says that evidence thrown up in the aftermath of the Oklahoma City bombing links McVeigh "in specific ways to a kind of fiction and fantasy that acts as a powerful drug to the scattered groups and embittered

individuals who embrace racism and bigotry." The article details the influence of *The Turner Diaries*, which has become "the Bible of the racist right," on McVeigh. It goes on to assert that "if the Oklahoma bombers drew direct inspiration from *The Turner Diaries*, they would not have been the first. The book served as a blueprint for a gang in the 1980s led by Robert Mathews, who bombed, murdered, robbed and forged."

In another program entitled "Patriots and Profits," the CNN – in November 4, 1995 – once again stressed the possible influence of *The Turner Diaries* on McVeigh and other acts of violence committed by the American right. The program was interrupted twice to break the news of the assassination of the Israeli Prime Minister, Yitzhak Rabin, by Yigal Amir, a right-wing Jewish extremist. Two days later an article by Patrick Cockburn in *The Independent* (November 6, 1995) reported that the police found on the killer's bookshelf a "work lauding Baruch Goldstein, the Jewish settler who killed 29 Muslims in the West Bank" as well as a copy of Frederick Forsyth's thriller, *The Day of the Jackal*. The novel published in 1971 has also been made into a film. In the story Colonel Marc Rodin, Operations Chief of the right-wing Secret Army Organization discovers that de Gaulle's policy no longer includes *Algerie Francaise* and is planning talks with Ben Bella and the FLN. When he realises that the heyday of French presence in Algeria was over, his world, hopes, belief and faith disintegrate: "… there was nothing left. Just hate. Hate for the system, for the politicians, for the intellectuals, for the Algerians, for the trade unions, for the journalists, for the foreigners; but most of all hate for That Man" whom he considers to be a traitor. He therefore plans to use an Englishman – code-named the Jackal – to assassinate General de Gaulle. Although the professional assassin fails in his attempt, it may be interesting to note that, like the Jackal in the novel, Rabin's assassin Yigal Amir – who had a copy of the thriller – also used specially prepared explosive bullets!

49   Cerasini, p.9.
50   Ibid., p.55. Clancy wrote some of his novels with the help of a former Naval Intelligence operative, Lary Bond. Bond created a war game called Harpoon which, Clancy acknowledged, inspired *The Hunt for Red October*. This game has been used by the American Navy as a "training tool," (see ibid., p.20).
51   Ibid., p.5.
52   Ibid., p.9.
53   Ibid., p.54.
54   Ibid.
55   Ibid.
56   Ibid., pp.54–55.
57   Johnson, "A Suitable Enemy for Crusaders."

58   Quoted by Saunders, *Who Paid the Piper?*, p.22 from Douglas Waples, Publications Section, OMGUS Information Control Division. 'Publications for Germany: Agenda for Psychological Warfare Division and Office of Warfare Information Conference', 14 April 1945 (OMGUS/RG260/NARA).

59   David Poyer, *Black Storm* (New York: St. Martin's Press, 2002). Poyer is a retired US naval officer who served in the Atlantic, the Mediterranean, the Gulf and other areas.

60   See Richard Beeston, "Hospital Search Fails to Find WMDs," *The Times* (9th June, 2003).

61   London: Secker & Warburg, 1976

62   Ibid.

63   It is rumoured that Saddam Hussein was given a copy of the novel which was translated for him. Whether this novel had an impact on his decision to attack and invade Iran, almost four years later, we can only probably guess. Whether or not this novel ignited Saddam's interest in fiction writing (he has produced four and was writing another in prison), is something we may never find out. For Saddam dabbling with the genre see "Saddam the Romancier," *Prospect* (July, 2004).

64   London: W.H. Allen, 1988.

65   Ibid., p.11.

66   John Burrowes, *Gulf: At Last the Real Story of Arabia as it Truly is in the Eighties* (Edinburgh: Mainstream Publishing, 1988).

67   David Poyer, *The Gulf* (New York: Saint Martin's, 1990).

68   Quoted in the introductory pages of Poyer, *The Gulf*, op. cit.

69   Terence Strong (London: Hodder & Stoughton, 1993). A best-selling author, Strong is claimed to have – as a freelance journalist and writer – "first-hand" knowledge of the Middle East. His main interests are said to include international relations, politics and military affairs, along with special forces. The theme of his novel is the subject of not only other works of fiction but at least one action film so far: *The Finest Hour*, produced by 21st Century Film Corporation directed by Shimon Dotan in 1991, starring Rob Lowe, Gale Hansen and Tracy Griffith. In Strong's other novel *The Fifth Hostage* (London: Hodder & Stoughton, 1983), the scene is set in Iran of 1980. The SAS are on a mission inside that country to rescue a British hostage and his "devastatingly beautiful" girl friend at all costs. The classified information – which the Iranians are trying to get – could "shatter NATO unity like megaton." Strong's *Conflict of Lions* (London: Hodder & Stoughton, 1985) gives an "inside account" of an SAS peace mission that finds itself pitted against "Libyan terrorists." His subsequent *Sons of Heaven* (London: Hodder and Stoughton, 1990) labours roughly the same theme: the *Pessarane Behesht* (the Sons of Heaven) are the new secret

sword of Islam, "nurtured in revolutionary Iran to wreak Vengeance on the enemies of Islam" by kidnapping and assassination.

70   (London: Bantam Press, 1994).

71   This is inscribed in Arabic on the cover of the book. Forsyth's other novel *The Negotiator* is set in the future. In it the two superpowers realise that oil reserves will be exhausted, and decide that Saudi Arabia must come under their direct control.

72   (London: Chapmans, 1992).

73   *Daily Mail*, Wednesday, 5th August, 1992.

74   McCormick and Fletcher, "Cross-Fertilization: the Relationship between Writers and the World of Intelligence," in *Spy Fiction*, p.297

75   See Masters, pp.114–133.

76   See Denis Smyth, "*Our Man in Havana*, Their Man in Madrid: Literary Invention in Espionage Fact and Fiction" in Wark, p.117.

77   Ibid.

78   Ibid. My emphasis.

79   Simon, p.v.

80   Hugo, p.285. After the 3rd of March 1996 cruise missile attack, code-named Desert Strike, and during a briefing of reporters at the Pentagon, the American Secretary of Defense, William Perry tried to justify the bombing of defense instillations in Southern Iraq. He described "Saddam's threat" as "clear and present danger." It did not escape the attention of commentators and even ordinary listeners that he used the title a novel by Tom Clancy, *Clear and Present Danger*.

81   See "10 Things You Didn't Know About Clinton," *The Guardian* (5th November, 1992).

82   Richard Clarke, *The Scorpion's Gate* (New York: G.P. Putnam's Sons, 2005).

83   McCormick and Fletcher, p.297.

84   Ibid., p.10.

85   Ibid.

86   See Graham Philips and Martin Keatman, *The Shakespeare Conspiracy* (London: Century, 1994).

87   See "Writers and Spies: From Geoffrey Chaucer to Graham Green," *Books Quarterly*, (2004), no.12, p.43.

88   See David Riggs, *The World of Christopher Marlowe* (London: Faber and Faber, 2004).

89   "Writers and Spies: From Geoffery Chaucer to Graham Green," p.43.

90   Masters, p.2. See also McCormick and Fletcher, pp.297–304. It is also a known fact that some poets have also worked for the secret service. Basil Bunting was a British Intelligence agent specializing in the Middle East: See Keith Alldritt, *The*

Poet as Spy: The Life and Wild Times of Basil Bunting (London: Aurum Press, 1998). Dylan Thomas, according to his biographer David Callard, may have worked for MI6: See Michael Smith, "Dylan Thomas 'spied for MI6 on mission to Iran'," *The Times* (January 1, 1999).

91 Masters, p.3

92 Ibid., p.2.

93 Ibid., p. vii.

94 See Earl Davies, "Howard Hunt and the Peter Ward-CIA Novels," *Kansas Quarterly,* (Fall, 1978), X, pp.85–95.

95 For details see "Howard Hunt: The Spy Who Knew Too Much," in Masters, pp.204–228.

96 McCormick and Fletcher, p.298.

97 For details see "Writers of Spy Fiction Worldwide," in McCormick and Fletcher, pp.286–290.

98 McCormick and Fletcher, p.298.

99 The full story of the CIA and modern art was told in a programme entitled "Hidden Hands" on Channel 4, October 29, 1995. A booklet entitled *Hidden Hands: A Different History of Modernism* by Frances Stoner Saunders was produced by Channel 4 to accompany the production. See also "Modern Art Was CIA 'Weapon'," in the *Independent on Sunday* (October 22, 1995).

100 Ibid.

101 David Caute, *The Dancer Defects: The Struggle for Cultural Supremacy During the Cold War* (Oxford: Oxford University Press, 2003).

102 Ibid., p.5.

103 Saunders, p.1.

104 Ibid., p.2.

105 John Blundell, "Waging the War of Ideas: Why There Are No Shortcuts" (The Heritage Foundation, n.d.), Monograph 254.

Crimean Tatar Revival

1 I. Aleksandrov, *O musul'manskom dukhovenstve i upravlenii dukhovnymi delami musul'man v Krymu posle ego prisoedineniia k Rossii* [On the Muslim clergy and the management of Muslim affairs in the Crimea after its incorporation into Russia] (Simferopol: Tipographiia Tavricheskogo gubernskogo zemstva, 1914), p.8.

2 A. Krichinskii, *Ocherki russkoi politiki na okrainakh. K istorii religioznykh pritesnenii krymskikh tatar* [Studies in Russian policy on the borders. On the history of religious pressure on the Crimean Tatars] (Baku: Izdanie soiuza musul'manskoi trudovoi intelligentsia [Publication of Muslim working intelligentsia union], 1919), p.43.

3   E. Avamileva, Nekotorye aspekty zemel'noi reformy v Krymu [Some aspects of land reform in the Crimea]. In *Problemy integratsii krymskikh repatriantov v ukrainskoe obschestvo* [The problems of integrating Crimean repatriates into Ukrainian society] (Kiev: Svitogliad, 2004),p.56.

4   V. Voronin, Realizatsiia zakhodiv derzhavy shodo integratsii v ukrains'ke suspil'stvo deportovanykh kryms'kykh tatar i osib inshykh natsional'nostei: sychasnii stan i perspectyvy [The realisation of state initiatives towards deported Crimean Tatars and other nationalities concerning their integration into Ukrainian society: the current situation and outlook]. In *Problemy integratsii krymskikh repatriantov v ukrainskoe obschestvo* [The problems of integrating Crimean repatriates into Ukrainian society] (Kiev: Svitogliad, 2004), p.25.

5   E. Avamileva, op. cit., p.57.

6   Ibid., 57–8.

7   M. Aradzhioni, Issledovanie sovremennogo urovnia tolerantnosti naseleniia poluostrova i istoricheskogo opyta mezhetnicheskikh i mezhkonfessional'nykh otnoshenii v Krymu (po materialam issledovanii 2001–2004 gg), [Research into the current level of tolerance among the population of the peninsula and the historical experience of interethnic and interfaith relations in the Crimea (based on the materials of 2001–2004)], in *Problemy integratsii krymskikh repatriantov v ukrainskoe obschestvo* [The problems of integrating Crimean repatriates into Ukrainian society] (Kiev: Svitogliad, 2004), pp.47–8.

8   Nikolai Kiryushko, Islam u zhitti kryms'kikh tatar [Islam in the Crimean Tatars' life]. *Liudina i svit* [The individual and the world], 2001, 1: 27.

9   *Kratkaia khronika deiatel'nosti Medzhlisa krymskotatarskogo naroda, ianvar'-oktiabr' 2001* [Short chronicle of Crimean Tatar Medzhlis activity, January–October 2001], (Simferopol: Odzhak, 2001).

Global Citizenry Ancient and Modern

1   Robert Wuthnow, et al., *Cultural Analysis: The Work of Peter L. Berger, Mary Douglas, Michel Foucault and Jurgen Habermas* (Boston: Routledge & Kegan Paul, 1984), p.25.

2   Mohammad Siddique Seddon, "'Some thoughts on the Formation of British Muslim Identity' – A Response to T. J. Winter," *Encounters: Journal of Inter-Cultural Perspectives* (September, 2002), vol. 8, no. 2, p.187.

3   Stuart Hall, "New Cultures for Old," in *A Place in The World?* Edited by Doreen Massey and Jess Pat (Oxford: Oxford University Press, 1995), p.178.

4   Kevin Robbins, "Tradition and translation: national culture in its global context," *Enterprise and Heritage*, eds. J. Corner and S. Harvey (London: Routledge, 1991), p.41.

5   Hall, in Massey and Jess, eds. (1995), op. cit., p.180.

6   Ibid., p.180.

7   Ibid., p.181.

8   Edward Said, "Narrative and Geography," *New Left Review* (March-April, 1990), no. 180, pp.81–100.

9   For a detailed discussion on national consciousness, see Benedict Anderson, *Imagined Communities, Reflections on the origins and spread of Nationalism* (London: Verso, 1983).

10   Enoch Powell, *Freedom and Reality* (Farnham: Elliot Right Way Books, 1969), p.245.

11   Paul Langford, "The Eighteenth Century," in *The Oxford Popular History of Britain*, ed. Kenneth O. Morgan (Oxford: Oxford University Press, 1998), p.410.

12   See, Bashir Mann, *The New Scots: The Story of Asians in Scotland* (Edinburgh: John Donald Publishers, 1992), p.203; and Mohammed Evans, *Islam in Wales* (Cardiff: Pawb for S4C, 2003), p.3; and Peter Fryer, *Staying Power: A History of Black People in Britain* (London: Pluto Press, 1984), pp.1–3.

13   Hall, in Massey and Jess, eds., 1995 op. cit., p.79.

14   See, Ashis Nandy, *The Intimate Enemy* (Oxford: Oxford University Press, 1983).

15   Stuart Hall, "Whose Heritage? Unsettling 'The Heritage', Re-imagining the Post-Nation," in *The Third text Reader on Art, Culture and Theory*, ed. Rasheed Araeen, Sean Cubitt, and Ziauddin Sardar (New Zealand: Continuum International Publishing Group, 2002), p.80.

16   For a detailed exposition in the wider British Muslim context, see Saied R. Ameli, Manzur Elahi, and Arzu Merali, *British Muslims' Expectations of the Government – Social Discrimination: Across the Muslim Divide* (Wembley: The Islamic Human Rights Commission, 2004), http://www.ihrc.org.uk/file/1903718287_content.pdf; and Saied R. Ameli, Arzu Merali, *British Muslims' Expectations of the Government – Dual Citizenship: British, Islamic or Both? Obligation, Recognition, Respect and Belonging* (Wembley: The Islamic Human Rights Commission, 2004). Also see *Muslims in the UK: Policies for Engaged Citizens*, 2004, http://www.eumap.org/reports/2004/britishmuslims

17   Seddon, in, Seddon et al., *British Muslims Between Assimilation and Segregation: Historical, Legal and Social Realities* (Markfield: The Islamic Foundation, 2004), p.131.

18   Leela Gandhi, *Postcolonial Theory: A Critical Introduction* (Edinburgh: Edinburgh University Press, 1998), p.126.

19   Tim Winter, "Some thoughts on the formation of British Muslim identity," *Encounters* (March, 2002), vol. 8, no. 1, p.4.

20   An extract from a speech by Her Majesty Queen Elizabeth II, delivered in

Islamabad, 8 October, 1997, cited in, Muhammad Anwar and Qadir Bakhsh, *British Muslims and State Policies* (Warwick: Centre for Research in Ethnic Relations, 2003), p.73.

21 Khizar Humayun Ansari, in *Muslim Identity in the 21ˢᵗ Century: Challenges of Modernity*, ed. Bahmanpour, M.S., and Bashir (London: Book Extra, 2000), p.97.

22 David Nichols, *Deity and Domination: Images of God and State in the Nineteenth and Twentieth Centuries*. Reprint (London: Routledge, 2001), p.129.

23 See Talip Kucukcan, "The Making of Turkish-Muslim Diaspora in Britain: Religious Collective Identity in a Multicultural Public Sphere," *Journal of Muslim Minority Affairs* (October, 2004), vol. 24, no. 2, p.244.

24 Ibid., p.250.

25 Tariq Ramadan, "Europeanisation of Islam or Islamisation of Europe," in *Islam, Europe's Second Religion: The New Social, Cultural and Political landscape*, ed. Shireen Hunter (Westport, Connecticut: Praeger, 2002), p.208. Also see Tim Winter, "Muslim Loyalty and Belonging: Some Reflections on the Psychosocial Background," in Seddon, et al., eds., *British Muslims: Loyalty and Belonging* (Markfield: The Islamic Foundation, 2003), pp.8–9.

26 Noha Nasser, "Expressions of Muslim Identity in Architecture and Urbanism in Birmingham, UK," *Islam and Christian-Muslim Relations* (January, 2005), vol.16, no. 1, p.61.

27 Ibid., p.63.

28 Malik, in, Seddon, et al., 2004, op. cit., p.147.

29 Ibid., p.147

30 Ibid., p.148.

31 Robert Colls and Bill Lancaster, eds. *Geordies: Roots of Regionalism* (Edinburgh: Edinburgh University Press, 1992), p.145.

32 Ibid., p.148.

33 Charlotte Seymour-Smith, *Macmillan Dictionary of Anthropology* (London: The Macmillan Press, 1986), p.281.

34 Ibid.

35 Paul Dresch, *Tribes, Government and History in Yemen* (Oxford: Oxford University Press, 1993), p.324.

36 Ibid., pp.328–29.

37 Ibid., p.331.

38 Ibid., p.346.

39 Richard Lawless, *From Ta'izz to Tyneside: An Arab Community in the North-East of England during the Early Twentieth Century* (Exeter: University of Exeter Press, 1995), p.39.

40 This population figure is taken from the 2001 Census data.

41 Betsy Hartmann and James Boyce, *A Quiet Violence: View from a Bangla-desh Village* (London: Zed Press, 1983), p.112.

Blinkered Politics

1 Thucydides' account of how speech was transformed during the sedition in Corcyra is all too apt for our times, especially his observation that the cause of such distortion "is desire of rule out of avarice and ambition, and the zeal of contention from those two proceeding." See *Thucydides: The Peloponnesian War, the Thomas Hobbes Translation*, ed. David Grene, intro. Bertrand de Jouvenel (Ann Arbor, MI: University of Michigan Press, 1959), Bk. 3, sect. 82; also sects. 70–85.

2 For example, when I defended Professor Sami al-Arian against the charges for which he was indicted and explained how the programs of WISE benefitted academics, in an exchange on a restricted list-serve, Martin Kramer denounced me on Campus Watch, albeit somewhat abashedly (www.campus-watch.org/article/id/557). Above a picture of me that I had never before seen was pasted one of the Lidd bus-bombing, suggesting it was my doing. Calls for my dismissal were numerous, heated, and clearly orchestrated. Fortunately, administrators at the University of Maryland adhered to the principle of academic freedom.
   Equally deplorable are the tactics of David Horowitz, the founder of www.FrontPageMag.com, especially his list of those professors whom he deems "the 101 most dangerous academics in America."
   Consider, too, the case of Douglas Giles as another instance of how free speech about the Middle East and US foreign policy has disappeared from the university classroom. An instructor on world religions at Roosevelt University in Chicago, Giles was forbidden by his department head to permit student questions about Palestine and Israel or mention in class, textbooks, or examinations that might bring criticism upon Judaism. A student asked about Palestinian rights, another complained, and Giles was dismissed. Henry Porter, "Comment: The Land of the Free – But Free Speech is a Rare Commodity," *The Observer*, August 13, 2006, http://www.guardian.co.uk/commentisfree/2006/aug/13/israel.usa

3 In "Campus Groups Brace For Anti-Israel Campaign," *The Jewish Week*, August 11, 2006, Gary Rosenblatt reports that "Jonathan Kessler, the leadership development director at the American Israel Public Affairs Committee, which organizes pro-Israel activities at universities around the country … and a number of other American Jewish leaders and educators said they are bracing for a surge of rallies, protests and campaigns against Israel's military conduct in Lebanon." To counter criticism of Israel, they plan to emphasize "Hezbollah's

responsibility not only for Israeli deaths with missiles aimed at civilians but Lebanese casualties as well, since the terror group positions itself among the populace." They "had to scramble to re-frame the focus of their attention from the Palestinian conflict to the war with Hezbollah over the last several weeks. AIPAC's long-planned four-day training seminar for 350 student activists from around the country, held July 23–26 in Washington, was 'recalibrated' only days before ... so as to reflect the current conflict. ... The main goal of the conference... was to deliver the college campus as an asset to the pro-Israel community, primarily by engaging in political activity."

4   *The Washington Post*, August 3, 2006, p.A27. Yaalon excused the Qana atrocity by asserting, against all available evidence, that "after launching missiles at Israel, the terrorists rushed inside a building. When Israel fired a precision-guided missile to strike at the terrorists, scores of civilians, including children, were killed." Not only did *The Washington Post* publish this mendacious account without comment or disclaimer, but followed it up with a front-page article that depicts Yaalon as conscientiously trying to limit collateral damage in Israeli targeted killings. Laura Blumenfeld ("In Israel, a Divisive Struggle Over Targeted Killing," *The Washington Post*, August 27, 2006, A1 and A12–13) examines in detail the argument between Yaalon and his colleagues over the size bomb to be used in their 2003 attempt to kill Hamas leaders at a meeting in a Gaza apartment building. In the August 3 article, Yaalon had argued that Israel's concern not to harm civilians sometimes works against its military goals: "We knew that a one-ton bomb would destroy the three-story building and kill the Hamas leadership. But we also knew that such a bomb would endanger about 40 families who lived in the vicinity. We decided to use a smaller bomb that would destroy only the top floor of the building. As it turned out, the Hamas leaders were meeting on the ground floor. They lived to terrorize another day." Neither Yaalon nor Blumenfeld say anything about how many civilians were killed in this particular action. Nor does either acknowledge the civilians killed in other targeted killings. In passing, Blumenfeld mentions the 2002 bombing of a Gaza apartment building that resulted in the deaths of 15 civilians, 9 of whom were children – an event that surely affected the 2003 decision. Yaalon, however, said nothing of this incident in the earlier article. The juxtaposition of the two articles and the common theme that links them causes one to wonder what standards of journalism guide the editors of *The Washington Post*.

5   In "Nasrallah Didn't Mean To," *Haaretz*, August 17, 2006, Amira Hass provides needed background to Yaalon's white-wash of Israel's aggression in Lebanon: "the claim that 'they' (Hezbollah and the Palestinians) cynically exploit civilians by locating themselves among them and firing from their midst

...is made by citizens of a state who know very well where to turn off Ibn Gvirol Street in Tel Aviv to get to the security-military complex that is located in the heart of their civilian city; this claim is repeated by the parents of armed soldiers who bring their weapons home on weekends, and is recited by soldiers whose bases are adjacent to Jewish settlements in the West Bank and who have shelled civilian Palestinian neighborhoods from positions and tanks that have been stationed inside civilian settlements."

6   John J. Mearsheimer and Stephen M. Walt, "The Israeli Lobby and U.S. Foreign Policy," Harvard University, John F. Kennedy School of Government, Faculty Research Working Paper Series, March 2006, RWP 06–011.

7   For a contrast, see John L. Esposito, "It's the Policy, Stupid: Political Islam and US Foreign Policy," *Harvard International Review*, http://hir.harvard.edu/articles/1453/. Moreover, the essays by Michael Scheuer, Peter Bergen, and Antony T. Sullivan in "9/11/06, Five Years on: A Symposium," *The National Interest* (September/October, 2006 [no. 85]), pp.20–35 offer a novel, thought-provoking analysis of the factors leading up to 9/11, especially the political ones. Although Alexis Debat and Nikolas K. Gvosdev try in their co-authored piece to buttress the idea that 9/11 resulted from envy about what the US has achieved, Scheuer clearly depicts the political reasons for the attack; unfortunately, his "might makes right" remedy is difficult to defend on any but narrow "America-first" grounds. It is cleverly countered by Bergen's compelling, deeply sensitive analysis. By far, however, Sullivan's vivid account of al-Qaida's potential to wreak havoc and thus counter US military adventures abroad makes the most powerful case for reconsidering the origins of 9/11.

8   See Condoleeza Rice, "A Path to Lasting Peace," *The Washington Post*, August 16, 2006, p.A13. Contending that the responsibility for Israel's most recent attack upon Lebanon lies with Iran and Syria while Hezbollah merely serves their purposes, she claims "for the past month the United States has worked urgently to end the violence that Hezbollah and its sponsors have imposed on the people of Lebanon and Israel" then insists that "while the entire world has spent the past month working for peace, the Syrian and Iranian regimes have sought to prolong and intensify the war that Hezbollah started." In other words, the US Secretary of State is unable to blame Israel in any way for the damage wrought by this war or even to see how Israel blew the original *causa belli* out of proportion. Yet any fair-minded person must understand that while a soldier may be put out of action by being killed, wounded, or taken prisoner, he may never – qua soldier – be "kidnapped." Seizing elected officials and cabinet officers, as Israel has done with 45 members of Hamas, does qualify as kidnapping, however.

9   Alan Hart develops the background to the thesis in a speech for the International Institute of Strategic Studies, August 10, 2006, "The Beginning of the End of the Zionist State of Israel?," http://mparent7777.livejournal.com/11313638.html. Hart argues that Hizballah's capture of the IDF soldiers was merely a pretext for a war long-planned, one designed to occupy and annex Lebanon up to the Litani River, and that Israel repeatedly seeks out regional confrontation so as to keep tension and fear of attack high among citizens and soldiers. Indeed, this is the means by which it maintains the deterrent power of the IDF. Meyrav Wurmser, director of the Hudson Institute Center for Middle East Policy and Israeli-born spouse of David Wurmser, a Middle East adviser to Vice-President Cheney, adds to Hart's contention. "The bottom line is that Israel's gripe is not with Lebanon; it [is] with Syria and Iran," she writes in *National Review Online (NRO)*, then draws the obvious consequences: "Given the explosive nature of the situation, Israel ought not let its adversaries define the battleground. Rather, it ought to carry the battle to them."

10   See, for example, his "Hizbullah's attacks stem from Israeli incursions into Lebanon," *Christian Science Monitor*, August 1, 2006: "Since its withdrawal of occupation forces from southern Lebanon in May 2000, Israel has violated the United Nations-monitored 'blue line' on an almost daily basis, according to UN reports. Hizbullah's military doctrine, articulated in the early 1990s, states that it will fire Katyusha rockets into Israel only in response to Israeli attacks on Lebanese civilians or Hizbullah's leadership; this indeed has been the pattern." Most important, Strindberg understands that "the fundamental obstacle to understanding the Arab-Israeli conflict is that we have given up on asking what is right and wrong, instead asking what is 'practical' and 'realistic.' Yet reality is that Israel is a profoundly racist state, the existence of which is buttressed by a seemingly endless succession of punitive measures, assassinations, and wars against its victims and their allies. A realistic understanding of the conflict, therefore, is one that recognizes that the crux is not in this or that incident or policy, but in Israel's foundational and persistent refusal to recognize the humanity of its Palestinian victims. Neither Hizbullah nor Hamas are driven by a desire to 'wipe out Jews,' as is so often claimed, but by a fundamental sense of injustice that they will not allow to be forgotten."

11   In a speech sponsored by the New American Foundation in Washington, DC, on July 31, 2006, Prince Turki began by firmly castigating Hamas and Hizballah: "Saudi Arabia holds firmly responsible those who first engaged in reckless adventure under the guise of resistance. They have brought much damage and danger to the region without concern for others." "However," he added, "these unacceptable and irresponsible actions do not justify the Israeli destruction of Lebanon or the targeting and punishment of the Lebanese and

Palestinian civilian populations. These actions are without consideration for international pacts, conventions, and norms. This is not the way of peace."

12 Almost every analyst recognizes that the war in Lebanon had a broader goal. Vali Nasr of the Naval Postgraduate School, Monterey, and adjunct senior fellow at the Council on Foreign Relations surmises that its goal was to emphasize to Iran the depth of US determination "to bring it into compliance on the nuclear issue." Because the war "not only failed to subdue Hizbullah militarily, but has made it politically stronger," Nasr urges "US objectives and interests would be better served by giving Iran a vested interest in stability... including [it] in a new regional security framework [while continuing] to demand that Iran curb its nuclear activities, abandon support of terrorism, and respect the democratic aspirations of Iranians;" see "After Lebanon, there's Iran," *Christian Science Monitor*, August 9, 2006. In "Israel's Broken Heart: Final Reckoning," *The New Republic Online*, August 15, 2006, Yossi Klein Halevi also notes that Israel had "an unprecedented green light from Washington to do whatever necessary to uproot the Iranian front line against Israel," then goes on to lament its failure to have succeeded.

13 The problem with "might makes right" is that it can easily turn on the perpetrator. As Jean-Jacques Rousseau noted so well, "the despot is master only as long as he is the strongest; as soon as he can be overthrown, he has nothing to say against such violence. The riot that ends up strangling or de-throning a sultan is as juridical an act as those by which the day before he disposed of the lives and goods of his subjects." See *Discourse on the Origin of Inequality*, anti-penultimate paragraph; also *Social Contract*, Bk. 1, ch. 3.

14 Consider the announcement accompanying a lecture by Shmeul Bar, "Conflict with the West: Religious Drivers and Strategies of Jihad" at The Heritage Foundation on August 17, 2006: "Dr. Shmuel Bar, Director of Studies at the Institute for Policy and Strategy, Interdisciplinary Center Herzliya, joins us from Israel to discuss the close relationship between religion and politics in Islam – and the predilection of radical Islamic organizations towards religious motivation – which makes it difficult to draw a picture of the political and military strategies which drive them as distinct from religious convictions. The use of religious authority through fatwas (Islamic rulings) of Islamic scholars to justify the very act of jihad and to regulate its scope and constraints is a pivotal force for motivation of the foot soldiers of the jihad, but also a serious consideration for the leaders. The use of apocalyptic rhetoric for motivation of followers is not easily distinguished from the real expectations and practical plans of radical leaders. Join us as Dr. Bar explains the strategic concepts of Islamic terrorists and the resulting ramifications for U.S. policy toward the Middle East and for coalition forces currently on the ground."

British Islamic Culture After 7/7

1   Nabil Matar, *Islam in Britain, 1558–1685* (Cambridge: Cambridge University Press, 1998).

2   Jorgen Nielsen, *Muslims in Western Europe*, 3ʳᵈ edn. (Edinburgh: Edinburgh University Press, 2005).

3   Ceri Peach, "Muslims in the UK," *Muslim Britain: Communities under Pressure*, ed. Tahir Abbas (London: Zed Books, 2005).

4   Tariq Modood, et al., *Ethnic Minorities in Britain: Diversity and Disadvantage – The Fourth National Survey of Ethnic Minorities* (London: Policy Studies Institute, 1997).

5   Tahir Abbas, *Muslims in Birmingham, UK*. Background paper for the University of Oxford: Centre on Migration Policy and Society, 2006.

6   Muhammad Anwar, Patrick Roach and Ranjit Sondhi, eds. *From Legislation to Integration? Race Relations in Britain from Integration to Legislation* (London: Palgrave, 1999).

7   Tariq Modood, "Anti-essentialism, Multiculturalism and the 'recognition' of religious groups," *The Journal of Political Philosophy* (1998), vol. 6, no. 4, pp. 378–99; P. Werbner, "Divided Loyalties, Empowered Citizenship? Muslims in Britain," *Citizenship Studies* (2000), vol. 4, no. 3, pp. 307–24.

8   Tariq Modood, *Multicultural Politics: Racism, Ethnicity and Muslims in Britain* (Edinburgh: Edinburgh University Press, 2005).

9   Tahir Abbas, "Recent developments to British multicultural theory, policy and practise: the case of British Muslims," *Citizenship Studies* (2005), vol. 9, no. 3, pp. 153–166.

10   Milan Rai, *7/7: The London Bombings, Islam and the Iraq* (London: Pluto, 2006).

11   Robert Dreyfuss, *Devil's Game: how the United States helped unleash fundamentalist Islam* (New York: Metropolitan Books, 2005).

12   Tariq Modood, "British Asian Muslims and the Rushdie Affair," *Political Quarterly* (1990), vol. 61, no. 2, pp. 143–160.

13   Gurchathen Sanghera and Thapar-Björkert, Suruchi "'Because I am Pakistani ... and I am Muslim ... I am Political' – Gendering Political Radicalism: Young Masculinities and Femininities in Bradford," in *Islamic Political Radicalism: A European Perspective*, ed. Tahir Abbas (Edinburgh: Edinburgh University Press, 2007); Marie, Macey, "Islamic Political Radicalism in Britain: Muslim Men in Bradford," in Tahir Abbas, ed., op. cit., 2007.

14   Mike Nellis and Richard North, "Electronic Monitoring and the Creation of Control Orders for Terrorist Suspects in Britain," unpublished paper, University of Birmingham, 2005.

15   Alan Travis, "Community relations hit by terror laws, says MPs," *The Guardian* (6 April, 2005).

16 Institute of Race Relations, *Arrests under anti-terrorist legislation since 11 September 2001* (London: Institute of Race Relations, 2005).

17 Mosques and National Advisory Board, *Best Practise Guide for Mosques and Islamic Centres* (London: MINAB, 2006).

Alternatives to Violence in Muslim History

1 Henry David Thoreau, "Civil Disobedience," 1849, http://thoreau.eserver.org/civil.html

2 Qur'an (91:7–10). Quoted from Yusuf Ali, translation.

3 Thoreau, 1849, loc. cit.

4 Qur'an (33:67–68).

5 Qur'an (7:38).

6 Qur'an (48:1).

7 Qur'an (48:4).

8 See, for example, Shall Sinha, "Books Which Influenced Gandhi's Life and Thought," (1/2/05) www.ssinha.com/bksmgrd.htm

9 Brad Bennett, "Arab-Muslim Cases of Nonviolent struggle," in *Arab Nonviolent Political Struggle in the Middle East*, eds. Ralph E. Crow, Philip Grant, and Saad E. Ibrahim (Boulder: L. Rienner Publishers, 1990), p.43.

10 Amitabh Pal, "A Pacifist Uncovered," *The Progressive* (February, 2002), http://progressive.org/?q=node/1654

11 Quoted in ibid.

12 Quoted in ibid. This was also Gandhi's view. See, for example, Maulana Abul Kalam Azad, *India Wins Freedom: An Autobiographical Narrative,* with Introduction and Explanatory Notes by Louis Fischer (New York: Longmans, Green & Co., 1960).

13 Michael M. J. Fischer, *Iran: From Religious Dispute to Revolution* (Cambridge: Harvard, 1980), pp.123–4.

14 Ibid., p.124.

15 Ibid.

16 Ibid.

17 Ibid., p.183.

18 Ibid., p.185.

19 Ervand Abrahamian, *Iran Between Two Revolutions* (Princeton: Princeton University Press, 1982), p.506.

20 Fischer, 1980, p.186.

21 Abrahamian, 1982, p.503.

22 Ibid.

23 Hossein Bashiriyeh, *The State and Revolution in Iran* (New York: St. Martin's Press, 1984), p.112.

24 Fischer, 1980, p.193.

25 Ibid., p.194.

26 Bashiriyeh, 1984, cited in ibid.

27 Ibid., p.113.

28 Ibid.

29 Ibid., p.198.

30 Ibid., p.199.

31 Ibid., p.202.

32 Lynne Shivers, "Inside the Iranian Revolution," in *Tell the American People*, ed. David H. Albert (Philadelphia: Movement for a New Society, 1980).

33 Abrahamian, 1982, p.518.

34 Bashiriyeh, 1984, p.204.

35 Abrahamian, 1982, p.522.

36 Ibid., p.523.

37 Bashiriyeh, 1984, p.226.

38 Philip Grant, "Nonviolent Political struggle in the Occupied Territories," in *Arab Nonviolent Political struggle in the Middle East*, eds. Ralph E. Crow, Philip Grant, and Saad E. Ibrahim (Boulder: Lynne Rienner, 1990), p.61. While Christians were an important part of the Intifadah, they were the tail on the dog; see F. Robert Hunter, *The Palestinian Uprising: A War by Other Means* (Berkeley: UC Berkeley, 1991), pp.115-6.

39 For a detailed analysis of the escalating oppression that formed the context of the Intifadah, see Don Peretz, *Intifada* (Boulder: Westview, 1990), ch.1, pp.1-38.

40 Grant, 1990, p.64.

41 Hunter, 1991, p.89.

42 Peretz, 1990, p.52.

43 Grant, 1990, p.64.

44 *Ṣaḥīḥ Muslim*, hadith no. 79, trans., Abdul Hamid Sidiqi (Lahore: Kashmiri Bazar, 1976), vol. 1, p.33.

45 Thoreau, 1849, op. cit.

46 Peretz, 1990, p.52.

47 Hunter, 1991, pp.110-112.

48 Peretz, 1990, p.56.

49 Hunter, 1991, p.112f.

50 Ibid., p.55.

51 Ibid., p.58.

52 Ibid., p.62.

53 See e.g., Hunter, 1991, p.88ff.

54 See Peretz, 1990, pp.47-52.

55   Hunter, 1991, p.92.

56   Peretz, 1990, p.139.

57   Ibid., p.140.

58   Hunter, 1991, p.225f.

59   Ibid., p.226.

60   Ibid., p.124.

61   Ibid., p.124.

62   Ibid., p.125.

63   Ibid., p.126.

64   Thoreau, loc. cit.

65   Hunter, 1991, pp.131–2.

66   Ibid., p.136ff.

67   Ibid., pp.132–6.

68   Ibid., p.116.

69   Ibid., p.117.

70   Ibid.

71   See, e.g., Peretz, 1990, pp.167–181.

72   See, e.g., http://ifamericansknew.org

73   Ibid., p.66.

74   Hunter, 1991, pp.226–7.

75   Ibid., p.227.

76   For a thoughtful analysis, see Michael C. Hudson, "The Palestinian Challenge to US Policy," in *The Palestinians: New Directions*, ed. Michael C. Hudson (Washington: Centre for Contemporary Arab Studies, 1990), pp.77–118.

77   Hunter, 1991, p.83.

78   Ibid., p.79.

79   Qur'an (8:63).

80   Bill Paxton, "Eyes Without a Country: Searching for a Palestinian Strategy of Liberation" (Weatherhead Centre for International Affairs, 1994), http://www.wcfia.harvard.edu/ponsacs/seminars/Synopses/s94dajan.htm

81   Noah Merrill, "Celebrating Nonviolent Resistance," *Peacework* (February, 2006), American Friends Service Committee, http://www.peacework-magazine.org/pwork/0602/060210.htm

82   Ibid.

Places and Perspectives

1   Maulana Rumi, quoted in R.A. Nicholson, trans. and ed. *The Mathnawi of Jalalu'ddin Rumi* (Karachi: Dārul Ishaat, 2003), p.72.

2   A. Chhachhi, "Identity Politics: South Asia," in *Encyclopedia of Women and Islamic Cultures*, ed. Suad Joseph (Leiden: Brill, 2005), vol. 2, p.286.

3   See Modood and Werbner, for a detailed discussion. T. Modood and P. Werbner, eds. *The Politics of Multiculturalism in the New Europe* (London: Zed Books, 1997).

4   Chhachhi, op. cit., p.286.

5   D. Massey and P. Jess, *A Place in the World* (Oxford: Open Univeristy Press and Oxford Press, 1995), p.1.

6   Ibid., p.217.

7   Ibid., p.218.

8   A.S. Roald, *Women in Islam: The Western Experience* (London: Routledge, 2001).

9   Riaz Ravat, *Embracing the Present, Planning the Future: Social Action by the Faith Communities of Leicester* (Bury St Edmunds: Leicester Faiths Regeneration Project, 2004).

10 Richard Bonney, *Understanding and Celebrating Religious Diversity in Leicester's Places of Worship since 1970* (Leicester: University of Leicester, 2003), p.v.

11 Ibid., p.4.

12 Ibid., pp.5–7.

13 Ibid., p.4.

14 Op. cit., p.6.

15 In Bonney, op. cit., ibid., p.10.

16 Ibid., p.17.

17 Ibid., p.11.

18 I.S. Gilani, *Citizens Slaves and Guest-Workers: The Dynamics of Labour Migration from South Asia* (Islamabad: Institute of Policy Studies, 1985), p.17.

19 Quoted in Bonney, op. cit., p.11.

20 Ibid., p.12.

21 Quoted in ibid., p.14.

22 www.about-leicester/demographicandcultural, p.5.

23 www.about-leicester/demographicandcultural, p.4.

24 Bonney, op. cit., p.33.

25 In ibid., p.40.

26 Ibid., p.42.

27 Ibid., p.59; and J. Martin and G. Singh, *Asian Leicester* (Gloucestershire: Sutton Publishing, 2002), p.65.

28 Bonney, op. cit., p.59.

29 In Bonney, op. cit.

30 www.leicester.gov.uk/councillors

31 I. Young, "Impartiality and the Civic Public: Some Implications of the Feminist Critiques of Moral and Political Theory," in *Feminism, the Public and*

the Private, ed. Joan Landes (Oxford: Oxford University Press, 1998), pp.421–447.

32   M. M. K. Saroha, *Heavenly Ornaments*, English Translation of Maulana Ashraf Ali Thanvi's *Bahishti Zewar* (Karachi: Darul Ishaat, 1991); and *Heavenly Ornaments, Bahishti Zewar, A Classic Manual of Islamic Sacred Law by Maulana Ashraf Ali Thanvi*, trans. M. Mahomedy (Karachi: Zam Zam Publishers, 1999).

33   M. Eliade, *The Sacred and the Profane: the Nature of Religion*, trans. W. Trask (London, Harcourt: Brace Johanovich, 1959).

34   D. Massey, *Space, Place and Gender* (Cambridge: Polity Press, 1994), p.1.

35   Ibid., p.2.

36   Ibid., p.2.

37   Ibid., p.3.

38   B. Metcalf, *Islamic Revival in British India Deoband, 1860–1900* (Oxford: Oxford University Press, 1982), p.11.

39   Ibid., p.76.

40   Ibid., p.82.

41   B. Metcalf, *Traditionalist Islamic Activism: Deoband, Tablighis, and Talibs* (Leiden: ISIM., 2002), p.7.

42   Metcalf, 1982, op. cit., p.85.

43   Ibid., op. cit., p.153.

44   Ibid., p.125.

45   Ibid., p.136.

46   F. Robinson, *Varieties of South Asian Islam*, Research Paper no. 8 (Coventry, CRER: University of Warwick, 1988), p.5.

47   Metcalf, 2002, op. cit., p.7.

48   B. Metcalf, *Perfecting Women: Maulana Asraf 'Ali Thanawi's Bihishti Zewar* (Oxford, University of California, 1990).

49   Ibid., p.12.

50   Ibid., p.vii.

51   Ibid., p.9.

52   Ibid., p.8.

53   Ibid., p.22.

54   Ibid., p.34.

55   Ibid., p.318.

56   Ibid., pp.318–327.

57   See op. cit., Saroha, *Heavenly Ornaments*, Metcalf, *Perfecting Women,* and Mahomedy, *Heavenly Ornaments*.

58   Metcalf, 1990, pp.108–110.

59   Saroha, 1991, p.342.

60 M. Hermansen, "Imagining Space and Siting Collective Memory in South Asian Muslim Biographical Literature *(Tazkirahs),*" *Studies in Contemporary Islam,* (2002), vol. 4, no. 2, p.1.

61 Ibid., p.2.

62 Ibid., p.2.

63 Ibid., p.3.

64 Ibid., pp.10–11.

65 Ibid., p.6.

66 P.H. Collins, *Black Feminist Thought: knowledge, consciousness and the politics of empowerment* (London: Routledge, 1991), p.206.

67 Ibid.

68 S. Harding, *The Science Question in Feminism* (Ithaca: Cornell University Press, 1986); and "Rethinking Standpoint Epistemology: 'What is Strong Objectivity?'" in *Feminist Epistemologies,* eds. L. Alcoff and E. Potter E. (London: Routledge, 1993), pp.49–82.

69 D. Haraway, *Simians, Cyborgs and Women: The Reinvention of Nature* (London: Free Association Books, 1991).

70 A.S. Roald, "Who Are The Muslims? Identity, Gender and Culture," in *Gender, Religion and Diversity: Cross-Cultural Perspectives,* ed. U. King and T. Beattie T, (London: Continuum, 2005), p.188.

Securing Civic Relations in the Multicultural City

1 The data presented in this paper was gathered during 2004–2006 as part of a doctoral research project. Interviews and observations were conducted in two British cities: Manchester and Stoke-on-Trent. The research focused particularly on transitions in leadership experienced by Pakistani Muslim communities in these cities.

2 Humera Khan, *Q-News* (July, 2006).

3 David Faulkner, "Civil Renewal, Diversity and Social Capital in a Multi-Ethnic Britain," Runnymede Perspectives series paper (January). (London: Runnymede, 2004), http://www.runnymedetrust.org

4 Nikolas Rose, "Government and Control," *British Journal of Criminology,* (2000), vol. 40, p.3.

5 M. Innes, "Reinventing Tradition: Reassurance, neighbourhood security and policing," *Criminal Justice* (2004), vol. 4, p.2.

6 Ulrich Beck, *Risk Society: Towards a New Modernity* (London: Sage, 1992).

7 Muhammad Anwar, "Muslims in Britain: Issues, Policy and Practise," in *Muslim Britain: Communities Under Pressure,* ed. T. Abbas (London: Zed Books, 1991).

8 Humayun Ansari, *The Infidel Within: Muslims in Britain since 1800* (London: Hurst, 2004).

NOTES

9   Donatella Della Porta and Mario Diani, *Social Movements: An Introduction* (Oxford: Blackwell Publishing, 2006).

10 Kingsley Purdam, "The Impacts of Democracy on Identity: Muslim Councillors and their Experiences of Local Politics in Britain." PhD dissertation (Manchester: Manchester University, 2003).

11 John Solomos and Les Black, *Race, Politics and Social Change* (London: Routledge, 1995).

12 Purdam, 2003.

13 Electoral Commission, Voter Engagement among Black and Minority Ethnic Communities: Research Report (July) (London: The Electoral Commission, 2002).

14 Akhtar Hussain, *The Four Tribes of Nottingham: The Story of Pakistanis and Kashmiris in Nottingham, England* (Karachi: Awami Publishers, 1999).

15 Pnina Werbner, *Imagined Diasporas among Manchester Muslims: The Public Performance of Pakistani Transnational Identity Politics.* World Anthropology Series (Oxford: James Currey Publishers, 2002).

16 F. Anthias and Nira Yuval Davis, *Racialised Boundaries* (New York: Routledge, 1992).

17 Harriet Cain and Nira Yuval-Davis, "The Equal Opportunities Community and the Anti-Racist Struggle," *Critical Social Policy* (Autumn, 1990), vol. 29, pp.5–26.

18 Peter Shirlow and Brendan Murtagh, "Capacity-building, Representation and Intra-community Conflict," *Urban Studies* (2004), vol. 41, no. 1, pp.57–70.

19 Werbner, 2002.

20 I use the term 'younger adults' to refer to the 18–30 year old age cohort, who often escape attention in discussions of community engagement.

21 Prime Ministerial Press Conference, 5th August 2005. URL: www.number-10.gov.uk/output/Page8041.asp

22 Blair, ibid.

23 Michalis Lianos, with Mary Douglas, "Dangerisation and the End of Deviance: The Institutional Environment," *British Journal of Criminology* (2000), vol. 40, no. 2, pp.261–278.

24 Multiculturalist policies have been described as dangerous by a number of non-state actors, but most significantly by the Chair of the government-established Commission for Racial Equality (The Times, 4 April, 2004) and in the reports which followed the disorders across Northern England in the summer of 2001 (Cantle 2001, Ritchie 2001, Ouseley 2001, Home Office 2002).

25 Ulrich Beck, op. cit., p.22.

26 Yasmin Hussain and Paul Bagguley, "Citizenship, Ethnicity and Identity: British Pakistanis After the 2001 'Riots'" *Sociology*, (2005), vol. 39, no. 3,

272

pp.407–425; Stacey Burlet and Helen Reid, "Riots, Representation and Responsibilities: The Role of Young Men in Pakistani-heritage Muslim Communities," in *Political Participation and Identities of Muslims in Non-Muslim States*, eds. W.A.R. Shadid and P.S. van Koningsveld (Kampen, The Netherlands: Kok Pharos, 1996), pp.144–159; Marie Macey, "Class, gender and religious influences on changing patterns of Pakistani Muslim male violence in Bradford," *Ethnic and Racial Studies* (September, 1999), vol. 22, no. 5, pp.845–866; and Colin Webster, "Race, Space and Fear: Imagined Geographies of Racism, Crime, Violence and Disorder in Northern England," *Capital & Class* (December, 2002).

27 Lianos and Douglas, 2000, p.263.

28 10 Downing Street. MP's Press Conference (5 August, 2005), http://www. number10.gov.uk/output/Page8041.asp

29 *Q-News* (July, 2006).

30 Ted Cantle, *Community Cohesion: A Report of the Independent Review Team* (London: Home Office, 2001); D. Ritchie, *Oldham Independent Review*, Oldham Panel, one Oldham one Future: Oldham (2001), http://www.old-hamir. org.uk/, and; Herman Ouseley, *Community Pride not Prejudice* (Bradford Vision: Bradford, 2001).

31 Home Office, 2005.

32 'Responsibilisation' is a term used by Rose (2000) to describe the promotion of prudentialism by advanced liberal states in which individual citizens are encouraged to provide for their own future and to secure themselves against and educate themselves about risks.

33 Data collected in Stoke-on-Trent and Manchester during the period 2004–2006.

34 Home Office, "'Preventing Extremism Together' Working Group Reports, August–October" (London: Home Office, 2005), p.73, http://www.raceand-faith.communities.gov.uk

35 Department for Communities and Local Government, 'Preventing Extremism Together' Progress Report (London: Home Office, URL, 2006), http://www. raceandfaith.communities.gov.uk

36 Ibid.

37 Convenor's foreword, 2005, p.2.

38 Rose, 2000, p.324.

39 Ibid., p.329.

40 Open letter from GMP Chief Constable Michael Todd, 20 July 2005.

41 Interviews were conducted with a range of political and welfare-oriented 'leaders' in Manchester and Stoke-on-Trent.

42 Anthony P. Cohen, *The Symbolic Construction of Community* (London: Tavistock, 1985), p.12.

Islamic Revivalism and the Elusive Ethical State

1   Said Amir Arjomand, *The Turban for the Crown: The Islamic Revolution in Iran* (Oxford: Oxford University Press, 1998), pp.182–183.

2   Gilles Kepel, *Jihad: The Trail of Political Islam*, trans. Anthony F. Roberts (London: IB Tauris, 2002), pp.367–8.

3   Olivier Roy, *The Failure of Political Islam*, trans. Carol Volk (Cambridge: Harvard University Press, 1994), p.12.

4   Ibid., pp.12–14.

5   Ibid., p.62.

6   Ibid., p.60.

7   Ibid., p.23.

8   H.A.R Gibb, "The Fiscal Rescript of 'Umar II," *Arabica* (January, 1955), vol. 2, no. 1, p.8.

9   Abd al-Aziz Sayyid al-Ahl, *Al-Khalīfa al-Zāhid ʿUmar ibn ʿAbd al-ʿAzīz* (Beirut: Dār al-ʿIlm li al-Malāyīn, 1969), p.202.

10 Gibb (1955), vol. 3, no. 8; and Hugh Kennedy, *The Prophet and the Age of the Caliphate* (London: Longman, 1986), p.107.

11 Sayyid al-Ahl, 1969, pp.128, 170.

12 Kennedy, 1986, pp.52–57.

13 G.R. Hawting, *The First Dynasty of Islam* (London: Croom Helm, 1987), p.77; and Sayyid al-Ahl, 1969, pp.60–63.

14 Mahmud al-Aqqad, Abbas, *ʿAbqariyyah ʿUmar* (Cairo: al-Maktabah al-Tijāriyyah al-Kubrā, 1943), p.223.

15 Martin Hinds, *Studies in Early Islamic History* (Princeton: Princeton University Press, 1996), pp.45–46.

16 Ibid., p.52.

17 Taha Hussein, *Al Fitnah al-Kubrā* (Cairo: Dār al-Maʿārif, 1947), vols. I–II, p.118.

18 Sayyid al-Ahl, 1969, p.107.

19 Ibid., p.128.

20 Abdelwahab El-Affendi, "Al-Shuʿarā' kānū Ajhizah Iʿlām al-ʿArab" [Poets were Arab Media Organs], *Al-ʿArabī* (December, 1976).

21 ʿAbd al-Raḥmān ibn Muḥammad Ibn Khaldūn, *Al-Muqaddimah* (Beirut: Dār al-Mashriq, 1967), I, pp.3–xxv–xxvii. We refer here to parts and sections in Ibn Khaldūn's *Al-Muqaddimah*.

22 Ibn Khaldūn, I, p.3–vi.

23 El-Affendi, 1991b.

24 N. Machiavelli, *The Prince*, trans. George Bull (Harmondsworth: Penguin, 1999), p.54.

25 Ibid., p.56.

26 Thomas Hobbes, *Leviathan*, ed. C.B. Macpherson (London: Clarendon Press, 1968), p.185.

27 Ibid., p.186.

28 Ibid., p.227.

29 Ibid., p.228–251.

30 Ibid., pp.363–377.

31 Sanneh, Lamin "Religion and Politics: Third World Perspectives on a Comparative Religious Theme," *Daedalus* (Summer, 1991).

32 Patrick Dunleavy and Brenda O'Leary, *Theories of the State. The Politics of Liberal Democracy* (Basingstoke: Macmillan, 1987), p.7.

33 Charles Tilly, "War Making and State Making as Organized Crime," in *Bringing the State Back In*, eds. Peter Evans, Dietrich Rueschemeyer and Theda Skocpol (Cambridge: Cambridge University Press, 1985), p.171.

34 Ibid., pp.171–173.

35 David Held, "Central Perspectives on the Modern State," in *The Idea of the Modern State*, eds. Gregor McLennan, David Held, and Stuart Hall (Milton Keynes: Open University Press, 1984), pp.51–59.

36 Tilly, 1985, p.185.

37 Paul A. Rahe, *Republics Ancient and Modern: Classical Republicanism and the American Revolution* (Chapel Hill: University of North Carolina Press, 1994), vol. 2, pp.215–231; and Danoff, 2000.

38 Quentin Skinner, *Machiavelli: A Very Short Introduction* (Oxford: Oxford University Press, 2000), pp.1–2.

39 Ruth W. Grant, *Hypocrisy and Integrity: Machiavelli, Rousseau, and the Ethics of Politics* (Chicago: University of Chicago Press, 1997), p.98.

40 Ibid., pp.98–99.

41 Ibid., p.100.

42 Bruno Latour, "What if We Talked Politics a Little," *Contemporary Political Theory* (July, 2003), vol. 2, no. 2, pp.3–4.

43 Ibid., pp.5–6.

44 Held, 1984, pp.31–32.

45 Ibid., pp.37–42.

46 Ibid., p.16.

47 Robert A. Dahl, *Democracy and its Critics* (New Haven: Yale University Press, 1989).

48 David Held, *Models of Democracy*, 2nd edn. (Cambridge: Polity Press, 1996), p.19.

49 Ibid., pp.16, 19.

50 David Beetham, "Liberal Democracy and the Limits in Democratisation," in *Prospects for Democracy*, ed. David Held (Cambridge: Polity and Stanford University Press, 1993), p.55.

51   Ibid.

52   David Held, ed. *Prospects for Democracy* (Cambridge: Polity Press, 1995).

53   Ibid.

54   Blondel, Jean, "Democracy and Constitutionalism" in *The Changing Nature of Democracy* eds. Takashi Inoguchi et al. (Tokyo: United Nations University, 1998), pp.71–86.

55   Ibid.

56   Latour, 2003, p.14.

57   Rueschemeyer and Evans, op. cit, 1985, p.47.

58   Przeworkski, Adam, "Democracy as a Contingent Outcome of Conflicts," in *Constitutionalism and Democracy*, eds. Jon Elster and Rune Slagstad (Cambridge: Cambridge University Press, 1988), pp.63–65.

59   Ibid., pp.64–66.

60   Schmitter, Philippe C., "Some Basic Assumptions about the Consolidation of Democarcy," in *The Changing Nature of Democracy*, eds. Takashi Inoguchi, Edward Newman and John Keane (New York: United Nations University Press, 1998), p.24.

61   Ibid., pp.23–24.

INDEX

Addendum

Images copyrighted.